Mission-Based Marketing

Mission-Based Marketing

Positioning Your Not-for-Profit in an Increasingly Competitive World

Third Edition

PETER C. BRINCKERHOFF

WILEY

John Wiley & Sons, Inc.

Published by John Wiley & Sons, Inc., Hoboken, New Jersey.

Published simultaneously in Canada.

For general information on our other products and services or for technical support, please contact our Customer Care Department within the United States at (800) 762-2974, outside the United States at (317) 572-3993 or fax (317) 572-4002.

Wiley also publishes its books in a variety of electronic formats. Some content that appears in print may not be available in electronic books. For more information about Wiley products, visit our web site at www.wiley.com.

Library of Congress Cataloging-in-Publication Data:

Brinckerhoff, Peter C., 1952-
    Mission-based marketing: positioning your not-for-profit in an increasingly competitive world/Peter C. Brinckerhoff.—3rd ed.
        p. cm.
    Includes bibliographical references and index.
    ISBN 978-0-470-60218-8 (cloth); ISBN 978-0-470-88984-8 (ebk); ISBN 978-0-470-88985-5 (ebk); ISBN 978-0-470-88986-2 (ebk)
    1. Nonprofit organizations–Marketing.—I. Title.
    HF5415.B667 2010
    658.8—dc22   2010013514

Printed in the United States of America
10 9 8 7 6 5 4 3 2 1

For my wife and best friend,
Christine Hargroves Brinckerhoff.
In a life filled with blessings,
you are the one for which I am most thankful.

Contents

Acknowledgments

When you sit down to write the third edition of your third book, you get the silly idea that you know what you are doing, and can handle the task at hand. Of course, you are wrong, or at least I was. I have many people to thank for bringing this project to completion, and the main recipients of my gratitude are the staff and volunteers of the nonprofits whose examples bring so much life and credibility to the ideas found in the following pages. Any good consultant learns while he or she teaches, and I like to think that all of my training and writing are a way of sharing what I have learned. It is certainly true here.

About the Author

Peter Brinckerhoff is an internationally known expert at helping not-for-profits get more mission for their money. Since embarking on his consulting career by forming his firm, Corporate Alternatives, Inc., in 1982, Peter has worked with thousands of nonprofit staff and board members throughout North America, Europe, and Australia. He is a widely published author, with over 70 articles on not-for-profit management in such prominent journals as *Nonprofit World, Advancing Philanthropy, Contributions, Strategic Governance,* and the *Journal of Nonprofit and Voluntary Sector Marketing.*

Peter is the award-winning author of seven books related to nonprofits: *Mission-Based Management (3rd Edition), Financial Empowerment, Mission-Based Marketing (3rd Edition), Social Entrepreneurship, Faith-Based Management, Nonprofit Stewardship,* and *Generations: The Challenge of a Lifetime for Your Nonprofit.* Peter's books have won the prestigious Terry McAdam Award from the Alliance for Nonprofit Management three times. The award is given annually for "Best Nonprofit Book." Peter is the only author to win multiple awards, and his books are used in the graduate and undergraduate nonprofit programs at over 100 colleges and universities worldwide.

Peter brings a wide array of practical hands-on experience to his writing, consulting, and training. He has served as a board member, staff member, and executive director of a number of local, state, and national not-for-profits. He understands all three of these perspectives and their importance in the nonprofit mix.

Peter received his Bachelor's degree from the University of Pennsylvania, and his Master's of Public Health from the Tulane University School of Public Health. He lives in Union Hall, Virginia.

Peter can be reached online through his web site, www.missionbased .com.

CHAPTER 1

Introduction

Chapter Thumbnail

➤ A Competitive and Always-Online World
➤ Who This Book Is Written For
➤ The Benefits of Reading This Book
➤ Preview of the Book

Overview

Return on investment; social enterprise; social marketing; competitive environment; social networks; market-based pricing; managed care—these terms are now nearly ubiquitous in the literature of the nonprofit world. But what do they mean to your mission, your staff, your board, and the people whom your nonprofit serves? Just as importantly, how does your organization react, respond, innovate, and, yes, *prosper* in an increasingly competitive and rapid-response environment?

And then there is technology: How do you find the people you need to find (like donors, volunteers, great employees) when some are online, some aren't, some are avid fans of social networking or texting, and some hardly check their e-mail once a week? If marketing is about meeting wants (and it is), the challenge of meeting technology wants (what I call *techspectations*) can, in itself, be overwhelming. But, if you aren't meeting those expectations, you are leaving huge and important age cohorts on the sidelines.

Since the second edition of *Mission-Based Marketing* was published in 2003, a great deal has changed, and yet the core issues and skills of marketing for a nonprofit have remained the same. There is more acceptance of nonprofit advertising, and of nonprofits using business skills to pursue their mission. There is the increasingly quick advance of technology in all facets of our lives. For certain things, such as printing your own marketing materials, it has reduced costs drastically; in other areas, such as maintaining an appealing and mission-valuable web site, it has increased costs in time, money, and the skill sets you need on staff. And, of course, there is increased competition for everything: good staff, good volunteers, donated dollars and goods, and, most importantly, grants, contracts, and people to serve.

As I write this, the world is (hopefully) starting to come out of the deepest financial crisis since the Great Depression. Thousands of nonprofits in North America have already closed, or are on the cusp of closing. Human services organizations are faced with unprecedented demand while funding from foundations, corporations, individuals, and governments has fallen. Arts organizations, on the other hand, are faced with too much capacity, as demand for tickets, classes, and the like have fallen simultaneously with outside funding. It's a hard time for all nonprofits—perhaps the worst of times.

On the other hand, legions of younger people have been raised in a volunteering culture, businesses are concerned about social impact in their community, and technology enables us to cobble together groups of supporters from all over the globe in a ridiculously short amount of time. The 2008 U.S. presidential campaign showed us all the incredible potential of large numbers of small donations, and the financial crisis we all face gives us a once-in-a-generation opportunity to reshape our organizations to focus on what we do best. Perhaps it's the best of times?

So, how should your nonprofit respond and move forward? Of course, you should always start with your mission. It's the reason your organization exists, and it's the most valuable asset you have in marketing. You also need to look at your values. While the mission is why your nonprofit exists, your values show you how you go about pursuing that mission. This is true in service provision, internal management, and, of course, marketing.

That's where we'll start, but there's much more in the following pages. I will show you how to react, respond, and reshape your organization into one that prospers using the best practices in today's nonprofit management. How? By becoming market oriented while remaining mission based; by using the well-established and time-tested methods of marketing to do more mission; by treating everyone who interacts with your organization like valued customers; by developing a team approach to marketing, where customer satisfaction is everyone's job; by asking all your customers what they want and trying your best to give it to them.

In my writing, lectures, and keynotes, I repeatedly contend that the skill of marketing is the most important business skill you can have to improve your mission capability and output. Many people are uncomfortable with the concept of marketing in a nonprofit because they see marketing as no more than crass sales. Sales (crass or not—your choice) is *one part* of marketing, but not the whole thing by any means. Here's the first takeaway of the book: Good marketing in a nonprofit is good stewardship, because good marketing enables more effective mission provision. Read on; I'll show you how to make this a reality in your organization.

In this initial chapter, we will look at why your world is "going competitive" and what the linkage is between competition and marketing. We'll look at who I have written this book for (the target market) and what the benefits are of reading the book and of investing your time with me. Finally, I'll give you a brief preview of each of the remaining chapters of the book so that you will know what the sequence of our time together will be like.

There is little if any rocket science in the following pages. But there are scores of solid, practical ideas on how to bring your organization into a marketing frame of mind that will keep you doing more and better mission for many years to come. In the chapters that follow, you will learn why marketing is so fundamental to your mission and how successful mission-based organizations are simultaneously market driven. You will view a marketing cycle and see how it can be adapted to your organization and your mission. You will learn how to identify and keep close to your customers, and how to identify and keep tabs on your competitors. You will see how technology has made marketing easier, cheaper, and much more challenging all at the same time. We'll walk through the key elements of incredible customer service and show you applications for your many and varied customers.

Marketing is not a discrete event with a beginning and an end. It is a continuing process, a cycle that becomes a discipline, part of your culture. To develop that culture may take months or even years in your organization, or it may be a very short journey. It will depend on your staff, your board, your funders, and your community, but most importantly on *you*, the reader. You will be the one who will have the tools to help the others cross the bridge from your current position to being mission based *and* market driven. It's a lot of work, but well worth it for your organization, your community, and the people you serve.

A Competitive and Always-Online World

Throughout the nonprofit community, the tide has been changing for the past decade. And, like tides, the changes are barely noticeable at first, and are more evident on some parts of the shoreline than others. But once the tide changes, the momentum is reversed and the outcome is irreversible. The forces at play are too big, too powerful, too global to resist.

In the nonprofit arena, just as in the rest of the world, the tide has changed and the trend is inexorably, irreversibly moving toward two things: more competition and ubiquitous technology. These two facts, both individually and in combination, are reshaping the way nonprofits do their work at every level, and make the need for rethinking your marketing more important than ever. Let's look at each separately, and then talk about what their combined weight will mean to your future.

Competition

This is not as new as it may seem at first glance. Your nonprofit has always competed—for the best staff, for great board members, for donated dollars. But more and more, you're also competing for people to serve. This is the result of two things: an increase in the raw number of nonprofits (particularly in the United States) and a change in funders' philosophy about our sector. Obviously, the more nonprofits there are, the more organizations there are needing boards, non-governing volunteers, funding, and staff. The issue of a change in funders' philosophy and its implications is a little more complicated.

Governments and foundations have come to the conclusion that competition works in the nonprofit world, and that freeing up this part of the economy produces lower-cost and better services just as in other sectors. And, as with other transitions from a restricted market to a free market, it always produces a market shakeout: Some organizations don't survive because they cannot adjust and compete.

I need to digress here for a moment. At the same time (1960–1990) that we were spending trillions of dollars fighting and ultimately winning the Cold War to keep the world safe for democracy and capitalism (or was it capitalism and democracy?), we prevented our nonprofit sector from benefiting from the open market. We had one of each kind of human services, or arts, or recreation nonprofit in each community and kept others out by not funding them.

 FOR EXAMPLE: Look at how we name our nonprofits: The Adams County Mental Health Center, Roanoke Symphony Orchestra, Denver Association of Retarded Citizens, Sacramento Animal Shelter. In our very names we declared a geographic monopoly for these groups and local donors, and then the United Ways and other funding entities kept out competition (by not funding other organizations), using the excuse of "duplication of services." ■

When you think about it, this is not only incredible, it's also very patronizing and demeaning to the nonprofits' staff and boards. It says, "We know you are nice folks, but you aren't very good managers and so you can't play by the same rules we do (the free market). But we need your services, so we'll protect you." It also resulted (sometimes) in less efficient and less flexible organizations getting funded.

In fact, in all of the major nonprofit arenas—the arts, research, the environment, human services, education, religion, and associations—only three areas were completely unfettered by this shackle of restricted markets: religion, private (usually higher) education, and associations. We see the best example of diverse organizations trying all kinds of ways to meet the diverse needs of the population in places of worship. With no restrictions on size, location, theology, or services, religion has become a truly diversified "industry," with an order and denomination (or "flavor" as my minister puts it) for everyone. Churches, temples, synagogues, and mosques are free to compete, and many choices have naturally evolved (no pun intended). Not so in the arts or in most human services, where most of the government money is spent. These groups have been, and in some cases still are, protected, and at a high price. And the good news (for some) and the bad news (for others) is the same: This protection is eroding as governments, stuck in a perpetual budget crunch, try to find new methods of paying for the increasing demand for social and educational services.

Part of this evolution has shown up in the outsourcing or privatizing of traditional government services, such as prisons or charter schools. As that action has become more and more accepted, funders have taken another look at how they currently fund the original "outsourcers"—nonprofit groups. The funders have realized that they can get more for less by allowing competition to enter previously sacrosanct areas, and, as long as their standards for quality are high, that it should be a win-win-win situation.

 FOR EXAMPLE: The federal government, long a bastion of continuing contracts, is now bidding most of its work annually, particularly in the human services area. They are looking more at outcomes than at process, and are allowing for-profits and nonprofits to bid on work that used to be set aside solely for nonprofits. ■

 FOR EXAMPLE: Ask any development officer of any organization whether the fund-raising arena is more or less competitive, more or less outcome-based, more or less driven by the needs and wants of the funder than it was 15 or 20 years ago. Their answer will be a resounding "Yes!" I recently saw an article that noted that the ratio of corporate dollars applied for to those granted went from 13,000:1 in 1995, to over 25,000:1 in 1999, and to nearly 50,000:1

(continued)

(continued)

by 2008. Certainly, the foundation staff that I know are deluged with applications from types of organizations that they had not even heard of five years ago. ■

This trend, from a taxpayer's or a donor's view, is good. We get more services, often of better quality, and usually for less money. And, competition should result in better mission on all fronts. But from the viewpoint of your nonprofit today, how does it look? Scary? Exciting? Dangerous? Like an opportunity? Probably a little of each.

One more note on the issue of competition before we tackle technology: Some funders, notably foundations and United Ways, and some academics in nonprofit management, have argued that there are too many nonprofits, that nonprofits that have similar mission should merge, and that, in general, we should consolidate the sector.

I could not disagree more.

I know I just told you that there's more competition, and that funders have found that services are better. But, it seems that with so many people knocking at the funders' doors, some have now looked out and said, "There are too many of you . . . go away." I am sure you've heard that history repeats itself. It is true here, too.

Let me tell you why forced consolidation is a *bad, bad, bad* idea. First, who among the funders can tell me how many nonprofits is enough? Which startup charity would they tell to close down? How can they tell which new organization will be the next Kiva, or the next Tom's Shoes, or the next Susan Komen Foundation, and which won't?

 FOR EXAMPLE: In the late 1970s, most existing low-income housing organizations *tut-tutted* the ridiculous idea of low-income residents helping build their own houses; and besides, they said, "We're already providing low-income housing services. This new group would surely reduce resources for everyone by sucking up much-needed funding. It should not be supported."

The nonprofit in question, of course, is still with us, and wildly successful. The world would be poorer without Habitat for Humanity, not richer. ■

Can you imagine a government telling Burger King or Hardees that there are too many fast-food restaurants, and that they should merge with McDonald's? Or Lowe's with Home Depot? Neither can I. But the situation is the same. With two home improvement stores in our community, we reduce the profits of each, stretch the resources of both, and—oh, yes—increase choice for the consumer, create jobs, and push both organizations to do better. Hmmm, and this is a bad thing?

New nonprofits push existing ones to make their case to donors with more passion, to provide new services, and to pay more attention to their communities and the people they serve. In marketing terms, by having competition, existing organizations need to stay in touch with their markets and give them more of what they want. This is a *good* thing, not a bad one.

Are some mergers and consolidations good in nonprofits? Of course, but only if *the nonprofits* decide they are, not some outside funder or government.

So, competition is good for mission—hard, exciting, and nerve-wracking, but good for mission. Now, let's look at our second trend, technology.

Technology

Let's start with the takeaway here: It is my passionate belief that the future of philanthropy is in the successful merger of mission and technology. This does not mean that we won't still hug people or read to second graders or counsel face to face. What it does mean is that nonprofits that do not *embrace technology for mission* will be less effective than they can be, and will perhaps fail.

Note that I said *embrace* technology. Not *accept* technology, not *use* technology, but rather wholeheartedly *embrace* technology for mission.

Nowhere is this more important than in marketing for your nonprofit. If you don't have an awesome web site, if you can't accept donations or guide people to volunteer opportunities online, if people can't deeply educate themselves about your organization's mission at your web site, or find out about careers in your organization online, you are excluding millions of people who will not, repeat *not, ever* pick up the phone or a piece of printed material. Good tech and good marketing go hand in hand in your nonprofit, and that's why we'll spend a whole chapter on technology.

More on both of these trends later, but let's revisit our initial metaphor: The tides have changed, and we need to adapt to the flow or perish. If your organization is not market driven, not ready for competition, not tech savvy, then these trends probably result in deep concern, as well they should. Hopefully, by reading this book and applying the ideas and techniques you will find here, you can turn the adversity into opportunity, and improve your organization's mission capability.

Who This Book Is Written For

This book is written for the management and board members of nonprofit organizations of all types. Whether your organization is in human services, environmental protection, the arts, education, religion, or an association, this book has something for you. And, if you want to promote your mission, hire better staff, get terrific volunteers, engage your community, provide better mission, increase your donations, and recruit and retain the best board members, this book will show you how.

Your organization needs to be more market driven, and, for many entities, that requires a culture change. Such changes are initiated only at the board and senior management level. And, changes of such importance need to be coached consistently over time to take hold. They need to be coached by those same board members and senior staff. Like so many other key facets of your nonprofit, good marketing needs to be led by example.

But, such cultural change will not be successful unless everyone in the culture adopts the new ideas, the new philosophy. As you will read over and over in the following pages, marketing is a *team* sport, and when one person doesn't play well the entire team loses. Thus it is essential that the key ideas in this book be transmitted to the entire team. As a former staff member, executive director, and board member of local, state, and national nonprofits, I try to provide ideas for all levels of your organization, not just for the executive director/CEO, or solely for the board. I believe that a strong marketing effort is put forth by a team—one of line staff, senior management, boards, and volunteers—since the more people there are who can see the ideas here, the easier and faster it will be to implement them.

The book is designed to give you practical advice on how to move your organization as a team toward a market-based philosophy. To help you, I have included dozens of real-world examples (which can be found by looking for the **FOR EXAMPLE** tag), and specific applications for you to apply, in some cases, the same day you read them (which can be found by looking for the **HANDS ON** tag). At the end of each of the following chapters, there is also a list of discussion questions that focus on the key points of the chapter. These questions are intended to help you generate discussion about the important issues raised in the book, and to provide a team forum to help you decide which ideas you can use right away, which will take some time, and which may not be appropriate for your organization.

The Benefits of Reading This Book

By buying and reading this book, I know that you are making an investment of time and money. So, what are the benefits of that investment? What will accrue to your organization? *I guarantee that you will get at least the following benefits from this book:*

- An understanding of why marketing is so crucial to being an effective mission-based organization

- An understanding of why marketing is so important to your continued competitiveness in every aspect of your nonprofit
- A new insight on what the marketing cycle is and how your existing and future services and customers fit into it
- A series of methods to help you and your staff treat everyone like a valued customer
- A clear understanding of the difference between needs and wants, which is crucial to a successful mission-based organization
- Ways to embrace technology in your marketing efforts at all levels of the organization
- Knowledge about the best ways to develop and conduct surveys and focus groups
- An understanding of how and why to write a marketing plan
- An understanding of why marketing principles are so important to more successful development efforts
- New insights on ways to improve your marketing materials (both paper and electronic) and focus them on your many markets
- An understanding, perhaps for the very first time, of who your markets really are
- A list of ways to provide excellent customer service
- Ideas on how to get your board and staff involved on your marketing team

By the time you finish reading this book you should have an excellent hands-on understanding of marketing, competition, and your role on the marketing team.

To get the most from this book, or from any management text, I strongly recommend that you read it as a team of board and staff. With team reading and team application, there is a much higher likelihood that the ideas included here will get implemented. That is why I have included the discussion questions at the end of the remaining chapters. Have your staff read the book, and then use the questions to generate a healthy discussion. Use their ideas to improve your efforts at all levels of the organization.

Preview of the Book

So now you know why you need to read this book, and what benefits will accrue to you because of your investment of time and money. But what is in the book? Let's look at how the book is constructed and then at a brief summary of the chapters.

I have split the book into two major areas. The first four chapters are really about philosophy and getting you to change your ideas about the intersection of marketing, competition, and your nonprofit mission. These chapters contain the big concepts, as well as some hands-on ideas for initiating needed changes in your organization.

Beginning with Chapter 5, we get into the more technical aspects of marketing and competition, including your markets, your competition, using technology, ways to ask, methods of improving your marketing materials, customer service, and developing a marketing plan. These eight chapters are the "how-to" part of the book, where I offer specific ideas to help you embrace the concepts provided in the first four chapters. Let's look at the chapters in more detail.

Chapter 1: Introduction

The present introductory chapter provides an overview, a method of getting the most from the book, and some focus for you on key nonprofit trends affecting your marketing efforts.

Chapter 2: Marketing: A Key to Better Mission

In this chapter, we will review why good, consistent marketing is a mission imperative. We will first review the seven characteristics of nonprofits that are truly market driven. You will see that market-focused organizations consistently meet customers' *wants,* not just their *needs.* You will get your first ideas on how to treat everyone (including your funders) like valued customers. We'll also take an initial look at how your organization can be better than your competition. Finally, we'll explore why marketing is truly a team effort and show you some ways to bring everyone in your organization onto that team.

Chapter 3: Being Mission Based and Market Driven

At some point your organization will be faced with a dilemma: Follow the mission or follow the market. What do you do? This chapter will deal with ways to decide what is the best path for your organization as well as for your own personal ethics and values. The chapter will cover how to move with the markets, but maintain your mission. I'll also show you how to delineate and then use core values to make staying on track easier. Another challenge is how to bring the rest of the staff and board along for the ride. This chapter will cover that by giving you some tools to motivate the staff and board, and will reiterate the six mission benefits of becoming and remaining market based and customer oriented. Also included are some suggestions for how to settle into the marketing culture for the long term.

Chapter 4: Being Flexible and Innovating with the Market

Flexibility is the key to marketing and competitive success. The wants of your markets will change—in unpredictable ways and not always on your schedule. This chapter will show you why you need to stay flexible, provide some examples of the pace of changes in the market, show you seven workable methods of becoming a change agent in your organization, and identify the ways that you can retain your organizational flexibility in the right-now environment.

Chapter 5: The Marketing Cycle for a Nonprofit

The cycle for marketing is endless, and it starts at a place that may surprise you. This chapter will show you in detail the proper sequence for marketing, and will also go through the marketing cycle of competitors. Additionally, we will review what may be the biggest barrier standing in your way to becoming a competitive marketer: the marketing disability of most nonprofit staff and boards.

Chapter 6: Who Are Your Markets?

In order to serve the many markets of your organization, you need to first know who they are. This chapter will walk you through the surprising process of market identification, and then will show you how to segment those markets to decide which ones you want to pursue most avidly. Once that is accomplished, it will be time for you to select and focus on target markets. The discussion here will show you how. You will see that you can use this technique both in the provision of mission and in your fund-raising activities. Finally, we'll make sure that you, your staff, and your board all understand why all of your markets (even your funders) should be treated like valued customers.

Chapter 7: Who Are Your Competitors?

The flipside of identifying your markets is to identify who is going after those markets—other than you. This is already occurring in fund-raising, volunteer recruitment, and hiring of good staff. How do you compete? You start by looking at your competition. This chapter will show you how to identify and continually monitor your competition. Then, we will review ways for you to focus on your core competencies so that you can successfully compete.

Chapter 8: Asking Your Markets What They Want

You need to give your markets what they want, within the constraints of your mission and marketing strategies. But you can't know what they want until you ask them. This chapter will cover asking in detail, including surveys, focus groups, informal asking (and common mistakes), and what to do after you ask. We'll talk about asking online, and how to ask your customers for key information about your competitors. Finally, you'll learn critical ideas on what to do *after* you ask.

Chapter 9: Better Marketing Materials

With as many markets as you have, it makes little sense to have just one or two pieces of marketing material. It makes even less sense to have those marketing pieces focus on your services rather than on your customers' problems. This chapter will show you some specific ideas on how to improve your marketing material, seven things to include in your material, seven things to *avoid* in your material, ways to customize your materials for various markets, and how to use the latest (inexpensive) technology to develop very focused and very inexpensive marketing materials.

Chapter 10: Technology and Marketing

If you need to embrace technology for mission, you certainly need to push your use of tech in marketing to the absolute limit. This chapter will show you how, starting with your web site and including discussion of online asking and social networking. Finally, since tech changes so quickly, I'll give you some great resources to use to keep current.

Chapter 11: Incredible Customer Service

When you have attracted people to your organization, whether as employees, volunteers, or consumers of your services, you need to keep them. To do that, you need to employ top-notch customer service methods. This chapter will reiterate the three core rules of customer service, show you how to empower all your staff to solve customers' problems *now,* help you instill the necessary attitude of what I term *compassionate urgency,* provide you with eight ways to do better customer contact, and show you tried-and-true methods of turning your customers into referral sources.

Chapter 12: A Marketing Planning Process

Like other key functions, marketing should be planned, with strategies, goals, and objectives. This chapter will show you how to develop your marketing team, plan your asking, target your marketing, and utilize the best current marketing planning software, and it will provide an outline that you can use as you develop your organization's marketing plan.

Recap

In this initial chapter, you have had your first exposure to the more competitive, always-online world in which your nonprofit serves. We have discussed ways of getting the most from the remainder of the book, and previewed the chapters for you.

There is no question that marketing and mission go hand-in-hand. If you don't know who your customers are, how can you find out what they want? If you don't know what they want, how can you attract and keep them as customers? The same holds true for staff, board, donors, and community support. You can't do much mission without them, and good marketing is the key to improving in these areas as well.

The challenge for you is to bring your organizational culture, which for a variety of valid historical reasons may have less than a fully focused marketing worldview, into a world where such an outlook is critical—essential to mission success and to organizational survival.

CHAPTER 2

Marketing: A Key to Better Mission

Chapter Thumbnail

➤ The Characteristics of a Mission-Based, Market-Driven Organization

➤ Meeting Customer Wants

➤ Treating Everyone Like a Customer

➤ What about Your Competition?

➤ A Team Effort

Overview

You have already read in Chapter 1 about the changing, increasingly competitive, and online world that your nonprofit organization will be working in for the remainder of your career. If you work for an organization that you consider competitive now, how can you stay ahead of the competition? However, as you look objectively at your organization, if you do not see a market-driven player, what do you do?

The answer to both questions is: You market. At its most fundamental level, marketing is the mission edge for nonprofits, and this chapter will start you on your journey to becoming a mission-based *and* market-driven nonprofit manager.

We'll begin with the seven characteristics of market-driven, mission-based organizations. These characteristics will allow you to look at your organization and discern some potential weak points that you can focus on as you read the remainder of the book. They are drawn from my experience with successful nonprofits in all parts of the nonprofit sector over three decades.

After we lay that groundwork, we will look at the difference between meeting needs and wants and show you a number of examples of how nonprofits are working hard to gear their services to wants instead of needs. Then, we'll go over tried-and-true methods of treating everyone, including your funders, like valued customers. Your attitude, and more importantly, your staff's attitude toward service recipients, donors, volunteers, and even other staff as customers is absolutely essential to your organizational transition.

Then we'll turn to ways to be better than your competition, and give you your first glimpse of how your competition views you and ways to measure yourself against competitors. Finally, I will show you how to start bringing everyone onto the marketing team. Marketing is everyone's job, not just for the executive director or the public relations manager.

By the time you finish this chapter, you will have a good initial handle on the principles that will guide the remainder of the book: that good marketers meet wants, not needs; that competitive organizations must market aggressively; that every one of the people in every one of your markets deserves and needs to be treated like a customer; and that everything that everyone does in your organization is marketing: Everyone is on the team.

The Characteristics of a Mission-Based, Market-Driven Organization

So, where do I want you to end up? How do I want your organization to eventually look? What comprises a market-driven, and yet mission-based, organization? Let's look at the seven characteristics of nonprofits that are successful at this difficult and challenging mix of high priorities. The characteristics listed here work together as a comprehensive whole. Don't delude yourself into thinking that if you pick 1, 3, and 7 you will be okay. You won't—you need to move toward complete implementation of *all* seven.

Nonprofits that are successful at marketing do the following:

1. Understand Their Markets

They realize that their markets extend beyond just the people whom they serve. They identify, quantify, and target the markets that they want to serve and can serve well. They study the markets as they are, and as they will be. They get to know the people who are in their markets, and constantly evaluate the regular changes in each market's wants. We'll investigate market identification and understanding in detail in Chapter 6.

2. Treat Everyone Like a Customer

Funders, board, staff, non-governing volunteers, and people who receive services are all thought of and treated like customers. Even difficult customers are treated as well as possible. Customer satisfaction, solving customer problems, and a sense of compassionate urgency are high priorities organization-wide. Customer satisfaction will be the subject of Chapter 11.

3. Have Everyone on the Marketing Team

They work hard to make sure that everyone, every staff person and every volunteer, knows that they are crucial to the success of the organization's marketing, its customer service, and its competitive edge. They know that the smallest mistake or indifference or lack of understanding can result in a lower perception of value from a particular market or customer. There will be more on the marketing team later in this chapter.

4. Ask, Ask, Ask, and Then Listen

You cannot know enough about what a customer wants until you ask, and ask regularly. Successful organizations shape their services to meet customer wants, and they are constantly asking so they can stay in tune with how those wants change and develop. We'll look at asking in depth in Chapter 8.

5. Innovate Constantly

They are flexible. To respond to constantly changing market conditions and customer wants, these organizations have to be extremely flexible, with staff and board encouraged to take reasonable risks on behalf of the people whom they serve. We'll look at innovation more closely when we consider flexibility in Chapter 4.

6. Promote and Protect Their Brand

They understand that their brand is crucial and that, in a low-attention-span world, brand recognition and a positive association with that brand is crucial to their mission success. They also protect their brand from abuse and infringement when necessary. We'll talk more about branding in Chapter 9.

7. Use Every Communication Medium Available

As this is written, nonprofits communicate through personal contact, paper materials, web sites, social networks such as Facebook, text messaging, phone calls, e-mail, and Twitter. By the time you read these words, those communications choices will have changed. Here's where the constant-innovation characteristic mentioned in point 5 meets the promotional part of marketing—you have to use all available media, not just those you are currently comfortable with. We'll discuss communications more in relation to your marketing materials in Chapter 9 and regarding technology in Chapter 10.

How do you feel your organization meets these benchmarks? If you feel pretty good about where you are, great! You will learn some excellent techniques about how to turbocharge your organization in the coming pages. If you feel that you don't measure up as well as you'd like, don't despair! All of the characteristics will be addressed in the remainder of the book with hands-on suggestions for you to implement.

Meeting Customer Wants

As I hope you have noticed, I have repeatedly used the term *wants* instead of *needs* when describing the target of your marketing interest. I have done this because there is a *huge* difference between needs and wants. You might do well to rethink your traditional view of working to meet customers' needs. What you must target is their *wants.*

Let me start by describing the difference between the two. We all have needs: to sleep, eat, breathe, work, socialize. We also have wants: chocolate, new clothes, time with our family, a new job. What is the difference? People *have* needs. People *seek* wants. There is no more fundamental concept for successful marketing than those six words: *People have needs; people seek wants.* Let's look at some examples of what I mean, for both wants and needs.

 FOR EXAMPLE: If you have ever had a friend, family member, or employee who abused alcohol or drugs to the point of becoming dysfunctional, you know that that person *needed* treatment, often intense and immediate treatment, long before he or she *wanted* it. In fact, everyone around the abuser—friends, family, employers, and neighbors—all knew what was *needed*. But as long as the abuser didn't *want* help, he or she wouldn't seek help. This is a sad example, but one that is played out every day in nearly every community. Wants rule. ■

FOR EXAMPLE: We all need water, or at least some liquid, to survive. In the United States, most of us get our drinking water from municipal water treatment systems or, in rural areas, from wells. Some systems have "hard" water, some "soft." But nearly all our water is safe to drink, and while the taste varies widely from system to system (as a frequent traveler I can attest to this fact), neither medical nor safety reasons mandate or even suggest that we avoid our tap water.

So why the incredible popularity of bottled water? This product is expensive, *unneeded,* yet obviously *wanted* by millions of American consumers, so much so that the product now comes in not only about 40 different brands, but five or six primary sizes and innumerable flavors. It's a case study in wants surmounting needs. Again, wants rule. ■

 FOR EXAMPLE: Think for a moment of a chocolate milkshake. Who needs one? Nobody. Who wants one? Millions of us, enough so that every major fast-food chain carries them, and in many other flavors and varieties. Those yummy wants get the better of us—and sometimes wind up as unwanted baggage around our waists! ■

 FOR EXAMPLE: I may have a need for transportation to school or work. But I decide from many choices which method of transportation I will purchase: car, truck, van, bus, motorcycle, bicycle, or rollerblades. And within those choices are many makes and models. I have a need, but I buy what I want, within my budget. In fact, many people *want* a particular car (that they don't *need*) so badly that they buy well above what they can afford. Again, wants rule. ■

I'm sure that you can come up with your own examples by the dozen of how people have wants that are not really needs, but for which they are willing to pay serious money. Now, what can you do to meet your customers' wants? How can you be competitive with other providers of services like yours or for each increasingly competed-for donated or earned dollar?

First you have to ask. The biggest mistake people make in marketing is saying, "I've been in this business twenty years and I know what customers want." That is almost never true. While I'll give your experience enough credence to admit you might know 70 percent of what your market wants, it's that last 30 percent that's constantly changing, that's focused on what people want *now,* that's the competitive edge. And you can't know that last

30 percent until you ask, and ask regularly. You need to develop a *culture of asking* in your nonprofit, and this cultural shift is so important that we will spend an entire chapter on ways to ask, when to ask, and how to ask.

Second, you listen, and try to meet as many wants as you can. This may mean providing services at new times, in different places, in new settings, or in different languages. Let's look at some examples.

 FOR EXAMPLE: Churches throughout the United States have developed more and more "family night" activities as well as expanded youth activities, and building the buildings to house them. Particularly popular are open gym times, volleyball and basketball leagues, family aerobics, and family activities. What wants do these activities meet? They address the wants of parents for a safe environment for their kids as well as a common ground for planned family interaction and time. Usually these activities have little if any religious content other than the location. Church and non-church members are welcome. The benefit for the church is straightforward: By meeting a want in the community they get people into their facilities, where inevitably some will take an interest and join the congregation. ■

 FOR EXAMPLE: Museums and zoos provide classroom "experiences" for elementary, junior high, and high schools. These traveling roadshows expose the students to art, history, archeology, and zoology in their schools. What are the wants that are met? Enhancements to the traditional curriculum without the cost (in both time and transportation) of a field trip. What are the benefits? Often the organizations are paid for this type of work, and it gets some of the kids interested enough in the museum or zoo to talk their parents into a visit. Fifteen years ago, you rarely saw these kinds of programs; now they are everywhere—because they meet a set of wants. ■

How did these organizations find out what their customers wanted? They asked, they observed, they read aggressively, they watched their competition as well as organizations that were not competing with them, and then they asked again. What they didn't do was assume that they knew what people wanted or, worse, what people *needed.*

Speaking of needs, we in the nonprofit world are so good at giving people what they need that we forget to worry about what people want. I call this the nonprofit *marketing disability,* and we'll cover it in detail in Chapter 5. Suffice it to say here that we have to break out of the mold of assuming that because someone needs something, or worse, because we "know" they need it or tell them they need it, that they will want it. Doing a needs assessment is not enough.

This brings up an interesting and important point. Once we diagnose, or test, or interview, or observe and decide what a person needs, many nonprofit staff have a moral and professional responsibility to see that the customer gets what he or she needs. Doesn't this negate the concept that you have to give people what they want? Not at all: Both the want of the customer and the responsibility of the professional can be met.

 FOR EXAMPLE: A psychologist has a patient who has been evidencing more and more erratic and sometimes self-abusive behavior. The standard medications and outpatient therapies are obviously not working, and the psychologist's professional opinion is that the patient *needs* inpatient treatment for weeks, if not months. Without the treatment, the patient may become suicidal or violent toward others. But the patient is an adult, and has the choice of being admitted or not admitted. And, at this point, he doesn't *want* to go into a treatment facility.

What should the psychologist do? All the professional knowledge of *need* is powerless in the face of the ability of the patient to follow his *wants*. But the psychologist does not turn away. She works to convince the patient that he *wants* to go into the facility. She does her best to turn the *need* into a *want*. By doing this, she is using an age-old marketing technique, the one that convinces people that they really want a product or, in this case, a service. The technique is called *sales*. ▪

I would not be surprised if you or others in your organization were uncomfortable with the idea of marketing, and this is often because "marketing" is often equated with "sales." While incorrect, this assumption leads to concerns about marketing being crass. "We are better than that," I've heard often throughout the nonprofit sector. "Our mission is so important, we don't have to sell it."

To help you get past this speed bump, let me describe needs and wants another way, one that may ease the discomfort a bit: For-profit organizations can and do spend marketing dollars to make us want what we don't need. We don't really *need* a new car (or SUV) every three years. My daughter doesn't *need* to wear only clothes from The Gap or Limited. No one, not even my wife, *needs* chocolate. Such mixing of needs and wants is understood and accepted in the free market. Buyer beware.

The difference between for-profit marketers and nonprofit marketers is crucial: Whereas for-profits make people want what they *don't* need, nonprofit marketers should always strive to make people want what they *do need*.

See the difference? And, just as importantly, do you see that the skills required are essentially the same? Good marketing *is* good mission. Organizations that have good marketing skills can do better mission. And it all starts with understanding—and accepting—the difference between needs and wants.

Work with your staff to help them understand that no matter how correct they are about needs, customers have the right to want something. Show them that marketing, turning needs into wants, can lead to *more* mission, not less.

This realization that people seek wants, even people whom we serve, is the first step in treating everyone like a customer, which is the subject of the next section.

Treating Everyone like a Customer

This is such an important concept that I will dwell on it more than once. Successful and competitive organizations realize that everyone in and out of the organization needs to be thought of as a valued customer (even if and when that customer is wrong). This is often tougher for nonprofits, for a variety of reasons that we should review.

The nonprofit community is the only market that I am aware of that often thinks of its biggest customer as the *enemy*. Those of you with a major percentage of funding from foundations or local, state, or federal governmental sources will know what I am talking about: You may well look at these payers as organizations to do battle with, to lobby with, to argue with. This perspective is, to put it mildly, shortsighted. The people who *pay you* are *customers*, and deserve to be treated that way. They may be the customers from hell, but they are still customers.

 HANDS ON: Look at your organizational attitude right now. Get out your income and expense statement. Look at your four largest sources of income. Now think of the people at those organizations with whom you deal the most. Is your image of them that of a valued customer or a pain in the neck? Are they, in your opinion, an opportunity to serve—or a barrier to service? For a real litmus test, consider this question: When was the last time someone from your organization visited that funder in her office and asked her "How can I make your job easier?" Not "Give us more money!" or, "Cut back on the ridiculous oversight," or "Don't make us prove what we do," but "How can I make your job easier?"

If you just laughed out loud and wondered why *anyone* would do that—it's exactly what the for-profit marketers do with their most difficult and most loyal customers: Solve their problems and make their jobs easier. What about you? ■

Now let's look at the other side of the ledger—the people whom you serve. If you are like most nonprofits, you don't call these people *customers*, which is fine. You call them *students, patrons, consumers, clients, patients, parishioners, recipients, tenants, the congregation*. Such labels are fine. However, if the labels are joined to an attitude that doesn't acknowledge that these people are also customers, and also have opinions that should be listened to, you've got trouble.

A competitive, market-oriented organization, whether for-profit or non-profit, thinks of *everyone* outside the organization, and as well as those *inside* the organization, as customers. We'll discuss this at greater length in Chapter 6, after we identify all your markets and their differing wants. Then, I'll show you how to provide every customer with "incredible customer service" in Chapter 11. For now, just remember (and begin to preach to your staff and board) that in today's environment *everyone* is a customer, and that those organizations that fail to appreciate this truth will not do as much mission as those that do. The techniques of marketing will help you tremendously in this effort, but the attitude that funders, staff, board, and the people you serve are truly customers has to come first, and it has to be believed, reinforced, and, like so many values, led by example— by you.

What about Your Competition?

But what about the other guys? In a noncompetitive environment, you don't need to worry about competition. Either there isn't any or there isn't much and you really are protected by your funders from worrying about the market's whims and changes. But this is no longer the case. Not only do you have to pay attention to your markets, ask what they want, and give it to them (as we will detail in Chapter 8), you have to compete for the good graces of your customers with other organizations that are trying to lure them away from you.

Competitors come in all shapes and sizes, provide great and innovative services and awful ones, have lots of money and are broke. For many nonprofits, competitors are other nonprofits—for donors, for the best staff, for great board members. For some, competitors are government organizations or for-profits. Obviously, knowing the competition is a critical component of both marketing and becoming competitive, and we'll spend an entire chapter (Chapter 7) just on this subject. Right now, I want to make two important points about marketing and your competition.

First, the competitive marketing skills you will learn by reading this book will go a great distance toward helping your organization maximize its effectiveness in a competitive market. This goes for fund-raising as well as service provision, and for employee retention just as much as for community outreach.

You can out-research, outsell, out-produce, outsmart, and be more responsive than your competition (even really well-run organizations) if you apply what you learn in these pages. However, if you ignore the marketing part of your job, if you don't ask your markets what they want, if you just decide that what you are doing is fine and that you know what's best for all the people you serve, then even the sloppiest competitor that applies some marketing smarts is going to eat your lunch. You can be better than your competition if you pay attention to what they are doing, if you innovate, and if you are willing to be flexible as the market changes. Most importantly, you need to be better than your competition—not just in your eyes, but *in the eyes of your customers.*

 FOR EXAMPLE: Assume you are trying to retain your physical therapy staff (which, for readers not familiar with the human services arena, is a *very* tough job; there are many more jobs than there are therapists). You check around and find that your salary is very competitive, and your fringe benefits are great. You thus assume that you are competitive, that you are giving the customers (in this case, the therapists) what they want. And then they leave for jobs at a *lower-paying* competitor. Why? Because the competitor has traditionally invested in regular staff training and has the best therapy equipment, which is what your therapists value. Why didn't you know this? Because you didn't ask; you assumed that money was the issue. You were better than your competition on the financial scale, but not on the scale that was important to the therapists: training and equipment. You lose, and more importantly, so do the people your organization serves. ∎

My second point is that you need to preach (or, if you are already there, regularly reinforce) the underlying philosophy with your staff that it is necessary to *compete.* Many nonprofit line staff, mid-management, and even senior staff feel that they are professionals and thus it is unseemly, undignified, and somehow *dirty,* to compete. "That's the director of marketing's job. I just do what I am trained for." "If I go after other organizations' clients (patients, customers, students, members), I will not only sully my reputation, I will anger all my friends at that organization." Does this sound familiar?

This was fine and honorable thinking in the past, but it's deadly in the current environment. Attitudes like that will keep staff from believing that they are on the marketing team; it will keep them from accepting the need for flexibility, accommodation, and rapid change to meet customers' wants; it will impede their thinking of everyone as a customer. And, since marketing is a team sport, it will cause the team to do poorly as a whole.

 HANDS ON: For many readers, this will be a tough cultural change. Here is how to start: Talk to staff in groups of 8 to 10 about the changes in the business environment, and demonstrate how what you have done in the past is competitive, and discuss how your environment is becoming even more competitive. Show them who your competition is and how the competition can now take away customers, clients, volunteers, and donated dollars. If you have had staff or customers leave (or not return) recently, use them as case studies. Then ask, "How can our organization respond?" Let the staff (hopefully) come to the realization that marketing and competition, while difficult and perhaps distasteful, is the only way that your organization is going to survive to *continue to do more mission.* As with so many other discussions of change, if you can emphasize the mission connection, that marketing is good mission—that competing is good mission—you will have a much better chance of convincing the skeptics. Repeat the exercise for the whole staff, and as you go through your sessions, note which staff are on board and which are holding back. Encourage the people who are buying in to coach and cajole their hesitant peers. Remember that cultural changes like this take time, and that slow and steady repetition, reminders, and training are the essential tools. In Chapter 3, I'll provide you with seven specific ideas on how to motivate and bring along your board and staff. ■

Repeat after me: *Competing is not bad. Competing is not immoral.* Competing means continuing to be there to do good works. Competing makes us better. Competing means doing more mission, in a more focused and effective way. But in the new, more competitive environment, you have to believe in your mission, your skills, and the quality of your outcomes enough to be *willing* to compete. Remember when you were called back inside from recess in grade school? Did you run faster to the door when you were alone or when you were racing one of your friends? Me too; competition does that—it pushes us to achieve things we couldn't on our own.

One other note: Competition does not always result in military analogies: conquest, vanquishing, total victory. Often it means carving out enough market share, enough customers—more importantly, enough of the customers that you can serve the *best*—to keep you financially healthy, innovating, and prospering in your mission provision.

You do not have to be predatory to be competitive. But you do have to be proud enough of what you and your organization do to *not be ashamed* to tell the customers of another organization how good you are.

 FOR EXAMPLE: An excellent demonstration of this is in America's places of worship. I have long contended that they provide an excellent example of what nonprofits can do where the free market exists. No United Way, foundation, or government funder says, "There are too many churches in this community; we have duplication of services." And thus we have lots and lots of spiritual choices, with more springing up every day.

I know a lot of ministers, rabbis, and priests. All of them devoutly believe in their place of worship's theology. Few of them would think of themselves as competitive (except against evil), but in truth all of them are competing to attract and retain members for their congregation. When we lived in Illinois, the church we attended completed a major building project, moving into a new sanctuary after four years of construction. In the first weeks that we were in the new facility, we had many more visitors than normal, as people came to see the new building. Our minister used the opportunity to give a series of sermons on "What We Believe," detailing the key points of our denomination's value structure. While he never derided other churches, he was performing another age-old marketing ritual—product definition. *Look everyone, here is what makes us different. We believe in it and we hope you will. If you share our beliefs, come join us.* ■

Were our minister's words from the heart? Absolutely. Was it sales? Without a doubt. Was the minister moving the mission of the church forward? Yes; you see, marketing does not have to be flackery. Just because you believe something deeply, that does not prohibit you from selling it, and to deny that you are selling is simply self-delusion. Once you accept marketing as mission promotion, you can study marketing (as you are doing by reading this book) and use the techniques to promote more mission. Once you realize that striving to be the best does not necessarily mean boasting about being better than your competition, you will have made the first big psychological leap toward becoming a mission-based competitor.

But you can't do that alone. You need help, and that comes from your staff, board, and volunteers. Let's look at their impact, and how you can get them to move with you toward a market-oriented future.

A Team Effort

You've heard this a lot already, but not enough: Marketing is a team sport. And, since competition is most often a win-lose proposition, your team wins or loses together. One of the major mistakes that noncompetitive organizations (both for-profit and nonprofit) make is allowing any of the employees to think that their job has nothing to do with marketing. These are the organizations where you call with a question and are left on hold for half an hour only to be connected to the wrong person, who says they know nothing about your problem. These are the restaurants that cannot accommodate someone with a special dietary need. These are the airlines where the baggage handlers are rude, or the grocery stores where the staff send you on wild goose chases looking for products that the store doesn't even stock.

The truth is that *marketing is everything that everyone in your organization does every day*. It is the way that the phone is answered, the grass is cut, the e-mail inquiry is handled, the building is maintained, the bills are paid, the bills are collected—not just how the services are provided. It is the way that customers' problems are solved, the way inquiries are followed up, and the way that the staff interact with each other. All staff need to develop a perspective that what they do, and how they do it, affects the whole team, not just the people within their immediate field of vision.

 FOR EXAMPLE: For those who cling to the idea that the senior management alone is responsible for organizational marketing, consider this: When you interact with a business organization, an airline, hotel, car rental agency, restaurant, or quick-lube shop, who do you come in contact with? What kind of people are responsible for ensuring that you are a well-served, happy customer? It's the *lowest-paid people in the organization,* that's who. At the airline, it's the reservation agent, counter staff, and flight attendant. At the hotel, it's the desk clerk, housekeeping, and restaurant servers. At the car rental agency, it's the bus driver, counter staff, and check-in staff. At all of these organizations, it is the people on the bottom of the organizational ladder who make or break your experience with the company. If any one of them screws up, the entire experience takes on a bad taste.

And, in each of these cases, there are people, also in the lowest-paid tier, who *never see customers,* but who also affect their satisfaction. For example, at a car-rental agency, the people who clean the cars and service them are critical. Get into a dirty car, or have a breakdown on the road, and you will not be a happy camper. At the airline, the baggage handlers, the operations

(continued)

(*continued*)

staff, and the aircraft service crews all go about their work anony-
mously, but have enormous impact on customer satisfaction. The
gate agent may bump you up to first class, and the pilot and flight
crew may get you to your destination on time (or even early!), but
if the baggage crew doesn't get your luggage on your flight, or if
they trash your bags, how happy will you be? ■

So, it is not just the people who deliver the service, nor is it the top
management who are in charge of marketing. Everyone is on the team,
everyone has impact, even those who don't deliver the mission in person.

But even though all your staff are on the team, many may not want to
be members. What do you do about them?

 HANDS ON: Some of your staff may not get the fact that they are
on the marketing team, or, as I say, they may not want to. They
will fear yet another addition to their job description, a function
that they aren't sure that they understand: marketing. Assure them
that they are probably doing many of the things that they need
to already. Are they polite and helpful to the people you serve?
Do they try to solve their problems? Are they making suggestions
to you about what they hear from customers? Are they watching what other organizations like yours are doing and bringing
the ideas to the table? Are they continuing to read and learn
about innovations in your field? All of these things are part of
the marketing continuum. The greatest resistance to being on the
marketing team that I see is people who assume that they will
have to *sell*. My advice is that you specifically tell your staff that
it isn't that their job will change, it is just that everyone needs to
realize that everything they do *matters,* both in terms of mission
and in terms of marketing. Helping your employees to understand
how their job impacts the organizational mission is crucial to both
better customer satisfaction and their own job satisfaction. So, it's
a win-win. ■

The question is this: Do your staff know, understand, and *believe* that
their actions affect the entire organization? If they do, then the way that they
do their job, their attitude and commitment, will carry them. If they don't,
no amount of marketing technique or training will help.

 FOR EXAMPLE: My late sister was a woman with severe mental
retardation who lived for 20 years in a small group home in northwest Connecticut. When I visited her at home, I looked at many
things: What was the physical condition of the building and the

yard? How well-dressed, clean, and healthy did *all* of the residents look (not just my sister)? How helpful were the staff to me, and to the residents? And, how did the staff get along with each other? All of these things were going through my mind before, during, and after a visit. So, a staff person who thinks I would be happy if my sister was neat, well-dressed, and happy (all of which were, of course, important to me) would have missed the boat if the rest of the indicators I listed were broken. Whereas the staff may not have agreed with me that whether the lawn was mowed or not mattered, it did (and still does) to me (as I believe that maintenance of a property is an indication of organizational commitment to total quality), and what *I* wanted as the customer is the bottom line. ■

Remember, the customer's *perception* of quality is what ultimately counts. In Chapter 5, we'll discuss the marketing disability that most non-profit staff suffer from—a disability that makes it hard to focus on what the customer wants. Your staff may be ignorant of how customers perceive your organization, or they may feel that, since no one has complained, customers are happy. This is another big mistake, and another reason to ask.

 HANDS ON: To get an idea of how customers perceive your organization, try this. *Phase One:* Find a good friend who can act as a potential consumer. Arm him with a few key questions, such as: "What services do you offer? What kind of payment do you accept? What are your fees? Are you accessible to people with disabilities? Do you have references that I can call? Why should I join (come, purchase, etc.)?" Have the friend first call your organization, and carefully record what happens from the most critical viewpoint possible. How many rings did it take before the phone was answered? How long was it before the caller was connected with someone who knew this basic information? If the caller was promised a call back, or was told information would be sent via snail-mail or e-mail, was he ever called, did the material ever arrive, and did it answer his questions? Was there follow-up? Ask your friend, "Based solely on this interaction, would you pursue using our services further?"

Phase Two: Have the friend present himself at your organization's door, asking the same questions, perhaps being a bit difficult, or asking unusual questions. Again, debrief the friend to find out the result of the visit. Was the information given in person and over the phone the same? What did you think of the part(s) of the facility you saw? How were you greeted? With a smile and a

(continued)

(continued)

welcoming word, or as if you were interrupting something *really* important (like the receptionist's coffee break)?

If you want, add questions for staff that would target a new market that you are after. For instance, if most of your clientele is paid for by Medicaid and you want to move toward people who are covered by private insurance, have your friend present himself as a "covered life." Try to have him pose a slightly different question, and see how your people respond.

Phase Three: If your wonderful friend is up to it, have him present his experience (good or bad) to your management team or marketing committee in person. Try to have him explain his perspective on the interaction. This is a scary but valuable exercise. You and your staff will learn a lot, and you will gain important insight into how things look on the other side of the admission desk or entryway. It will also reinforce the fact that everyone is on the marketing team, all the time. ■

What about your board members, and your other volunteers? Are they on the team? Of course; boards are representatives of the community to your organization, and they are also ambassadors back to the community. How they act and interact is important, both at board meetings and elsewhere. Volunteers are also involved in many key tasks—ones that, if done well, enhance the mission and the reputation of the organization. But they also can be done badly, or with a poor attitude, or with the feeling of "I'm just a volunteer...."

 FOR EXAMPLE: In the mid-1990s, good friends of ours began looking for a new church. Their current church had grown too big for them, and they focused their search on smaller, more intimate congregations. Denomination was not as important to them as how much opportunity there was to get to know the people, to participate in community outreach, to sing in an active choir, and to have group discussions rather than lectures in Sunday School classes. Over lunch, I asked the couple which churches they were considering, and they rattled off four or five that they had visited, and two or three more that were on their list. I suggested one more church that was in the geographic area of their search and met many of their criteria, and got an immediate and vehement response: "No way, their board of elders is the most divisive, political group we have seen. We know three couples there and they constantly talk about the infighting at the governance level and how much friction and tension there is." That church, despite its small size, active volunteer program, and excellent music ministry, was a nonstarter. Why? Because the board couldn't get its act together. ■

Everyone is on the marketing team—the executive director, the receptionist, the janitor, the volunteer, and everyone in between. Make this your mantra. Repeat it until you, your staff, and your board instinctively act that way.

Recap

In this chapter, we have covered some key preparatory ground. We first looked at the seven characteristics of a market-driven, mission-based organization:

1. Know your markets.
2. Treat everyone like a customer.
3. Have everyone on the marketing team.
4. Ask, ask, ask, and then listen.
5. Innovate constantly.
6. Promote and protect your brand.
7. Use every communication medium available.

After this initial benchmarking, we went over why marketing and all of its components are such a critical edge in the increasingly competitive world you will inhabit. We then discovered the core truth about marketing: *People have needs, but people seek wants.* Meeting needs is not enough in a competitive world. Finding out what the wants are and meeting them should be your organization's focus from this day forward. We also discussed the ways that you can turn a need into a want, a particularly important skill for some readers.

Next, we looked at ways to change your mind-set about some of your markets so that you can develop a culture where everyone is treated like a customer. This includes your funders, which I acknowledge may be a stretch for many readers. We went through your internal and external markets and discussed why all of them are customers.

We then turned to the issue of your competition, and why "better" needs to be defined by your customers, not just by you. I showed you some examples of how organizations that compete do not have to be predatory, but how all of them have to meet wants by listening to their markets and responding.

Finally, we discussed how marketing is first, last, and always a team sport. Everyone in your organization must play, and be aware that they are always playing, if you are to compete successfully. In a competitive world, there is no sideline, no injured reserve. Everyone is always on.

Mission-based organizations can use marketing as their mission edge. The tools you will find in the rest of this book can help you do more mission, more efficiently, more effectively. And remember that your competition will make your organization a better one, but only if you survive to get better. Good marketing will give you the edge, and the time—not merely to survive, but to thrive. Effective marketing is not just haphazard selling. You need to move your organization from what may well be its current monopoly status (or attitude) to being market based. That's not easy, but it needs to begin now. It's the subject of the next chapter.

Discussion Questions

1. How does our staff view marketing? How can we make ourselves more market driven while remaining mission based?
2. Do we have some, all, or any of the characteristics of a market-driven organization? Which ones? How can we improve against this benchmark?
3. Do we meet needs and wants, or just one or the other? Do our staff and board know the difference between needs and wants?
4. Can we really compete? Are we of a mindset to be competitive? Do we say, "Oh, no!" or "Bring it on!" when confronted with a competitor? Do we understand all the ways we currently compete?
5. What percentage of our staff and board and non-governing volunteers understand that everyone needs to be on the marketing team? How can we improve/maintain that percentage?

CHAPTER 3

Being Mission Based and Market Driven

Chapter Thumbnail

➤ Which Is Right, the Market or the Mission?

➤ Moving with the Market and Maintaining Your Mission

➤ The Never-Ending Marketing Cycle

➤ The Results of Becoming Market Driven

➤ Motivating Board and Staff

➤ Holding On to Your Core Values

Overview

As you read this, you are probably in one of two positions. You are ready to move toward becoming market driven, convinced that a competitive and increasingly online marketplace is here to stay and that the only way for your organization to survive is to listen and respond to the marketplace. Or, you are still hesitating, unsure of whether becoming market driven is the right thing for your organization at this time, unconvinced that you can bring your board and staff along.

In both cases, you should be asking these questions: Can we *really* be both mission based *and* market driven? Can my organization be responsive to the whims, trends, and even the folly of the marketplace and still be considered true to our mission? Can we even hold onto our identity, much less our core values, over time?

All of these are important questions, and ones that I want you to carefully consider, even if you are convinced that market-driven operations are the path to the future for your organization. In this chapter, we will discuss them, and give you some tools for wrestling with these dilemmas as they come up, because they will. Today, tomorrow, next week, or next year, you will have a market opportunity that pulls you away from your mission. What will you do? Now is the time to set the guidelines.

First, we'll look at which of the two powerful forces is correct: the market or the mission. One is always right, but one should be your focus and your guide, and I'll show you which is which. Then we'll look at a number of examples of nonprofits that have moved with the market while maintaining their mission, and use their experiences to guide you as you proceed. You will see how some organizations adapted their mission to the market, and how others bent the market wants to meet their core mission.

Also in this section, we'll review the important ways that you can use your mission to strengthen your market-driven efforts and to keep you on course. Next, I'll show you why the marketing cycle never really ends; why you never truly satisfy all the market wants; and how you can constantly challenge yourself, your staff, and your organization to attain new heights of quality and customer satisfaction.

We'll continue by figuring out how to make sure that your board, staff, and volunteers are enthusiastically contributing to the transition. You need to motivate them, and I'll show you how. Then, we'll examine the positive results of becoming market driven while continuing to be mission based. This list will be one that you will want to discuss thoroughly with your board and staff, as will our next topic, the results of staying where you may be now, a service-based organization. Finally, we'll go beyond the mission, to your core values. Each organization has them, and you should be able to list yours and refer to them often as you try to ensure that you don't stray too far from what you believe. Here, too, we'll look at some examples of organizations that had to decide whether to accept the market wants or to say no.

By the time you are through with this chapter, you will be able to start the transition to being mission based and market driven, which I believe is crucial to your organization's continued survival and ability to continue providing its important mission.

Which Is Right, the Market or the Mission?

If your organization moves toward the market, if it listens to what the market wants, some day, some week, some month you will be confronted by a market want that conflicts with your mission, your organizational history, or even your personal values. What are you to do? What should be your guide? Which, in such a conflict, is "right"—the market or your mission?

Let me put it as succinctly as I can in three sentences:

1. The market is *always* right.
2. The market is *not always right for you.*
3. The *mission* should be your organization's ultimate guide.

The market wants what it wants, and there is no denying it, no ignoring it, no *trying to make it not so.* The people whom you serve want what they want, but you can, and in some cases *should,* give them only so much. The people who fund you want what *they* want, but you can, and in some cases *should,* give them only so much—even to the point of turning down their money.

And here is the point: *The choice is always yours as an organization.* You can choose not to meet a market want whenever you feel that it is in conflict with your organization's mission or values, or that trying to meet the want would mean providing a subpar service. And, further, you have to evaluate whether such a market move is in conflict with your personal values and ethics.

 FOR EXAMPLE: A good friend of mine was the director of patient education for a set of rural health centers in the Southwest. As she did her market surveys, talked to patients and community members, and reviewed data from focus groups, she repeatedly saw that the community was concerned about a rapid rise in teenage pregnancies and what seemed to be an epidemic of girls dropping out of high school to care for their babies. She brought this information, along with the other identified concerns, to her marketing committee and eventually to the board of directors.

The board decided to expand the organization's already broad educational role in the community by working with the community's public and private schools to offer more effective classes and counseling on pregnancy prevention, to both boys and girls. This supported the organization's mission of primary care prevention, treatment, and community education, and its core value that prevention was a priority. This was fine with my friend. The idea was good, it was something that she could do well, and the board had given her the resources she needed.

But the board had added one point she could not abide. In working with the teens, the board directed (after a long and acrimonious debate) that *all* options should be discussed—that all choices, including terminating an unwanted pregnancy, should

(continued)

(continued)

be presented objectively and without endorsement. My friend has very strong personal feelings about abortion, and she stated that she could not endorse, encourage, present, or even develop such a presentation. After a great deal of personal soul-searching, she resigned her position. ■

Whether or not you agree with my friend on the very controversial subject of abortion, you have to admire her willingness to sacrifice her job to preserve her own sense of morals, ethics, and values. Two key markets, the board and the community, had indicated their wants, so the market had spoken. The board's method of meeting the community's wants was not the only choice, but it was the option that they selected. And my friend thought it through and said, "I cannot, in good conscience, do that."

My point here is that if you find yourself being drawn into territory where you feel uncomfortable, stop. Talk it through with friends, coworkers, family members, or a spiritual counselor. Don't let the market drag you into a place where you no longer feel good about yourself. As a nonprofit manager, you have to feel good about what you do; you must exude enthusiasm and commitment to the mission to do your job well. It is that selfless, idealistic energy that makes nonprofit staff special. It's that same enthusiasm and commitment that gets the organization over the hurdles and barriers it confronts, and that keeps everyone on the team we discussed in the last chapter. If you feel you are being forced into a position of doing something wrong, even if your competition is doing it, even if the markets are screaming for it, you will lose that edge—that extra effort, extra sacrifice—you are now willing to make to pursue your mission. Don't lose that by following the markets into a dark place. You *can* say no. Others, in other organizations, will be there to meet the want, and that's fine. You need to do, first and foremost, what you feel is *right*.

That having been said, how do you decide? Look at the sequence shown here. Use these checkpoints to assure yourself that you are not being drawn into a place that is wrong for you or your organization:

Checkpoint 1: How does this change fit with our organizational mission and values?

Checkpoint 2: How does this change fit with my personal ethics and values?

Checkpoint 3: How does this change coincide with and support our organizational strategic plan? Can we do this well?

Notice that the first checkpoint is your mission, the second checkpoint is your personal values, and the third is an organizational capability check.

While I think that this is an appropriate ordering, you really can answer the questions in any order, because if you find that the answer to *any* of them is negative, you should not proceed. So if you are more comfortable putting the personal issues first, that's fine. If you feel that they should be the final checkpoint, then that works as well. Just check *all of them*.

> **HANDS ON:** For a new service or even a major service expansion, run through the following checklist:
>
> - Does this action support our mission?
> - Does it support or conflict with our organizational values?
> - Does it support our strategic planning goals and objectives?
> - Does the action wind up with net income or net cost? If it is a loss center, can we afford it?
> - Is this something we can do well?
> - Is this action something I can personally support?
>
> If there are other issues that are important to you, add them to the list. Go through the list considering the mission, values, and ethical issues carefully. ■

The bottom line in this discussion is that, to be effective, you need to move with the markets whenever you can, but you need to use your mission, your values, and your personal ethical compass to guide you and set appropriate limits.

Don't let your mission be the excuse to *never* change. Something new or different is not by definition *anti-mission*. If you hear yourself saying, "We've never done it that way," that doesn't mean you shouldn't. *Use* your mission, don't hide behind it.

Moving with the Markets and Maintaining Your Mission

So what are some practical ways to move with the market and still maintain your mission? The most important skill in this area is learning how to say "no" to a good idea, and even to a real need. Even though a market may want you to provide a service, you need to back away if you can't do it well, or if doing the service would jeopardize everything else you are doing. More and more nonprofits are learning that they cannot be all things to all people, that they cannot solve all the problems in their community, and that they need to focus on what they do well and what they can afford, and not just chase every dollar out there.

FOR EXAMPLE: How often has your organization faced a dilemma like this: You are awarded a $1 million contract for services. Not often enough, you say? Well, read on. Let's assume that the contract is for one year, and is designed to reimburse all your costs, and thus is a financial breakeven. The funder wants you to start the first of next month. You have no startup expenses and can just open your doors on the first day and start doing business. (Having no start-up costs would be *extremely* unusual, but it makes the example more understandable.) You will bill the funder monthly on the first of the month and the funder will take 45 days to pay. Is this great, or what? Only if you have $125,000 to invest. That's the cost of the contract for the 45 days that you have to operate before the funding kicks in. You are lending the funder $125,000 *interest-free* for the year of the contract—real money that really disappears for that time.

What do you do? The markets (the funder and the service recipients) really want this contract to take place. It supports your mission. But it does not support your organizational value of at least breaking even on every piece of work, and your strategic planning goal of not letting your cash on hand drop below 40 days' operating expenses. Since this contract does not recognize the expense of the "loan" to the funder, you lose money (the opportunity cost or interest that you can earn on the $125,000 for the year). And the use of that money to finance the contract draws down all your cash reserve. ■

The market said "move." The mission said "move." But your values and goals said "stop." Frankly, this problem confronts nonprofits every day. Should you take the money or not? The market says "yes." What do you say?

A second challenge in following the market is that you may not realize the problem until you are already deeply involved with the market change. None of us can predict the full outcome of implementation of new methods of service, different payment methods, or new strategies for identifying and meeting community needs.

 FOR EXAMPLE: In the health-care field, managed care puts health-care providers into the incentive/risk loop, pushing them to keep people healthy and to treat them faster, with more outpatient care. It is a payment strategy that has literally swept away old concepts in medicine and dramatically changed the relationship between providers, insurers, employers, and patients. Managed care has moved the markets—seismically.

Most hospitals and physicians grudgingly accepted managed care, convincing themselves that the quality of care would not suffer too greatly. And they jumped into programs wholesale. The managed care intermediaries looked first at where the greatest savings were to be found, and it was easy to identify hospital inpatient costs as a huge percentage of overall health-care expenses, and a place where significant savings could be quickly realized. So admissions were questioned, stays were shortened, and the hospitals and physicians went along.

Then the insurers crossed an invisible "morality" line, one that no one could have foreseen: They started limiting new mothers to 24, even 18, hours in the hospital after the birth of a child. This policy generated a huge number of complaints, which were picked up by the media and outraged the public. Money had overcome basic mission, and people were angry. But what could the hospitals and physicians do? They were contractually obligated to follow the managed care intermediary's rules. Yet they felt morally and mission obligated to do *something*. Some hospitals let mothers stay and didn't charge for the extra day or two. But there is only so much uncompensated care that any hospital can absorb. So, the hospital and medical industries lobbied Congress and state legislatures to change the law and set low-end limits that everyone could live with. They met their mission benchmark, the market want of their patients, *and* the market want of the funding intermediary. ■

Your next challenge is to make sure that when you move with the market, you don't lose your organizational identity. If you move too far afield from the service, group, or community that people identify you with, you can put your organization into a bind, particularly in fund-raising and board recruitment. No one will know who you really are; no one will be able to join you to a core cause.

 FOR EXAMPLE: United Ways are a great example of this. Originally formed to provide a collaborative fund-raising organization for most nonprofits in a community, many United Ways have sought to expand beyond what the public perceives as their role. Most United Ways did this in response to requests from their communities' nonprofits; some did not. But the result is a hodgepodge of United Way services, such as training, technical assistance, consulting groups, and even acting as de facto community foundations. The result in many towns is that you ask a citizen what a United Way is, and they'll answer something to the effect of: "Fund-raising for charities." One thing. One identifiable thing. Now, go ask the

(continued)

(continued)

United Way staff, and they may rattle off four or five different services that the organization provides, but these are so far outside popular perception that no one outside the organization knows about them. ■

Don't follow a market want either into anonymity or far enough afield to fundamentally confuse people; but, again, don't automatically discard any idea that changes your traditional services or service population.

 FOR EXAMPLE: A good example of success in such an identity transition is the YMCA (remember, the *M* stands for "Men's"), which moved across gender lines in the 1950s to expand its potential customer base. (I should point out that the age and religious labels have also been surmounted. You don't need to be under 30 or a practicing Christian to use a Y, be on its staff, or volunteer for a board position.) ■

Thus, identity-drift is okay, but you need to carefully think through how people think of you now and how they will think of you as you change. And, in some cases, it won't matter.

 FOR EXAMPLE: Chaddock is a residential school in Quincy, Illinois, that serves children who come from broken or abusive homes, and who have not been able to succeed in a family foster care environment. Its original name was Chaddock College, and it has gone through a series of name and service changes since its incorporation in 1853, including the Chaddock Methodist Boys School. It ceased using this name in 1983 when it admitted girls for the first time. Yet, in 1995, Chaddock received over 100 donations where the check was made out to "Methodist Boys School." It didn't matter that the organization now serves boys and girls, or that it is no longer closely affiliated with the Methodist Church as it was in its early years. Its image and its identity have remained the same. ■

Finally, I want to show you a tool with which to maintain your mission while you move with your markets. You don't even have to go to a hardware store to purchase it. It's in your office right now. It's called your *mission statement.*

Successful managers use all available resources to get the job done. Our mission statements are truly our central tool, our most valuable asset. So why don't we use them more? Here are some ways that you can get more use out of your mission, and have it help you keep your organization mission based, even while you are in the heat of discussions on how to meet the changing wants of your target markets.

Have the Mission Visible—Everywhere

If you don't already, discuss your mission at every staff and board meeting, by reviewing a short (1 minute, max) mission-success story. Put the mission on your screen savers and hand out copies to staff and board. Put it front and center on your web site and in the e-mail signatures of your staff. Print it first in your strategic plan, annual report, and in your newsletter. Have it relentlessly around, a constant reminder of what the point of your organization is.

Constantly Use the Mission Statement at Management, Board, and Committee Meetings

Now that it's around, you need to put it to use. If you don't, the mission will just become another essentially invisible wall or computer screen decoration. So, make copies of your mission statement and have them literally *on the table* at all board meetings, committee meetings, and staff meetings. Then talk up the mission. In staff meetings, when there is a program or policy choice to be decided, ask, "Which one of these choices is more mission based or makes us more mission capable?" Lead by example and show staff that you rely on the mission to help make your decisions, and that you expect them to do the same. Duplicate this action at board and committee meetings. Will having copies of the mission end all disputes? Hardly; but it will help to make sure that everyone in the organization is mission focused.

Use the Mission in Your Decisions about New Markets and New Services

Working with the checklist detailed earlier in this chapter, use the mission as one of your most important benchmarks in deciding when (or when not) to move toward a new market, provide a new service, or serve a new clientele.

You already have the entire organization invested in the mission. That's why you are all there doing the good works that you do. So, use the mission as a tool to help you keep your organization on track. Not only will it help guide you in marketing, but it will get you into the habit of using the mission in all of your major decision making, in your staff and board meetings. It's a good mission-based habit to get into.

The Never-Ending Marketing Cycle

Where does all this lead? When do you get to the Promised Land of becoming a mission-based and market-driven organization? How do you know when you have arrived? And, when you arrive, can you stop and rest a bit?

Not really; once you embark on this journey, it becomes a philosophy as crucial to the performance of your charitable purpose as any other part of your mission statement. For example, you may, as an organization, believe in prevention, early intervention, a particular method of education, or in a particular environmental cause. Those beliefs are closely related to your organizational identity; they describe in large part who you are. Now you need to become a *market-driven organization* that also has those same values, one that puts credence not only in your own beliefs but also in the beliefs and wants of your many markets.

How will you know when you have become market driven? You will know when you can quickly tell me how your five most important funders feel about you, based on survey or focus-group data. You'll know when you can rattle off the four or five most recent adjustments you have made to your service array, or to the delivery of services, based on information gathered from your customers. You'll know when I can walk into your organization and you are sure that I will be greeted with courtesy on my arrival and asked about my experience on my departure. You'll know when your web site is awesome, with targeted information for your many markets, and when you and your key staff can quickly list your target markets, your key competitors, and your areas of organizational core competence.

But even when you can do all this, you won't yet have *arrived.* There is always a little further to go. Your markets are always in flux; there's regularly a new want in development, a new competitor to face. Marketing is a tease, really, a horizon that you can see the shape of but that is always just out of reach. It is moving ground, constantly reshaping itself in ways that you can't really predict until you are there.

So, you never really arrive, but you still cannot afford *not* to embark on the journey.

The Results of Becoming Market Driven

What good things happen when you go through all the work, effort, and discipline to become and remain market driven? How can you tell if it is worth the investment? There are some real and tangible results from making this change, and the six listed here are the ones I see most often.

1. You Will Have Happier Markets—Particularly the People You Serve and Your Key Funders

If you ask and listen, ask and listen, ask and listen, and then make a reasonable effort to accommodate the wants people have, they will have a better feeling about you. They will feel better, first, simply because you asked. That action shows that you care, are businesslike, and, in the case where there has been a poor historic relationship with your funders, want to improve the relationship. Second, they feel better because you take action and try to accommodate them. Happier customers mean more return customers, more referrals, fewer hassles from funders, more sweep-up funds and pilot project grants, and being given a little slack in a crisis. You want happier service customers and happier funders. Marketing can help you get both.

2. Your Organization Will Have a Better Image in the Community

People will talk about you as a "mission-based business," one that is using what they rightly perceive as their money (from donations or taxes) in a more efficient and effective manner. You will have higher visibility in the community, because you will be out there asking all the time. You will gain a reputation as a responsive organization, not one of those nonprofits that hasn't changed since the first Bush Administration. This image will mean more customers, more donations, better morale for the staff and board, easier board recruitment, more designated donations through United Way, better online buzz, and easier staff, volunteer, and board recruitment.

3. You Will Retain Your Current Markets

If it is not already happening, it will soon: Someone will show up to compete with you for your core business or your best staff or even your top volunteers. They may, as we discussed earlier, just "cream" your organization, taking the most lucrative funders, donors, families, or service recipients. But come they will. By doing good marketing starting *now,* not after the competition shows up, you will cement the long-term relationship with many of your core markets. And, by competing and being responsive to changing wants when the competition does arrive, you have a much better chance of keeping those customers on board and loyal. If you think that this doesn't apply to you, ask your development staff if they need those donors who reliably contribute every year—those people who are retained customers. You don't want to lose them.

4. Your Organization Will Be More Efficient and Effective in the Provision of Services

By definition, if you are a market-driven organization, you are doing things that your markets want, and not doing things that they don't want. This will allow you to focus more and be more efficient and effective in what you do. You'll get more mission for the money, because you will be putting your money where it has the most impact.

5. You Will Develop New Revenue Sources

Success breeds success. You will find that happy customers (staff, volunteers, funders) will tell others, and this will result in more business, more customers, and new funders. Organizations that are good marketers attract new revenue like a fully pollinating flower attracts bees. Your business skills will be tested, deciding which work to take and which not to, and it will be important to stay focused on your core competencies. But I have seen organization after organization reap the financial rewards of marketing by having new and previously untapped sources of funding within 18 to 24 months of kicking off their marketing effort.

6. Your Organization Can Become and Remain More Financially Stable

As a result of being more focused and effective, and as more funding sources are developed, you can become much more financially stable. Notice that in the five previous points I say you "will," but here I say you "can." That's because just having more income doesn't mean you will be more financially stable. More income gives you the means to stability, but you still need to manage those funds well, ensuring your growth doesn't outstrip your cash, that your new expenses don't exceed your new income, and that you put some money aside for capital improvements and repairs. But good marketing gives you the opportunity to become financially stable. (For a whole book on this subject, see my book, *Financial Empowerment, More Money for More Mission,* Wiley 1996.)

If you do your marketing well, consistently, and with the entire staff and board on the marketing team, all of these results will accrue to your organization. These are the tangible benefits of all the work and money that you will put into your organizational change. Some are measurable, some are not, but if you are sensitive to them, you will be looking for the rewards in the right places.

Motivating Board and Staff

You cannot make this change alone. For some people in your organization (perhaps including you), this will be the first time they have ever encountered or had to deal with competition. For others it will be old hat. For some, there will be an easy transition. For others, there will never be complete acceptance that the "charity" days are long gone and will never return.

But you can do it. Your organization, if well led, can make the transition to a mission-based and market-driven entity. Look around. You have lots of company.

FOR EXAMPLE: Thirty years ago, American hospitals had a pretty good deal. In most communities there were a stable number of hospitals, with a slowly growing number of beds. They often shared physicians, and even certain resources. Rarely did hospitals openly compete; certainly they never advertised. There was often an esprit de corps and an elitism at a larger institution that perhaps was associated with a medical school, but, in general, a hospital was a predictable entity: a nonprofit, community-based organization that provided a wide range of different inpatient care and was a user of community resources, including donations and volunteer time. Walk into a primary-, secondary-, or tertiary-care hospital in New York, Des Moines, or Phoenix, and you would see basically the same array of services, the same equipment, and the same approximate size.

Just ten years later, it was anything but the same. Over 20 percent of American health care was delivered in for-profit hospitals, when it was delivered *in* the hospital at all. The number of hospital beds shrank in relation to population.

In this century, hospitals have merged, acquired, and been acquired to meet the wants of the markets, who in their cases are not only their patients, but also their physicians (the classic model of a referrer), the insurers, and even some tough-to-recruit staff, such as physical and occupational therapists.

The hospital that you and your family visit now is by definition market driven. I can say that with assurance, because the ones that are not market driven are gone.

Was this an easy transition? No; but the change was coupled with a huge increase in the business expertise and education of hospital administrators. Dozens, even hundreds, of master's programs in hospital management and administration sprang up all over the country as people worked hard to learn how to manage these multimillion-dollar nonprofit businesses in a competitive environment. ■

 FOR EXAMPLE: If you are as old as I am, you can remember "the phone company." AT&T was "Ma Bell," a complete monopoly. The phone in your house was owned by AT&T, and came in one color (black) and one style. Then came deregulation, and AT&T had to learn to compete. Think of this: a company with 300,000 employees and *no,* repeat, NO *marketing budget.* And, just when AT&T adjusted to the fact that Sprint and a now-long-dead

(continued)

(continued)

company named MCI were in their face, along came the cable
companies and then the biggest change of all—the Internet. AT&T
is now a wireless company, having gone through wrenching
changes multiple times in just over two decades. ■

These examples have themes similar to the dilemma you face: These
organizations had a staff and board that had been raised in a monopoly, not
in the more frantic, more variable competitive arena. Just like your organization, they had a choice: Adapt or die. Just like your organization, they
were faced with the possibilities of merging, or acquiring, or even of being
acquired.

And there was one other thing that these industries did: They got outside
help. Hospital administrators hired marketing staff from the for-profit arena.
When that didn't always work, they set up master's programs in administration to learn from within. The phone companies relied heavily on consultants
and outside hires who understood the whims of the marketplace. They spent
a great deal of money retraining employees, focusing on customer service,
and learning how to solve problems quickly, efficiently, and *even politely*.

The point is this: You can too. As you enter the competitive arena, many
of your staff will seize up and resist the change. They will bemoan the fact
that they took their job to serve, not to sell. Many, in fact, sought the shelter
of the nonprofit environment precisely because they did not want to enter
the hurly-burly of the business world.

However, some of their resistance will not be solely for philosophical
reasons. Many staff will correctly assume that they don't know *how* to act
competitively. And, like most people, they would rather do nothing than
mess up. So they will resist.

 HANDS ON: Get your staff and board the help that they need.
Specifically:

- Send people to in-person or online courses on marketing, customer service, quality control, surveying, focus-group
  development, and improving your web sites and paper
  materials.
- Have an outside marketing consultant come in and provide
  you with a competitive assessment. Have him or her tell you
  what you need to improve, and where your strengths and
  weaknesses are in terms of expertise and readiness.
- Hire from outside your discipline. Particularly in the marketing
  area, a fresh set of eyes, a fresh perspective, can be invaluable.
  Having this new expertise in-house will be vital in the coming
  economy.

If they feel that they are properly equipped to compete, most of your staff and board will do just fine. But you have to provide them with the "equipment." ■

What else can you do to motivate the staff and board and get them over the inertia of resistance?

 HANDS ON: Try one or more of these ideas:

1. *Talk to them about the reality of competition.* Engage the staff and board early and often in discussions about competition. Show them information about the competitiveness that is occurring in your sector. Target your information as closely as you can to your own discipline, and your income and service array. For example, if you get 25 percent of your income from small donations, you can show your staff and board members information on how many groups in your community have increased their development efforts. If you only get 1 percent of your income from fund-raising, don't bother with making a case for more competition in that arena.

   Have senior staff and your board read this book, and then use the questions at the end of each chapter to walk them through topics relevant to the issues developed in the book. This will allow you and your management and policy team to more easily coalesce around the reality of increased competition as well as the need for increased marketing efforts.

2. *Talk about your mission.* Discuss the people that your organization has helped. If you can, use real names of real individuals to highlight the value of what your organization does. Note that if you don't compete there is a good chance that you will not be around much longer to help those people who depend on you. If you have a much-disparaged competitor, talk about what happens if the people you serve must start going to them because you are no longer around. Use your mission as a tool for reflection on your value, and for motivation to try competing.

3. *List organizations like yours that are in trouble or out of business.* If you can, prepare a list of organizations in your area of work that are in financial trouble. National examples are good, but local or state ones are much better for underscoring

(*continued*)

(continued)

the potential outcome of not paying attention to the market forces that are shaping the future of your organization.

4. *Get them comfortable with the idea of marketing.* Review with them who your markets are, using the chart in Chapter 6. Help them understand that everyone, including your funders, are really your markets. Remind them that while mission is always first, if there is no money, then there is no mission!

Most importantly, help them see that they are already marketing, and have been for many years. This will help remove some of the "change" and "new" labels from the idea. For example, if you have "nontraditional" hours for services designed to meet the needs of two-income families, you are marketing—designing a service distribution to meet the wants of the market. If you already ask about customer satisfaction in any way, you are marketing—testing the wants of your customers. If you have started up a new service, or opened a new location in response to a customer-stated desire, you are marketing—responding to the markets. I'm sure you have some examples with which to allay the fears and concerns of your staff. Use them.

5. *Get them comfortable with the idea of competition.* Show them areas where you are currently competing: for the best staff, for board members, for volunteers, for donations, for community support. Ask, Is this kind of competition bad or good? Does it help the mission?

Go through the exercise of developing a list of the competition using the sample tables in Chapter 7. Make sure you emphasize your organization's strengths at some point, or your board and staff will think that you are facing unbeatable competition.

6. *Recognize and acknowledge their fears and concerns and admit your own.* Acknowledge that this is new turf for all of you, and that many staff and board did not come to the organization to take part in the competitive marketplace. Talk about your fears, concerns, and the need for more training and help. Note that change is inevitable and that, while you don't have the power to change the marketplace, you do have the power to shape your own destiny within that market. Discuss your options and your choices, and then look at the result of becoming market oriented and the fallout that will occur if you stay service oriented.

7. *State clearly and forcefully that you need to move ahead and do it now.* After this discussion is complete, end on a firm, forceful, and assured message: We need to move the organization ahead and get ourselves ready to compete. Look for agreement, and if you sense that it is not there, note that you are regrettably sure that this direction will alienate some members of the staff and board. And, for those whose discomfort is too severe, you would recommend that they go elsewhere with their time, energy, and skills.

This is a hard part of the discussion for most of us. You are embarking on a long and difficult journey through a countryside that many of your staff and board never thought they would set foot on. Dragging them along against their will slows everyone down, distracting you from the job at hand, which is to lead your organization through the change. It is better to make the hard choices now. As for people who you feel will not come along and support the new direction, it is better to recommend that they get out now. The train is leaving the station. Better to have these folks leave voluntarily now than to have them derail the train later on (or for you to have to throw them off). ■

These seven steps, if discussed with empathy and understanding, but with a clear sense of where you are going, will bring on most of your staff and board. Is there any other information that you can give these good people that might motivate them? Certainly, and in the next section I've listed several examples of the results of becoming market driven. Show them to your staff and board and ask whether these are outcomes that your organization would like to see.

Holding On to Your Core Values

We've already talked endlessly about mission, mission, mission, and markets, markets, markets. Ask, ask, ask; listen, listen, listen. There's more on all of these to come in the rest of the book.

Obviously, you can see I believe in the value of repetition. I have learned other things to value in writing: the use of examples in trying to give readers ideas that they can put into immediate use (Hands On), and telling the readers the whole truth, not just the parts that they might want to hear. I value clarity and brevity, but even though they are values and things that I value and aspire to, I do not always attain them to the level that I would like. I get distracted, get lazy, or just like a certain story too much to cut it short. My writing values are not always as tightly held to as I would like.

The same is true for your organization. Beyond your mission there is a set of core values that guide the way that you do the things you do. If you are a school, you might put a high value on teaching the students to work in teams, or on high discipline, or on faculty esprit de corps. As a place of worship, you might strongly value community service, political application of your spiritual beliefs, a literal interpretation of your scripture, or the support of overseas groups. As an art museum, you might focus on the avant-garde, or on traditional masters, or on teaching children, or on reaching out through the schools. Your organization may put a high value on teaching people to help themselves or on a certain therapeutic approach.

These values take you part of the way to the implementation of your mission. They give you guidance on the more practical month-to-month and year-to-year implications of how to stay true to your mission.

 FOR EXAMPLE: Here are the mission and values of a state child welfare agency that I helped the staff to develop a number of years ago:

> *MISSION: The Department of Child Welfare, in partnership with others, will provide services to children and families to protect and advocate on behalf of children and youth who are, or who are at risk of, being abused, neglected, or removed from their families.*

Values

- That children have a right to a safe, secure, permanent living arrangement, preferably with their own family
- That we should act quickly, competently, and professionally to protect children, prevent harm, and advocate for their well-being
- That children and families are served best in homelike settings in their own community
- That we should recognize the humanity and importance of each individual, and treat them honestly, with fairness, dignity, compassion, and cultural competence
- That we should foster a stable, supportive workplace that will allow for each employee to grow, develop, and participate in the fulfillment of the mission
- That we are accountable for the work we do, and thus must effectively and efficiently utilize all available resources to carry out the mission of the department ▪

You can see that the values in the previous example spoke not only to the mission, but also to the staff, and to the way the mission would be accomplished (not in institutions), and made it clear that everyone should be held accountable. This is a good set of values for a public organization.

 FOR EXAMPLE: National Public Radio's Mission and Values Statement reads as follows:

> *The Mission of National Public Radio is to work in partnership with member stations to create a more informed public—one challenged and invigorated by a deeper understanding and appreciation of events, ideas, and cultures.*
> *The fundamental values that guide our mission are:*
>
> - *Reporting with accuracy, thoroughness, and fairness;*
> - *Using sound creatively to engage the intelligence, curiosity, and imagination of listeners;*
> - *Encouraging innovation;*
> - *Honoring cultural diversity;*
> - *Upholding the tradition and prerogatives of public radio as a local medium;*
> - *Making the most of advances in audio technology; and*
> - *Encouraging the talent, dedication, creativity, and productivity of our staff.* ∎

The uses of these values in your marketing are many. They can help you select a core market to serve, avoid a funder, take a certain spin in your public relations, and focus on certain organizational outcomes.

They can also help you solve the painful puzzle of which tug to follow—the market or the mission.

 FOR EXAMPLE: Local nonprofit community hospitals throughout the nation are in a terrible moral bind. There are more and more people with no insurance (and few funds) who are presenting themselves at the emergency room door with real (and sometimes life-threatening) injuries or illnesses. If the hospitals let everyone in (regardless of their ability to pay), they will be out of business and of no help to anyone. However, the mission of hospitals is to help the sick and injured. How can they turn people away?

This dilemma is exacerbated in small towns, where it seems that everyone knows everyone. Thus, as they set the policy for what is called "uncompensated care," the board and staff are well

(*continued*)

(*continued*)

aware that they may be taking an action that will result in refusal of service to a friend, neighbor, or relative. How do values help? In most of the hospitals where I have helped board and staff through this moral mire, there was a value of "maintaining fiscal stability" that balanced the "ease the pain and suffering" value. ■

Often values do keep each other in balance. I have long held that the first rule of nonprofits is "mission, mission, and more mission." And the second, *balancing* rule is "no money, no mission." The same is true for your organization: You can have "competing" values.

 FOR EXAMPLE: In our jurisprudence system we have many values (mostly listed in the Bill of Rights), such as the right to an impartial jury of our peers, the right to a fair and speedy trial, and the right to face our accusers. In certain situations, though, we violate these values to meet more compelling values, such as the right to life, liberty, and the pursuit of happiness. For example, in the case of an abused child, certain courts have allowed the child to act as a witness against a defendant without actually doing it in the same court in which the accused appears. The value of the child's wellbeing and mental health takes precedence over the value of the right of the defendant. ■

In all of these examples, the values of the organization (or system) helped people to decide which path was right for them. And, in these examples, there was a lot of wiggle room to let different circumstances result in different interpretations.

 HANDS ON: If you don't have a set of organizational values, now is the time to develop them. With your board and key staff (and an outside facilitator), look at your mission statement, and then make a list of the key things that set your organization apart, that make your organization special, that you believe in. Print this list with your mission statement and use it along with your mission in management and policy discussions. ■

Your values are important guides in solving the moral, ethical, and mission quandaries that inevitably result from change, especially if that change is externally initiated. Formalize your values and use them as the moral and mission compasses that they are.

Recap

In this chapter, you have learned the methods—and the dangers—of being simultaneously market driven and mission based. You have seen the temptations that will tend to draw you into the world that chases money rather than mission, and I hope you now know the techniques to resist those temptations.

First, we went over the crucial question of which is right, the market or the mission? You learned that, at least in my opinion, the market is always right, but that responding to that market in the way that it wants will not always be the right thing for you. I showed you that your mission should be your guide, and that, while you need to listen and respond to the market whenever you can, the ultimate limit on your flexibility should be your mission. I also cautioned you not to let your mission be the rationale for rejecting any response to the market. What the market wants will mostly be very appropriate for you, and you shouldn't hide behind the mission.

Next, I told you how to move with the markets while maintaining your mission. I showed you some examples of organizations that are doing just that, and gave you some management ideas of how to get more use out of your mission statement to help you reinforce, remind, and refresh the mission every day.

We turned to the issue that moves past your mission and into your core values. I suggested that you list those values, discuss them, and use them as an additional framework within which to operate. We looked at examples of organizations that rejected new market opportunities that conflicted with their core values, and I provided you with a checklist that your staff and board can use to measure your comfort with a new or modified service based on your values.

Then we looked at the never-ending cycle of marketing, noting that your move from being service based to being market driven is really not a move; it is the beginning of a philosophy of action—an endless process that constantly adapts, changes, improves, and adjusts to the changes of the marketplace. In short, you are starting a journey that never ends.

We next covered some important ground by reviewing the benefits of becoming a market-driven organization. You can use these points in your discussion with board and staff to motivate and convince them that competition is real and marketing is a mission-based strategy. The six results were:

1. You will have happier markets—particularly the people you serve and your key funders.
2. Your organization will have a better image in the community.
3. You will retain your current markets.

4. Your organization will be more efficient and effective in providing services.
5. You will develop new revenue sources.
6. Your organization will become and remain more financially stable.

After that review, we talked about ways to motivate staff, board, and, yes, even yourself, to make that journey. First, we talked about team development and I gave you seven discussion threads with which to convince any hesitant staff or board that you are going in the right direction. These discussion topics can also help make them more comfortable with policies that they may know are correct, but do not yet feel are *right*.

To review, these seven ideas are:

1. Talk to them about the reality of competition.
2. Talk about your mission.
3. List organizations such as yours that are in trouble or out of business.
4. Get them comfortable with the idea of marketing.
5. Get them comfortable with the idea of competition.
6. Recognize and acknowledge their fears and concerns. Admit your own.
7. State clearly and forcefully that you need to move ahead and do it now.

By using these topics steadily, and with some empathy for the massive change you may be embarking on, you will bring most, although probably not all, of your staff and board along.

Now you know the yin and yang of making the change to a market-driven nonprofit. You have the skills and the techniques in front of you to convince your staff and board that it is the right choice. But, even after all of this work and motivation, you still have one more issue to think through before we move on to identify your markets and look at ways to deal with their wants. The question is: Are we flexible enough to meet the wants of so many different customers? That's the subject of our next chapter.

Discussion Questions

1. Are we mission based? How can we be more so?
2. Are we market driven? Can we improve our response to the markets? How?
3. What are the biggest barriers we face in achieving and maintaining market-driven status?
4. What are our core values? Should we add them to our mission? Who should be involved in setting them?
5. What are our core competencies? What is it that we do really well? Do these things enhance our mission or distract us from it?

6. Do our board members feel competition is a real concern? Why or why not?

7. Do all of our staff members feel that competition is a real concern? How can we regularly underscore this issue?

8. Do board and staff feel that marketing is related to mission? How can we do more to make the connection?

9. Can we take the actions suggested to make staff and board feel equipped to compete? How? When?

10. Looking at the benefits of being a market-driven organization, if these came true for us, what would it mean to our mission delivery?

CHAPTER 4

Being Flexible and Innovating with the Market

Chapter Thumbnail

➤ The Need for Flexibility

➤ Retaining the Capacity for Flexibility

➤ Being a Change Leader

➤ The Pace of Change in a Competitive Environment

Overview

If you use the ideas presented in this book, you should wind up asking all your customers what they want, and asking regularly. If you do that asking well, you, your staff, and your board will be constantly confronted with small, medium, and even large changes in the wants of your many markets.

Here is the problem: Can you adapt to these changes? Can your staff and your board? Are you flexible enough that your organization can reshape itself constantly to meet the changing environment outside your doors? In the old order, the protected economy, change came slowly and you had lots of second chances. The community, the funders, and the people you served all gave you a break since you were a nonprofit. No more. You need to adapt, adjust, change, improve, and innovate constantly to keep up with (if not ahead of) your competition. There is no point in going through all the marketing rigmarole that fills these pages if you are not going to change based on the information you have gathered.

Can you change? If you are like most readers, you probably have your doubts. Some of you are concerned about whether you can drag your organization kicking and screaming into the *1990s,* much less into the second decade of the 21st century! Others see a problem not only with staff being willing to change, but with the board acquiescing to fund the changes.

Additionally, there hangs over all of us the common wisdom that "we all resist change." This "wisdom" has been pounded into our heads for so long that we have all accepted it as profound truth, and that "truth" has become the number-one excuse of managers who don't want to make the effort. Get over it. Yes, it is tough to overcome inertia, but once you do, and the momentum is in your favor, it gets easier and easier.

In this chapter, I'll show you how to overcome that inertia, and how to develop and use the momentum you need to be constantly changing and improving your organization. First, I'll try to make a strong case for the need for flexibility, providing you with examples that you in turn can use with any staff or board members who are indeed resistant to change. Next, we'll go over some important things your organization needs to do to retain its flexibility. As we get older, we get less flexible. I'll show you how to stretch organizationally. Then, in the third section, I'll provide you with six specific ideas on how to be a change agent for your organization, showing you some hands-on ideas for keeping change moving throughout the organization. Finally, I'll really get your attention by showing you the increasing pace of change in a competitive environment. As I said earlier, in the old order we could slog along, but not anymore.

By the end of the chapter you should have a feel for ways to keep that momentum going. You'll need to. Outside your organization, the inertia has already been overcome and the changes you will need to adapt to are occurring right now. They will occur with or without you. As a good friend of mine likes to say, "The train is leaving the station. You are either on it, or under it."

The Need for Flexibility

"So what is all this talk about change? Why do we need to be changing all the time? What's wrong with what we're doing now? Change is such a hassle, and there is no guarantee that when we change we're going to be any better. I like things the way they are. If we do good work, people will continue to use us. What choice do they have? We've done just fine doing the things we've been doing. If it's not broken, don't fix it."

Does any of this sound familiar? Have you heard this from your board, your staff, yourself? You probably have. And, you have a choice: You can be flexible and survive to do more mission another day. Or you can be inflexible and not be around very long. In today's increasingly competitive market, flexibility—the capacity to regularly, and on increasingly short notice, adjust your directions, methods, service mix, and size—is essential.

In discussing change and flexibility, I am not always talking about huge changes, epic conversions such as new buildings, or massive changes in program methodology or reimbursement methods. More often we are talking about small, steady, regular improvements in services—adaptations to the changing wants of your markets. These are what I call small improvements around the edges, and these incremental changes provide most of the increased value for your markets—and with the least change pain for you and your staff.

Most people see the word *change* as

☹ CHANGE!!!!!!! ☺

Change is rarely that dramatic. Nor is seismic change always good. There is a Japanese philosophy of 100 percent improvement—1 percent at a time. This is the core of what used to be called Continuous Quality Improvement (CQI). It doesn't focus on wholesale change, discarding all the old ways to embrace the new. In fact, it builds on the best of the old, making steady improvements every day, every week, every month.

There are many, many examples in the nonprofit sector of incremental flexibility based on changes in market wants. Let's look at a few.

 FOR EXAMPLE: All of us know that nonprofits should be transparent and accountable to their communities. Today, we can go to an online watchdog such as GuideStar.com and see lots of information on most U.S. 501(c)(3) organizations. That's how it is today, and we all pretty much accept the fact that we're on display. But in the late 1990s, funders started to demand something called *outcome measures* from nonprofits, and, oh, you should have heard the wailing and gnashing of teeth. "The good we do is immeasurable," "You can't measure art appreciation (educational attainment, spiritual benefit, social justice)," and on and on. In truth, measuring *is* hard, and requires collection and analysis of a variety of data. Further, some things that funders want to measure are flat-out dumb and useless. But over time, the sector figured out (1) that a key market wanted outcome measures, and (2) step by step how to meet that want. But once the market wants changed, there was no convincing them to go back to the old ways. ∎

Once the market has made up its mind, for whatever reason, you are simply wasting your time whining about the philosophy or the change. You can't worry about what might have been. You need to deal with what *is*. The train is leaving the station.

 FOR EXAMPLE: In an earlier chapter, we discussed the many roles that United Ways have tried to play over the past two decades. But now, with direct online giving the preferred method of choice for millions of Americans and for nearly every donor born after 1970, the United Way has to figure out how to retain its relevance. Combine that trend with the fact that most Americans now work in smaller workplaces, which directly hurts United Way's model of large-workplace giving campaigns, and you have two direct challenges to the business model of this nonprofit icon. How will United Way respond? I don't know, but it's going to be very interesting to watch. What they can't do is wish away the Internet. The tech train has left the station. ■

 FOR EXAMPLE: Community colleges across the country have traditionally been a terrific option for a college student who either needs to live at home, or doesn't know what he or she wants to study, or wants to go back to school after starting work, or isn't quite ready to commit to a four-year college or university. All that is well and good, but the best and brightest college-bound students have usually looked past the community college (or looked down on it). That's changed in the past few years, as the cost for a year at a four-year college or university has skyrocketed. Now community colleges (which have ramped up their educational offerings) are appealing to the best students in their community to enroll for the first two years of college to save serious money. The CC system has been flexible and has adapted. ■

All of these examples point to the constant adjustment, accommodation, and willingness to be flexible in successful organizations in both the for-profit and nonprofit sectors. And, it gets us to a crucial point (and secret) about change:

It's the steady changes, the small improvements every day, not the huge makeovers, that make the difference. Not only are they more effective, they are easier for staff and board to accommodate.

Put another way:

Incremental change is less painful. Less pain means less resistance.

Why is this true? Because if you are market driven, if you are asking, listening, asking, and listening with relentless persistence, then you will hear of a thousand small ways you can make your customers happier for every one major change. If you change 1 percent a day, in just 100 days, or one-third of a year, the entire organization is renewed, but at a pace that your staff can adjust and adapt to. Steady change is the secret.

But you do need to make that change within the context of a plan, to make sure your improvements and changes are moving you toward your overall organizational goal. Otherwise, your 1 percent daily improvements can wind up with you going in circles.

Has your organization already changed while you weren't looking? Of course; you should not think for a moment that you are not changing. You are. And your staff is. And your board is. You have made accommodations to market changes, and you need to feel good about the changes you have made.

 HANDS ON: To emphasize how many changes you have made in your organization in the recent past, do this exercise with your staff and/or board members: Look at your organization five years ago. If you have pictures, policies, staff lists, board lists, marketing material, audits, and annual reports, use them to make a comparison of then versus now. Specifically, look at:

- *Size:* How much income do you have per year now versus five years ago?
- *Programs:* Do you have more programs? Are the ones that you have provided in the past different now? How?
- *Location:* Have you moved? Have you purchased or sold a building?
- *Staff:* How many new people have been added to the staff? How many of those on staff five years ago have left?
- *Board:* What changes in the board have you seen?
- *Policies:* How have your personnel, financial, quality assurance, and other policies and bylaws changed?
- *Funders:* What is your funding mix? Do you get funding from different sources than five years ago? What changes have there been in reporting and accounting? In auditing and oversight?
- *Technology:* How did your web site look five years ago? How many iterations of your web site have there been in the past five years? Did you accept online donations or reservations back then? What about your current online capabilities to accept donations and be more transparent? What did you think social networking was? How about Twitter?

As you answer these questions as a group you will see that you have changed *a lot*. Talk about these changes. Some were easy, some were painful. But reinforce the fact that your organization has *successfully* changed in many, many ways and that you can continue to do so in the future. ■

Feel good about how far you have come, and don't feel that you have been static while the world has moved on. You may very well feel that you have not kept pace adequately. And, it is true that the pace of change is accelerating. But don't for a minute let yourself, your staff, or your board think that you are going to start changing from a standing start. You are already moving. But how do you stay flexible while you are moving?

Retaining the Capacity for Flexibility

All of us are born flexible. As we age, we all lose our flexibility. I'm sure you have watched toddlers bend in ways that would put you or me in the hospital. As we get older, we have to work hard on flexibility or it disappears, much to our disadvantage.

Mentally we can get inflexible as well. By not continuing to learn, not continuing to consider new ideas or new ways of doing work, our mental processes get set in a rut just as surely as our muscles, tendons, and joints. When you hear yourself saying (or thinking), "Ah, that new stuff doesn't interest me. We're doing just fine," that should set off all the alarms. Sometimes the "new stuff" *is* questionable, but more often there is progress there to be embraced. Even if all of a new idea, process, or protocol is not completely applicable to your organization, some of it may be, and thus regular study and reading to both stretch your brain and learn something that may be of value to you later is important. Fight mental rigidity.

 HANDS ON: Here's a win-win for you: One of the best ways to improve your organizational flexibility is to keep pouring information into your staff and board. Being a lifelong-learning organization (one of my characteristics of successful nonprofits in my book *Nonprofit Stewardship,* Fieldstone Alliance, 2004) is a way not only to keep up on best practices, but to generate discussion and consideration of new ideas. As I said earlier, not all new ideas are right for your organization, but by exposing people to new stuff and then talking about it, you keep people's minds open and also reduce the idea that you "know it all" because you've been in business for 20 years.

Think of lifelong learning as regular mental stretching for your nonprofit—keeping you flexible today so that when you do need to change, you won't pull something. ■

Whereas mental inflexibility is the first problem, organizational inflexibility is a problem as well. We get invested in our buildings, a syndrome that I call the *edifice complex*. This complex results from having so much of our assets invested in our building that the building *becomes* the organization. We become product-oriented, and the product is what we do in the building. If we have classrooms, or inpatient beds, or display space, or even offices, we *have* to fill them—whether or not the market wants what goes into those spaces.

 FOR EXAMPLE: I'm sure you can think of any number of nonprofits that have provided services out of a particular location for years. In many cases the building is deteriorating (another problem, but not the point for this example), and the neighborhood has changed, perhaps for the worse, perhaps for the better. But in either case, it is no longer the ideal place from which to reach people. What do most for-profits do in this situation? The successful ones move. They realize that if their customers are not going to come into the neighborhood where they are located, there soon will be no business at all. So, even if the sale of a piece of property means taking a loss, a loss with the realistic expectation of meeting customer wants is a good move.

What do the nonprofits do? They come up with excuses about why they should stay where they are. Again, in the old economy this was fine, because there was no competition for their clientele. In the new economy such rigidity is a quick but painful method of organizational suicide. ■

You need to remain flexible as an organization, and not just in your buildings. You need flexibility in your programming, your service array, your methods of reaching people, and your methods of recruiting, managing, and retaining staff.

But how do you, your staff, and your board attain and maintain that flexibility? I've already shown you some suggestions on being a change agent, and I have some more ideas in this area.

Retain Financial Flexibility

Earlier, I mentioned the edifice complex, that terrible financial disorder that requires organizations to feed their buildings rather than pay attention to the marketplace. Part of financial flexibility is having the cash that will enable you to make strategic and tactical moves promptly. Part of financial flexibility is not having all your assets in your buildings. Part of it is making money each year as an organization so that you can reinvest in your mission. Part of it is starting and maintaining an endowment.

But financial flexibility empowers other kinds of flexibility, including risk taking, which we will cover in a moment. Suffice it to say here that financial decisions need to be looked at not only through the lens of getting enough financial and mission return on investment, but also with the idea of retaining enough flexibility to allow you some wiggle room later. (There is much more on this subject in *Mission-Based Management*, Wiley, 2009.)

 HANDS ON: Take out your most recent balance sheet and a calculator. Look at your fixed assets, and divide them by your total assets. Are fixed assets more than 75 percent of all your assets? Now, look at your cash and cash equivalents. Does it exceed 60 days' operation? If you have too many fixed assets and too little cash, you are hamstrung when it comes to quickly accommodating changes in the market. ■

Use Risk Taking as a Flexibility Tool

Social entrepreneurship, taking risk on behalf of the people you serve, is another of the nine characteristics of successful nonprofits that I examined in *Mission-Based Management,* and expanded on in *Social Entrepreneurship, the Art of Mission-Based Venture Development.* This important characteristic can be used here to retain flexibility.

One of the things that people don't like about change is that it is a threat: There is danger in the unknown. The Chinese symbol for change has two parts: one meaning "danger," the other meaning "opportunity." The Chinese got it right; there are both in any change. But where I see people putting up the most resistance is in regard to the danger of the unknown, the entering of a dark room with only a puny flashlight.

In going through change, we are taking risk. That means we are almost certainly going to make mistakes. Everyone does. Mistakes by themselves are no big deal. We all learn better from our mistakes than from our successes. But if your culture is one where anyone who makes any mistake is punished (a blame-friendly environment), people will not want to try anything new. This is because there is a higher likelihood of error in doing new things than there is in doing things that are already known and practiced. If error, any error, means getting chewed out, why take the chance?

Are you risk-averse as an organization? Do you have a mantra of 100 percent quality? While I have nothing against high-quality services, you need to remember: *Organizations that have a zero tolerance for error also have a zero tolerance for innovation.* Innovation, that essential competitive skill, is all about risk and reward. You try something new (a change) and you risk failure. But you also may succeed and then get rewarded.

You need to encourage prudent risk, regular innovation, and trying new things. Once your staff and board get the idea, you will see them stretching more and more. What do I mean by "stretch"? That's my next suggestion.

Stretch: Make Regular Small Changes

We talked earlier about regular organizational stretching as a flexibility tool. I know about this personally, since I'm a runner. Before I run, I stretch. Every time. If, for some reason, I forget, I can really tell the difference. You and your organization need to stretch as well, and do it regularly. How? By making small regular changes *and noting them.* Remember the exercise I suggested of listing all the changes that have occurred in staff, board, service, location, and the like? From here on out, not only make the small changes but make note of them, so that people get used to hearing the words, and will realize not only that things are changing, but that they are not getting hurt by those changes. What you want to seek is a culture that is constantly refreshing itself, trying new things, and taking on a new look.

Here are some small changes that you can make without too much trouble or expense. *Don't* do all of them at once! Dole them out over time, so that some change is *always* going on. I've divided the changes into two groups: *Low Impact* and *High Impact.* Changes in the first group are generally less expensive and less threatening to staff or board members; those in the latter are more so.

 HANDS ON: Try these changes:

Low Impact

- *Change your letterhead.* Not now, but when your supply runs out. (I know that could take a while, since you are certainly sending out fewer paper letters.) I'm not talking about changing the logo or the entire look (which may be timely as well) but rather moving the lines, changing the color, and so forth. I know that this may require changes in business cards and perhaps your web site, but those can be phased in over time.
- *Repaint, repaper, put down new carpet.* Don't ever think that a change of appearance is unimportant. If you have the money, give staff an allowance to buy wall decorations for their offices.
- *Upgrade your software.* You should be doing this anyway, but if you've let it slide, do it soon. It is often not expensive, sometimes even free, and you can be more productive after the change.

(continued)

(continued)

- *Rethink your meeting schedules.* Do you need staff meetings every week? Team meetings every month? Are the location, duration, and content of the meetings appropriate? Ask those who regularly attend, and make the changes that they suggest.
- *Start with your own environment.* Move your own office furniture, add a plant, remove a picture. Buy a new coffee mug, eat lunch at a different time each day, drive a new route to work. I work out of my home, in a very spare office that is also a workshop in our basement. As I wrote the third edition of this book, I moved my laptop and other work papers to a new location in another room for the duration of the writing, one with a different ambiance and view. The difference in my work attitude was amazing. For you, leading in this area by making changes yourself is crucial.

High Impact

- *Change offices.* Whoa! Here is a big one. Perhaps a change of location will help some people, or be an avenue for better communication, more effective supervision, or improved access to your clientele.
- *Change titles.* Start with your own. Perhaps you have been thinking of moving to a corporate model where the executive director has the title of CEO and where people who were directors become vice presidents. Is now the time to implement that change?
- *Reorganize your table of organization.* Not just to do it, but if you have been putting off a needed change, get on with it. Perhaps there will be a major reorganization; perhaps just a few people will be affected.
- *Change your committee makeup.* On the staff level this is pretty easy. I have always encouraged organizations to have representation on their committees from all levels of the organization both vertically and horizontally—this means from all levels of management and all parts of the organization. If you haven't done that, start now. If you have, shuffle some staff from one committee to another (asking them first, of course, if they have any preference). At the board level, talk to your board president about implementing a needed new committee, or changing the job descriptions on existing ones, or moving board members around, or even changing the staff who are responsible for particular committees. ■

Please, don't misunderstand me. I am not urging you just to stir things up. Don't make changes just to make changes. Any of these that you do implement should be done for a reason, and thoughtfully considered before starting. But a pace of regular change keeps the organization stretching, and thus more flexible.

Don't Always Call Change "Change"

Change is what it is—and it is inevitable. But if the word *change* really gets in the way, if when you say "change" the staff or board hear "trouble," switch the nomenclature. Use terms such as *improvement, adjustment, innovation, refinement, shift,* or *variation.* There is only so much cajoling, training, coaching, and being helpful that you can do. Some people get very hung up on words, hung up to the point that their engines seize. If that is true for you, go around the barrier instead of through it. Use different terminology, and perhaps it will help.

A final note about the retention of flexibility and change advocacy. Despite all of your efforts, all of your enthusiasm and spirited advocacy for moving your organization ahead, it is inevitable that some people just won't get it. They will continue to resist, or they will act out in other ways, some passive-aggressive, some morale-killing, some even outright rude.

When you have given your best effort to bringing these people on the team and they have decided, for whatever reason, not to join, it is time for them to leave. Once the organization has made a decision to go in a certain direction, it is up to them, whether they be staff or volunteers, to get with the program and support it, or find other things to do in another organization. What happens when a basketball player refuses to run windsprints, or a cellist refuses to play a certain piece with feeling? He or she is off the team or out of the orchestra. The same is true with your organization.

If you have read *Mission-Based Management,* you know that I am a great believer in participatory, inclusive management, a system where ideas flow from the point of service to the managers, and where decisions are made as close to the point of service as possible. That having been said, I do not in any way support staff insubordination or refusal to follow policy. Decisions still need to be made. And if we have trusted those decision makers, whether they are the board, executive team, or line workers, to make a decision, it is up to the rest of us to support it. Those who can't need to go elsewhere.

In *Leading Without Power* (a book I highly recommend to you), Max DePree discusses nonprofit decision making with this terrific insight: "We spend too much time looking for consensus, when we should be looking for agreement." I love that, and what it means is that, yes, you should get input, but committee work is not jury deliberation; you don't want to let one person who doesn't want to move forward control the organization's destiny. Rather, you ask for input from everyone, decide, and then ask if that support I discussed earlier will be there. The train is leaving the station—are you on it or under it?

Being a Change Leader

As a key staff or board member, you need to lead in terms of the changes your organization pursues. You need to develop plans that outline the way your organization is going, and then delineate what needs to happen to get there. You need to set internal policies that support those plans. You must identify issues and discuss them fully, including staff, volunteers, and even the community in those discussions when appropriate.

But when all is said and done, when all the dust settles and the decisions are made, you need to *lead* on the changes you have just initiated, not just tell people to go do them. You want to be not just the initiator of change but the facilitator of it. A change agent is someone who helps people through the process, overcoming the barriers to change. To do this, I have found that the following six steps are essential:

1. Show the Mission Outcome of the Change

We're back to the mission. Some people will resist new stuff. We all know it. But if you can show a relationship between the change and doing more and better mission, *some* of the resistance in *some* of your staff and board will be eliminated. Notice that I did not say *all* of the resistance in *all* of the people. But showing the mission connection will help. And, if you have been with your organization long, I'm sure you have dozens of human interest stories or success stories that you personally savor and that keep you motivated from day to day. Share them. John Kotter, who writes terrific books on change management, has a name for the first step in change—he calls it "Develop a sense of urgency." For nonprofits, nothing is more urgent than doing more or better mission, so share your stories.

2. Go Through the Change Together

Here's the lesson in a nutshell. People will change much more readily *with* you than *for* you.

 FOR EXAMPLE: Imagine yourself brought into a large room that you have never seen before. The room is an office for 10 people, and thus full of furniture. There is no one else there except you and your supervisor, who brought you in. The supervisor points to a door on the far side of the room and says, "That is where we're going now. Get there." And then he or she turns the lights out and leaves. You have to negotiate the new terrain in the dark. You decide not to move at all. You don't want to get hurt, and you didn't really get a good look at the location of all the furniture before the lights were turned out. An hour later, your supervisor returns and says, "Why haven't you done what I asked? I showed you what to do!" ■

The new room is the change. When you tell people what to do and then leave them to their own devices, if they have never been there before, they will naturally be concerned about making mistakes. If, however, you are there for them, and you show them how to make the change, they are much more likely to comply, and with much less resistance. Imagine that same supervisor offering to come with you across the dark room and, better yet, bringing the flashlight of your experience to light the way.

Stay with people through change. Check in. Be available. Do your changing as a team.

3. Point Out Changes Outside the Organization

Stay informed. Read widely. Pay attention to the outside environment, the world in general, and not just your industry. Learn to make connections between the changes in the outside world and your organization. Then, share this information with staff. Be a role model for them of lifelong learning.

4. Don't Wait for Big Changes to Make Any Changes

We've already discussed making many small changes as a starting point. Remember, if the only change your organization ever makes is monumental, you won't do it very well, because you won't have practiced much. Don't save up all your changes to "do it all at once." Incremental regular change is much less threatening. Remember the exercise I wanted you to do with your staff so that they would realize how much you had changed? If you did that, people probably said things to you like, "I had no idea we had come this far." Why didn't they notice? Because the changes were incremental. Now, use that low-profile, incremental approach to make your own organizational changes less threatening. If you do have a big change, can you break it down into more steady, small changes? If you can, it will lower anxiety and resistance.

Step 5. Don't Criticize the Past—Look to the Future

When you announce a change, do it positively, not negatively. Too often I hear people say, "Now, we're *finally* going to get it right," which of course implies that your people have been doing something *wrong* up until now. Talk about fostering resistance! Instead of criticizing the past, talk about how this will be even better, do even more mission, help in your continual quest for higher quality. Look forward, not back.

Step 6. Be Patient

Change takes time. Nearly any change you initiate, from a large one like a modification of your program policies, to a small one such as a change in a reimbursement form, requires a behavioral change on someone's part. And behavioral change takes time, a lot of time. You need to use your coaching skills to keep people on track. You need to be around so that you can catch small mistakes before they become big ones. You need to encourage and cajole and not expect perfection the first time out. Be patient.

These six elements, when used together, will make for a much easier change process for your organization. And, the more your leadership team, managers, and supervisors practice them, the better.

The Pace of Change in a Competitive Environment

"The hurrieder I go, the behinder I get" is an old saying that describes the feeling we all have at times about the world we live in. No one can possibly keep up with the changes in their profession, workplace, fashion, sports, music, technology, entertainment, politics, and local, national, and international events. So we have a tendency to throw up our hands and say "*overload!*" and find excuses not to pay attention.

In the old days, you could get away with that for a number of reasons. Change was slower paced, you got a break from people if you weren't "cutting edge" since you were a nonprofit, and, most importantly, you probably had a relative or virtual monopoly. Thus it didn't matter how much you accommodated to changes in the outside world. You could accommodate at your own more leisurely (more "professional") pace. Remember when attorneys and physicians berated those in their professions who advertised? It was unseemly, unprofessional. Now, you go online and see ads for law practices, medical groups, clinics, hospitals, and even individual practitioners. Remember, too, that some of those who refused to advertise are out of business, or have been bought out by their competition.

There are two key points I want to make here and they are both contained in the header of this section. First, there is the *pace of change*. It is accelerating with the explosion of available information, the speed of communication, and the general pace of our lives all being more and more intense. Second, is the *competitive environment*. This environment is one that your organization may already be in or may just be entering. But you and your organization cannot avoid it.

Imagine you are at a huge airport. You are walking down an immense concourse to your plane. Suddenly you come upon a moving walkway, and are forced by the crowd to get on. Your pace has just picked up. Now the walkway speeds up ever so steadily until you are nearly racing. Things go by faster. You have less time to study them before they are behind you. And the end of the walkway comes up very, very fast. That is the transition from noncompetitive to competitive environments and from the slower pace of yesteryear to the rapid pace of today.

So, both affect you, as do the following five cultural shifts:

1. The Average Attention Span Is Down

There's lots of data to back this up. We're a remote-control society. *Click.* Let's see here ... no, I'm bored, *click.* Let's look at that ... *hmmm*, not too interesting ... *click.* Why doesn't that webpage load ... *click.* ...

You see this everywhere. Look at the length of the average television advertisement, the shortening of the average article in newspapers and magazines (or the entirety of *USA Today*), the shorter stories on cable news. We are a short-attention-span, immediate-gratification society. What does this mean for you? People don't just lose this characteristic when they get up from their television set or turn off their computer. They bring it with them when they seek the services you provide. How many Americans would wait weeks or months for surgery? In Canada and much of the U.K., people are used to it. How many people do you see frustrated at not being the first in line at the checkout counter in the grocery store? I see lots, including myself. We *hate* to wait.

The issue here for you is that everyone wants what they want, now.

 FOR EXAMPLE: You meet me at a party and we start to talk. I ask what you do and you tell me you work for your nonprofit. I'm mildly interested, and know enough to ask this question: "What's your organization's mission?" You recite the mission, which takes 30 seconds, and then explain what the mission means, which takes four more minutes. You lost me 15 seconds in. *Click.* ■

 HANDS ON: Your mission statement needs to be short and sweet—in the parlance of marketing pros, an elevator message. I would add that the elevator is in a building that's only 10 stories

(continued)

(continued)

high ... not the Empire State Building. You need to get people's attention, and make them be willing to put the remote control down and ask for more. ■

2. Louder, Brighter Advertisements and Media

This is directly related to cultural shift number 1. If you saw a retrospective on television ads from 10 to 15 years ago, you would be bored silly. Those ads were, by comparison to today's machine-gun-style messages, bland and *long* (one whole minute!). You get inundated with ads on nearly every web site, on the shelves and carts at the grocery store, on your phone. Today, you have to nearly grab people by the throat to get their attention. And with the explosion of inexpensive PC-based design and printing software as well as dirt-cheap, high-quality color printers, the spread of really bright, classy-looking material is everywhere. The issue for you in a competitive environment is that your marketing, advertising, and promotions have to look "current," which means constantly updated. If they don't, you won't get people's attention. If you don't get their attention, they won't use your services. "It was boring"—referring to your marketing material or your services—is the ultimate pejorative, and a deadly one in a competitive world.

3. The Product Cycle Is Now Down to Months Rather Than Years

Used to be that the time from "Eureka!" to the marketplace was many years. Now, the turnaround is much, much faster. Just look at the rapid pace of "apps" for web-enabled phones, or updated hardware and software. They are often literally outdated when they arrive on the shelves. When you buy a new computer, you log on to download updates and patches—which often takes an hour.

The point for you? Just like their attention spans, people bring their *focus on the new* to your organization. Is what you do *exactly* as it has been for many years?—strike one. Is your pace of change so slow that you could gear up now for a service adjustment to meet a market want in *two fiscal years?*—strikes two and three. People won't wait that long, because your competition won't and then they will have choices of places to go other than yours. The assurance from you—"We'll be right there!"—doesn't work any longer. *Click.*

4. The End of Annual Cycles

In the old economy, people in the nonprofit world lived on an annual cycle, usually based on their state's or the federal fiscal year. We had annual budgets. We knew what our year "looked like" well in advance. No more.

Now we're asked to give quarterly updates to many funders, we live from big fundraiser to big fundraiser, and our outcomes are online and updated regularly. The annual work plan is increasingly a thing of the past.

5. There Is Much Less Sympathy for the Nonprofit That Can't Keep Up

I've touched on this a number of times already, but it has impact here as well. In the past century, when you had crummy service (or a pitiful web site, or obsolete buildings), people said, "Oh, well, they are just a nonprofit. What do you expect?" Now? Now, they expect *much, much, more*. People see the funds you use as *theirs,* and they have a valid point. The money may be from tax revenues or it may be from donations, or both. And people want outcomes from their investment in you. So, you don't get the break you did before. You need to compete, and more importantly, you need to be seen by your community as competitive, up-to-date, and fully professional.

Before we move on, I would be derelict if I did not discuss two important points. Up to here, I have been making the case for new, new, new. To some of you this may read as "trendy, trendy, trendy." In some cases, there is a real and valid reason for not constantly reinventing yourself, for *not* having the latest and greatest. Let's look at two such situations:

1. THE CASE FOR STABILITY   In some organizations it is important to have at least the appearance of sameness, of stability. For example, if your organization treats chronically mentally ill individuals, a predictable, comfortable, consistent environment is often important. If you go changing the office decor every six months (as if you could afford it), you could hurt your mission quality, rather than help it. In other cases, donors want to give to the "same" organization as they always have, and a major change in appearance of logo, stationery, or other materials could negatively affect that. In both of these cases, the stability of the appearance or of the program is important to key market segments. Respect that. Again, I don't advocate change for change's sake. But I want you to be aware that your organization is being held to an increasingly high standard to keep up with the rest of the world. And a change of availability—for example, adding evening hours to accommodate new customers—would not offend people who are used to being served during the daytime. Again, ask your markets, and adapt. But don't let the adage "But we've always done it that way" allow stability to overcome market sensitivity.

2. THE BELIEF IN POVERTY-CHIC   Poverty-chic is the still widely held belief that it is unseemly, if not immoral, for nonprofits to have any appearance of wealth. Another way of putting this is, "You can't do well doing good." There is a *long* story behind why this unfortunately still common belief is

out there, but it does present real conflict with all of the exhortations that I have just given you about being up-to-date, professional, and responsive. For example, if you are like most of my clients, you have been criticized at some point about your technology. Your computers are too fancy, too expensive for an organization like yours, some say. And the *same* machines get criticized by your accountant or board members for being so out-of-date. You can't win. If you have great marketing materials or a cool web site, some people assume you have lots of money and don't need donations. If you have new carpet in the lobby, you are seen as frivolous; if you don't, you are hassled for having crummy space.

It seems you can't win. Well, you can, but it takes some time. First, you need to have your board and staff behind you when you upgrade. By *upgrade* I mean the carpet, your vehicles, your computers, your office furniture. The staff and board have to agree that this is a good, mission-related investment. You have to have the people inside the organization on your side. Then, you can begin to make the case outside, but at least your staff and board shouldn't be taking shots at you.

It's a slow process to convince our friends and neighbors to let us be part of the rest of society. As long as they continue to treat us as poor brothers and sisters, we will, at least in part, act that way. And that way is not good mission.

But enough with the evangelism—let's get on to what a real marketing cycle is. It's much more than just a promo message or a web ad. That's the subject of Chapter 5.

Recap

In this chapter we have covered an important facet of competitive marketing: flexibility. Maintaining flexibility and welcoming positive change are difficult organizational skills, and I showed you a number of things that may help attain and maintain them.

First, we looked at the need for flexibility, and I provided you with a number of examples of organizations that were and were not flexible in the face of changing market wants. Second, I showed you some methods of retaining organizational flexibility, including retaining financial flexibility, using risk taking as a flexibility tool, stretching by making regular small changes, and not always calling change "change." We reviewed the fact that incremental change is less painful and thus often less resisted.

Third, we examined six specific ways for you to be a change agent:

1. Show the mission outcome of the change.
2. Go through change as a coach.

3. Point out changes outside the organization.
4. Don't wait for big changes to make any changes.
5. Don't criticize the past—look to the future.
6. Be patient.

We spent some time going over the pace of change in a competitive environment. The pace is picking up, and I pointed out that in the old days, people would give you a break because you were a nonprofit, but those days are long gone. You need to keep pace because, as the environment becomes more competitive, people will have more choices and they may just choose to go somewhere else.

There is no substitute for flexibility. Remember the old story about the grasses on the shore during a storm. They are flexible, they bend, and they survive the storm. The strong, inflexible oak can survive many a wind, but will eventually meet a storm that will knock it down. The storm of change that you are in is bigger than you are. Market wants change as fast as winds in a swirling gale, and you need to be flexible to remain standing.

Finally, flexibility is not something that we naturally get better at with time; we get worse. Both as individuals and organizations, we get set in our ways; we have our traditions ("the way we do things here") and our investments in certain paths. The older our organization gets, and the bigger it becomes, the more difficult it is to change the path. But you must be able to change direction promptly and with a positive attitude if you are to succeed in the markets of tomorrow.

Now that you know how to retain your flexibility, we've really covered most of the preparatory steps of good nonprofit marketing. Now let's get to the technical stuff, starting with the real markets you are serving.

Discussion Questions

1. How averse are people here to change? Why? Do we as managers lead through change?
2. How much can we morally change with the market? Are there things that we do now that we couldn't have considered five years ago? Why are they okay now?
3. Are we a lifelong-learning organization? Can we be better in this area?
4. Do we encourage or discourage prudent risk taking? How?
5. Is the pace of change in our markets accelerating or stable? What can we do to accommodate it? Can we encourage regular, persistent improvements?

CHAPTER 5

The Marketing Cycle for a Nonprofit

Chapter Thumbnail

➤ The Marketing Cycle That Works
➤ The Marketing Disability of Most Nonprofits
➤ The Marketing Cycle and Your Competitors

Overview

Marketing is not an event; it is a process, and one that never ends. Unlike a linear process with a beginning, middle, and end, marketing is more cyclical, with familiar steps repeated over and over as the organization regularly responds to changes in the markets, customer wants, competition, and innovations in strategy and best practices.

And, even though it is important to know that the marketing cycle is just that, a cycle that goes around and around, it is even more important to understand the hub on which the cycle spins. That axis is the people you are in business to serve. *First, last, and in between, the marketing cycle for your organization should revolve around the people you serve*—not around your existing services, not around your current building or staff or board, but around your ultimate customers.

This chapter will show you how the cycle works, and why it is important to attend to each part of the cycle in the prescribed order and with regularity. I will cover a marketing process that I like and then move our discussion to the marketing disability that really impedes most nonprofits as they market. This disability is a longstanding one that has been well ingrained in the minds of most nonprofit staff and board members, and thus will be difficult to dislodge. If it cannot be overcome, however, the organization that you work for may be permanently behind the competitive curve.

In the final section of the chapter, we'll look at the marketing cycle and how it affects some of your for-profit as well as your nonprofit competitors. You will learn how they view your organization, how they think about competing with you, and, most importantly, how you should view them. In Chapter 7, we'll cover the competition at much more length, but in this chapter we'll limit our discussion to your competition and their reactions to and interactions with your marketing cycle.

By the end of the chapter, you will have an excellent understanding of a marketing cycle that can work for your organization for existing products and services as well as for start-up ideas, new ideas, and even the business development cycle. You will know more about the marketing disability you have to overcome, and that knowledge will be the first step in successfully responding to it. You will be able to see the markets through the eyes of your competitors, a key competitive advantage in an increasingly competitive world.

The Marketing Cycle That Works

Most people seem to think that the marketing cycle starts with the product or service. If I know what I am selling, the theory seems to go, then I start from there. I then can decide how to sell, whom to sell to, how to convince them, and how to price. As noted in the introduction to this chapter, that sentiment is wrong, wrong, and wrong again. Marketing doesn't start with the product, or the service. Marketing starts with the *market:* the people to whom you are trying to sell, or whom you serve. If you start by deciding who it is you are serving, and follow that by asking those people what they want, and then respond by giving it to them, that's marketing.

 FOR EXAMPLE: Marriott is a great example of successfully adapting this method of satisfying customers. Their Courtyard brand was designed from the ground up by business travelers in the early 1980s and, as a result of that customer input, was an immediate success. A low-end brand, Fairfield Inns, followed. On the high end, Marriott Resorts and Ritz Carlton meet the wants of more affluent customers.

And, the process never ends. In 2007, Courtyard announced a major change in their facilities to accommodate the wants of a younger generation of travelers: more common workspace (with wireless and lots of electrical outlets) for work in the evenings. GenX wants to work in groups, whereas the Boomers have preferred working in their rooms. Wants change. ■

If you start without asking your markets what they want, if you just design a product or service and back into a market by asking, "How can I sell this wonderful product or service to these people?" you are destined to succeed only for a very short time and then only if you are a superb salesperson.

Marketing (the verb) has to start with the market (the noun) to be effective over the long haul. Only then, by putting the appropriate marketing activities together in the correct sequence, can you change the way your organization thinks of its markets and ultimately the way those markets think of you—hopefully for the better! The marketing cycle we'll review works for new products and new services, as well as for honing and improving existing products or services. It works in human services, the arts, education, religion, environmental action, and legal aid. It works, because at its core it is sensitive to people's wants, not their needs, and it puts those wants first.

With no further delay, let's review this marketing cycle. Exhibit 5.1 depicts the cycle at its purest and simplest, in a generic form that can be used across disciplines. Later, we'll apply it in a few examples.

As you can see, the cycle starts with the identification of the markets, works its way through asking about the markets' wants, and only then designs or modifies the product or service you are going to provide.

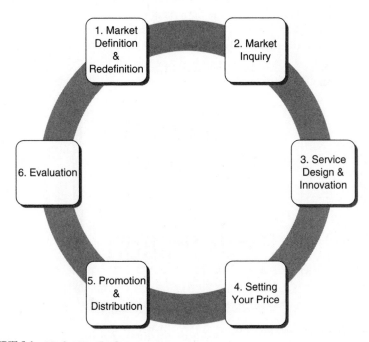

EXHIBIT 5.1 Marketing Cycle

Nowhere in the display do you see the word *need*. There's a reason for that, and you should know the answer if you have read Chapter 2: Needs are different from wants, and wants are what people buy, not needs.

As I said earlier, this cycle works for just about everything important in your organization: improving services, recruiting and retaining great staff, board, and non-governing volunteers, fund-raising, staff satisfaction, and on and on. I think you'll see that as we go through the cycle, but let's start by dissecting it and going through it item by item, discussing each point in some detail. Then we'll reassemble the cycle and look at its application in some real-world nonprofits.

Define and Redefine Your Market

This first step sounds so basic that it creeps up on people (see Exhibit 5.2). But the first question to ask is, who am I serving? Who are the people, the individuals to whom I am selling? How many of them are there? Where are they? Are they as a group, as a market, growing in numbers or waning? As you approach this question, do not get sucked up into what I call "the census trap." You get caught in the census trap when you assume that your market is all the people in a geographic area. It never is. This assumption comes from historical nonprofit monopolies. Many organizations had (and some still have) cachement areas, areas that were their "territory," their monopoly. In many cases, funding for these organizations was based on population (capitated) so that the illusion that an organization worked for everyone in the cachement area was reinforced.

1. Market Definition & Redefinition

EXHIBIT 5.2   Define and Redefine

Nothing, of course, could be further from the truth. Your market is not everyone; it is a much more defined group of people. If you are a private school, it is the parents of children in the age groups you teach, who are interested in non-public education and who have the resources to send their children to your school, and who can make the needed commute. If you are a health department, for health screenings it might be just people who don't have private physicians, or if it was for lead screenings, just people with very small children who lived in older homes with lead-based paint. If you are a church, while your doctrines may suggest that the world is your market, in reality, you are most likely going to appeal to people within five to eight miles of your church who are looking for a church and who do not already have a church home. This is a much smaller number than "everyone" in the community, or even within your five- to eight-mile radius.

Also, remember that in a larger market (such as "my donors") there are very important submarkets, such as online donors, annual donors, large-gift donors, special events attendees, and so forth. Each of these submarkets has its own special (and regularly changing) set of wants. Thus, you will probably want to go through the marketing cycle a number of times for the most important subsets.

Defining a market is pretty straightforward: You identify who it is you are going to serve. But what do I mean by *redefining*? It is an important term, because for most readers it will be the more common task. Redefining your market(s) means that you periodically go back and look at your markets, assuring yourself that they are still there, that they are the ones you want to serve, and that they still have wants you can meet. For example, if you are a YMCA and one of your markets (for your athletic summer camps) is kids from 8 to 18, you might reexamine this market and redefine it to be *kids from 8 to 18 from homes with incomes over $30,000,* or *kids from public schools* as opposed to private schools, or *kids who played in your regular youth athletic leagues.* This regular redefinition is crucial since conditions change: Markets mature, and wants change along with them. Only by regularly reviewing and redefining who it is you are serving can you accurately ask those whom you hope to serve what they want.

I hope that you get the idea that you need to identify your target markets carefully, developing as detailed a definition, as particular a description of them, as you can. The more accurate and finite your definition of your market, the more accurate your market projections will be, and thus your estimates, assumptions, and plans. This technique should be used for all of your services, and for all of your markets, so that you can recognize the many different markets that you serve. This activity is so important that we will spend the entire Chapter 6 solely on this subject.

Market Inquiry (What Does This Market Want?)

Having identified your market(s) as closely and finitely as you can, what is next? Is it to figure out how to sell your product or service to this newly identified group? Is it to blanket them with literature so that they will want what you have to sell? Is it to offer coupons to entice them into your doors the first time? No, not yet.

What is next in the marketing cycle is to figure out what the market wants (see Exhibit 5.3). How do you do that, you ask? By doing just that—*asking.* By asking *regularly,* and then, of course, *listening* and *responding,* you will find out what most people want. Remember our discussion in Chapter 2: People seek wants, so meet those wants and people will seek out your organization.

You can ask formally or informally. You can ask in surveys, in focus groups, in interviews, in one-on-one conversations. You can ask in person, or online. However you do it, you need to ask, and ask, and ask again. Asking once is not enough, since people's wants change *regularly.* This is also a critical issue, and we'll spend Chapter 8 entirely on asking in a variety of ways.

Suffice it to say that you cannot meet markets' wants if you don't know what those wants are. And, while you may have been in this field for 20 years and think you know it all, you don't. As I said earlier, I'll give you 75 percent, but the other 25 percent is the new stuff, the critical stuff, the competitive stuff that you simply cannot know unless you ask. The biggest mistake you can make in marketing is to say, "I've been in this business

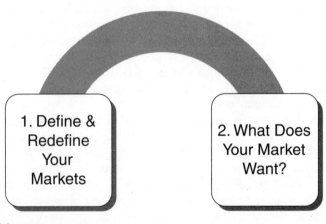

EXHIBIT 5.3   Market Inquiry

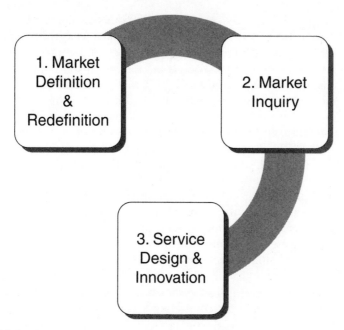

EXHIBIT 5.4   Shape and Reshape Your Products and Services

twenty years and I *know* what customers want." That's wrong. You cannot know everything you need to until you ask.

Shape and Reshape Your Products and/or Services

Only now that you know who your target market is, and know what they want, *only now* can you shape (or reshape) your product or service to meet the wants of your target market (Exhibit 5.4). This may mean starting from scratch to develop a new product or service, or, more likely, the constant amendment to, innovation in, and improvement of products and services already in place. Remember, not only will you be redefining your markets regularly, but wants change with time. Even within static markets, wants change. As a result, you need to assess and *reassess* your services again to ensure that they meet the current wants of the markets.

 FOR EXAMPLE: The staff of your organization is a market, and one that you should pay close attention to. Let's assume that you are going to survey staff about what kinds of benefits they would like as a precursor to making changes in your benefits package. What a great idea! You are asking a key market what they want! The survey asks each respondent to rate each of 20 potential benefits on a scale of 1 to 10. You collect the information and make the changes, trying your best to fit the benefits package to the wants of the staff. Now, go five years into the future. Assume the unlikely, that every staff person who took the previous benefits survey is still there, and no new staff have come on board. You repeat the survey. Would the answers be the same? Of course not. People's wants change as they age, and everyone in the market is five years older. Let's change the assumption. What if you have had normal turnover in the five-year interval since the first survey? If you readminister the identical survey, would the answers be the same? No, because the market has changed in composition. In both cases, you would need to change the benefits package to continue being market sensitive. ■

You cannot reasonably meet *every* want of *every* market. For example, if one potential customer for counseling services says that he or she can come in only between midnight and eight in the morning, it is probably not reasonable or cost-efficient to have a counselor on site overnight just for one customer. However, the information is important, because it may point out a previously hidden market—those who work second-shift jobs and are ready to seek services at night rather than during traditional hours. Is there enough of a market to support a reshaping of your services to accommodate this want?

You need to be sensitive to regular changes in market wants by making adjustments in the way you provide your services. However, you need to cushion your desire to fully meet every customer's wants with prudent business assessments and financial planning to ensure that you meet the wants you can afford to and defer on those that you cannot do efficiently, effectively, or with a high degree of quality.

Setting Your Price

A sensible price is one that: (1) recovers all of your costs of providing a service or manufacturing a product; (2) adds a profit to that price; and (3) meets the realities of the market. The first and second parts increase the price. The third part usually reduces it (Exhibit 5.5).

Let me focus you for a moment on the first part: full cost recovery. I know far too many organizations that are convinced that they must underprice their competition at any cost, and that cost is all that motivates a customer. Thus, they often juggle their costs around so that their sales price

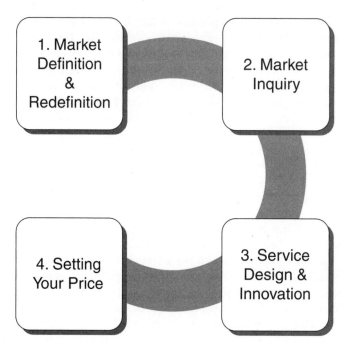

EXHIBIT 5.5   Setting Your Price

appears to be one that ensures full cost recovery but really doesn't. In this way they feel that they are assured of getting the work, of locking in the customer. What they are *really* doing is ensuring that each time they provide the service they *lose* money—such a deal!

It is crucial in price setting to remember that people don't buy based on price—they buy based on *value*. Price is a variable component of value. For some people, price is 99 percent of value; for others, it's just a small amount. If price were the only issue, there would not be any luxury products or services, no first-class seats on airlines, no Ritz-Carlton hotels, and no limousines clogging up the streets in our big cities. If price were everything, we would send all of our correspondence first-class mail. Federal Express would be shut down in a day. So would Gucci, Saks, and most of the stores on Fifth Avenue in New York, or Rodeo Drive in Beverly Hills.

So, don't just think about price. Think about value. And never tell people what they should value—that's giving them what they *need*. Ask them what they value, and then give them what they *want*. Do people highly value your service, or the way that you deliver it? If so, they will be willing to consider paying more for it. If they don't value your services, then even a lower price may not bring them on as customers.

FOR EXAMPLE: An organization that I work with provides inter-
pretive tours of historic districts in their city. They are devoted
to historic preservation and use their net revenues to fund historic preservation efforts. Their problem was that their tours
were too popular. They only had so many really good tour
guide/interpreters, and they knew that they could not train more
very quickly. So, to reduce demand, they raised the price, by
doubling it. Their rationale was that if they could not train more
excellent guides (and they couldn't in the short two-year term),
they would do only what they could do excellently. By raising
prices, they would reduce demand naturally, instead of making
people mad by having groups too large, or by turning people
away completely.

It was a gutsy call, and one that most nonprofits would not be
comfortable making. Other organizations would have rationalized
that since their costs had not risen, their prices should not. They
would assume that their status as a nonprofit did not enable them
to make a profit, and would not react to the market demand. But
this group did, and with *very* unpredictable results.

Demand went way up. It doubled in the first six months.
Why? Because people assumed that a tour that cost a lot would
be good—and thus desirable. The tours *were* good, and got rave
reviews. But the increase in price did not decrease demand. So
what did the organization do? It limited the size of tours, and
set up a reservation system including advanced payment (so that
it got to use the money early), but did not do more tours per
day *than it could do well*. Yes, that disappointed people, but five
years later the tours are still sold out five months in advance,
and, as another benefit, donations from tourists are way up, again
based on the perceived value of the service and the quality of the
organization. ∎

Never assume that price is everything. Recover your costs, add a profit,
and then listen to the markets. This is another really important issue, and
I have included a complete chapter on the subject in my book, *Financial
Empowerment*.

Promotion and Distribution

By now you know your market. You know what they want, you know what
you are providing, and you know the price (Exhibit 5.6). That's great, but
does your market know about you? Do they know that you are in business,

that you have this wonderful product or service that is shaped to meet their wants? This area is what is called *advertising*. It is cold calls, warm calls, direct mail, word of mouth, in-person sales, referrals, and public information. Don't just shotgun your information. Carefully gauge how and what you tell your markets. Track how they find you, and use only those methods that work. Experiment with new ones, but drop them if they are not delivering for you. A great example of this trial and error is your web site. While a web site is essential, many nonprofits don't really look at the desired outcome of their site, nor do they have any real goal for it other than "to be online." Has the web site resulted in clients? Has the organization improved its fund-raising and its volunteer recruitment? For some organizations, the answer is yes; for some, no. As all of us know, the Internet offers access to huge markets, but are they the people you want to seek? In my mind, yes, absolutely, but perhaps not in yours.

You need to promote to customers, to people whom you serve, as well as to people who send you customers—your referral sources. For a rehabilitation hospital this might be neurologists, for an ex-offender program it might be court adjudicators, for a wildlife preserve it might be travel agents

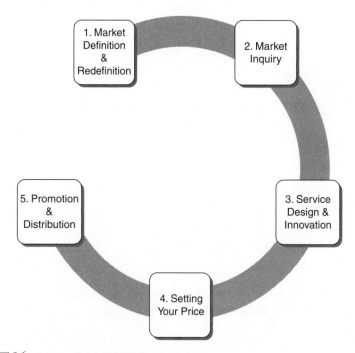

EXHIBIT 5.6 Promotion and Distribution

or local hotels and restaurants. You need referral sources, and you need to give them information that helps them understand what you do and why they should send people to you.

Here again is a very important issue. You need excellent marketing materials, and, in my mind, a top-flight web site, and you need to put them in front of the right people at the right time. So, we'll look at your marketing materials in Chapter 9 and better web sites will be included in our discussion of technology in Chapter 10.

Distribution is a common marketing term, but it may be easier for you to think of it as service delivery within the following contexts: *who, when, where,* and *how.* Remember that all of these context items weigh heavily on market satisfaction. A simple example is day care. If the *who* is not people who relate well to children (and parents); if the *when* is not at hours that meet parents' work schedules; if the *where* is not in an accessible location perceived as open, airy, pleasing, and safe; and if the *how* is not seen as beneficial to the children, then the services will not be patronized well enough to do the community any good.

By asking your customers what they want, you will learn a great deal about how they want the services provided. This cycle of asking and providing is yet another case of constant refinement. If there is a change in the wants for delivery, try to meet it if you can do so sensibly. To use the day care example, if your community's largest employer (a factory) suddenly went to a second or even a third shift, you might need to rethink the hours that you provide services. But if only one or two families out of a hundred need the extended hours, you might offer them in-home sitting rather than keeping the entire facility open all night.

Just because the *what* of your services is excellent doesn't mean that you don't have to pay attention to the *who, where, when,* and *how.* They are also part of the marketing mix, and the constant cycle of asking, innovation, and improvement.

Evaluation, Evaluation, Evaluation

As you have already seen, the markets and their wants change constantly. You need to be evaluating the effectiveness of your efforts as well (Exhibit 5.7). Customer satisfaction surveys are one way, as are regular interviews with funders, service recipients, staff, and board members. But you also need to be watching competitors, and tracking where your customers come from. All of these evaluation tools are important. In later chapters, we'll cover how to choose and segment markets, follow the competition, and ask customers what they want, but the essential thing here is to remember that evaluation and improvement are critical parts of the competitive marketing cycle.

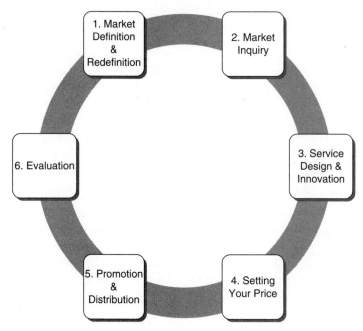

EXHIBIT 5.7 Evaluation

You can see that once you evaluate, you start over again; as I said earlier, the marketing cycle never ends; it just keeps going, helping you focus ever more resources on markets that want them.

Now let's look at two applications of this cycle in real nonprofits. This should illustrate more fully the applications of the marketing cycle and its usefulness to you and to your organization in your marketing efforts.

FOR EXAMPLE: A symphony wanted to expand its offerings to the local community, but found through surveys of ticket purchasers (particularly season ticket holders) that the current number of full symphony concerts was really all that the community could afford. However, the survey did produce some interesting comments (read: *wants)* from customers. They wanted concerts closer to downtown, and they wanted more intimate music, closer to the musicians. This was a result of the performance hall being a huge auditorium at a local university, 10 miles from the center of

(continued)

(continued)

the city. People also noted that they would like to come earlier than the traditional 8:15 P.M. start. The symphony already had a small chamber orchestra, but it played to small audiences at the symphony's admittedly too-large auditorium. The board and staff identified their market: new ticket holders with children, as well as those who had responded to the survey. They had asked what this market wanted and the answer was clear: more small, intimate concerts closer to downtown, starting earlier. They took an existing service, chamber orchestra concerts, and adapted them to meet these wants. They changed the distribution—the *where* and the *when*. The next season they held four chamber orchestra concerts in a historic church (with excellent acoustics) in the downtown area. They started on Friday at 7:00 P.M. rather than Saturday at 8:15. The concertgoers in the first pews could be close enough to the performers to read the music as it was played!

The price was also lower than at the large auditorium (the symphony's costs were down due to fewer musicians to pay and lower rental fees). The symphony promoted the idea heavily through music teachers in the public schools ("Get your parents to take you to a concert"). The result was an immediate success, with each concert a sellout. The next season the organization provided eight such concerts and they not only sold out, but allowed the symphony to retire a burdensome debt. ∎

What is the lesson here? Even adapting existing services can be a winning strategy when you ask your markets and listen to them.

 FOR EXAMPLE: The donations to a thrift store were down. And, the thrift store needed a continuing supply of quality donated goods to meet the constant demand from customers. (As an aside, thrift stores are excellent examples of organizations that work for two *widely* different markets: the donors of the goods and the purchasers of the goods.) The thrift store already had collection boxes, and would arrange to pick up goods if called. But still it wasn't enough. They decided to administer a survey in the local community, and found that what people wanted most was to simply get rid of excess "stuff," but only when they were (a) cleaning out their garage, attic, or basement, and (b) having a garage sale. A garage sale? It made sense, and the organization moved to adapt its existing pickup service to meet the wants of the customers. Staff watched the papers and, every morning, they went to houses that advertised garage sales. They talked to the homeowners and left leaflets noting that instead of the owners needing to pack up and retain the household goods that remained after the sale, the thrift shop would stop by, do the packing, and take some, most, or all of the leftovers. ■

What had they done? They had identified the market, asked for wants, adapted to meet those wants, and changed both their promotion and distribution to meet those wants—and it worked.

 FOR EXAMPLE: A Midwest state government department, a funder of human services that we will call HHS, had decided to, yet again, change the way that it organized, planned for, and funded the provision of services throughout the state. Over a period of two years, HHS floated policy papers, researched what was going on in other, similar states, met with legislators and the direct (nonprofit) providers of service, and then announced its sweeping changes. No longer would providers be funded on grants, but rather based on outcomes and on the number of people served (a modified managed care approach). The providers who could come up with the most innovative, cost-effective ways to provide services and still reach desired outcomes not only would be allowed to provide the services, but would be encouraged to expand to other communities, even if that meant pushing out current, in-place organizations.

What response did the providers have? About 80 percent screamed that the new system would not work, would hurt people who were being served, and was unfair to the provider system as well. About 20 percent quietly tried to figure out how to do what the funder, the customer, wanted. First, they looked at whether HHS was still a customer that they wanted, and saw that it was. Second, they looked at what HHS wanted: innovation, cost containment, and outcomes. Third, they asked themselves whether they could reshape their existing services to meet the wants of HHS and still meet their mission and values. It was not going to be easy, but they decided that they could. Fourth, they looked at their costs, and tried to reshape their services along with reducing their costs, again to meet a customer want. They looked at the way they delivered the services, the *who, what, where,* and *when.* Finally, they developed a promotion campaign for the funder, for HHS.

Which agencies were successful here? Did all 20 percent of these agencies succeed in making the changes? No; a number felt

(continued)

(continued)

that they could not do what HHS wanted. And some of the 80 percent stopped whining and followed the lead of the innovators. But many did not, and three years after the introduction of the new system, over half of those organizations were no longer eligible to provide services to HHS. Why? Because they didn't listen and respond to their market. ■

Use this marketing cycle to start up new services or adapt your existing ones. In either case, it will help you and your staff become and remain more market oriented, and thus more competitive.

The Marketing Disability of Most Nonprofits

You now know that asking, listening, and responding to the wants of your many markets is the core of good marketing. That doesn't sound too hard, right? I agree, and while marketing is certainly work, it is not particularly difficult work, just disciplined work. However, in my years of training and consulting with nonprofits, I have noticed that it seems to be more difficult work for staff than it should be. Staff either don't ask, don't listen, or don't respond. Over time, I have come to understand why.

Most nonprofit staff have a *marketing disability.* A real and severe disability. One that needs to be addressed and overcome for them to succeed in a competitive environment. Let me explain.

Most staff of nonprofits come from what I call a service background. They are curators, teachers, social workers, nurses, activists, ministers, scientists. They are trained to meet people, talk to them, test and observe them, and, as a result, be able to diagnose their *needs.* Or they are trained to assess a situation, or a community, and discover or reason out its *needs.* They are trained to know with confidence that they are "the professionals." They spent countless hours and lots of money in school learning this diagnostic skill. And, as valuable as that skill is, as necessary as it is in what the organization does, it becomes a disability as soon as the staff person says: "I know better than they (the customers) do what is *needed,* so I don't need to listen to what they *want.*"

Do you see the problem? By focusing on and reacting to their training, nonprofit staff members negate the key transaction in good marketing: asking customers what they *want* and valuing the answer enough to respond. By centering solely on their own expertise, these staff discount or even ignore completely the value of their customers' opinions. Therefore, they don't *listen.* They often don't even ask! Thus, they *can't* respond to the wants of the customer, and they are *doomed* in a competitive market. But asking, combined with listening, with a measure of diagnostic expertise works. Remember, nonprofit marketers give people what they *need*, but in a manner that they *want*.

 FOR EXAMPLE: A food bank in New York City provided food to hungry community members in the traditional way: having staff and volunteers pre-load boxes of food from their inventory that, together, provided good nutrition. A nutritionist helped develop checklists to insure that the combined food was healthy. One of item A, two of item B, and so on. Food recipients lined up and were handed a preloaded box of food to take home. People were grateful, and the food bank thought it was doing a good job.

That is, until it asked recipients some follow-up questions. It turned out that since the food recipients didn't pick their own food, they were throwing away the items that they didn't care for. This resulted in wasted food (not good), and in their constituency not getting a good nutritional balance (even worse). The staff were concerned, but until they began asking their constituents for ideas (a practice called *co-creation with constituents*), they were stumped. The discussions were energized, and the final solution both innovative and successful.

The entire food bank was reorganized. Recipients could come and shop for themselves and take a box of food, but it needed to be somewhat nutritionally balanced. Nutritional education was ramped up. Food was not wasted and the food recipients felt empowered. A win-win-win that started by asking the people served by the food bank what they wanted, and not merely telling them what they needed. In fact, this is a great case study of a nonprofit giving people what they need in a way that they want. ■

 HANDS ON: Talk to your staff, particularly your highest-trained staff, about the importance of listening to the wants of the people you serve. Remind them that listening is not an inherited skill, it is a *practiced* one, and that listening, really listening, is not just waiting their turn to talk! Finally, work with them on how to see things from their customers', their clients', and their students' perspectives. The more they can do that, the more value they will attach to the opinions, the complaints, the concerns, the *wants* of the people that your organization serves. ■

To overcome this disability, you need to constantly remind yourself and your staff that the people you serve have the right to have wants, and that those wants are important. Your skills as a diagnostician should not be diminished by this attention to wants. In fact, training yourself to listen in a new way may actually enhance your sensitivity to what your service recipients are saying. As a result, you may be able to serve them in new and better ways.

Remember the marketing disability. It is with you always, and you need to overcome it if you are to be successful, competitive, and market sensitive.

The Marketing Cycle and Your Competitors

You have read the marketing cycle that I want you to use. You know that it starts with the target markets, asks for wants, and then shapes (and reshapes) both services and products to meet those wants, including market-sensitive pricing, distribution, and promotion.

Where in this mix are your competitors? What about those people who want to take away your donors, staff, great board members, or, of course, the people you serve, and make them theirs? How do they fit? How can you adapt and respond to the competition?

As I said in the Overview, your competition is so important that we will spend Chapter 7 entirely on just that subject. Here I want to go over the parts of the marketing cycle and examine what your competition is doing. I hope to highlight a key point, and one of the characteristics of a market-driven organization:

Embrace competition—it will make you better at what you do.

Should you pay attention to your competitors? Certainly! Should you respect them? Yes, *if* they deserve respect. You certainly should respect the marketplace and its forces. Should you fear competition? No; if you do excellent work, if you ask your customers what they want and solve their problems, if you focus on customer service and let the markets lead you, in most cases, competition will not be life-threatening. Competition hones you, making you more efficient, effective, and focused on what you really do well. And that's good for you, for your organization, and for the people you serve.

So, know your competitors, learn from the good ones, and be aware that new competition can show up at any time, but don't live in fear. Put your energy into constructive avenues. Let's start by seeing how your competition reacts to the marketing cycle.

Defining/Redefining Your Market

As we have seen, for you this means figuring out who it is you are going to serve (or who you already serve in a more defined way). For your competition, it means the same thing, but perhaps in a different way. They may look at who you serve and try to take away only the most lucrative segment, or only the one closest to them. This is called *creaming* (as in skimming off the cream), and it happens in a lot of areas. Private schools may take only the best (or richest) students; museums seek to focus on kids (since parents will follow); environmental groups target people who want to buy "green" products and thus might be the most likely to donate to their causes, usually to the detriment of some other nonprofit that will not get that donation.

Any kind of shortage will do this as well. I've referred to shortages in physical and occupational therapists, and wealthier organizations often offer recruitment bonuses for individuals with such skills.

As I have said over and over, you have competition. Are you doing something for someone that your competition can do as well or better? Then watch out, because they are watching you! You may need to redefine your market to accommodate the competition.

Market Inquiry

Ask, ask, ask, and then listen! You've read that already. But you can also learn from your competition's asking and play off of what they learn.

While this may seem like a great, cheap way to find out things, do not fall victim to just being a copycat. You cannot always depend on the end product of others' marketing. What if they are making a mistake? What if their core clientele is fundamentally different from yours? Be a prudent observer, but make sure you do your own research.

You can be sure that your competition is watching you and asking your customers, volunteers, and employees how you do what you do, how much you charge, and what you do well or poorly. Depend on it. Little if anything in today's world is secret for long.

Service Design and Innovation

Your competition, in observing you, may steal your ideas (which, in nearly all cases, are fair game unless you can copyright or trademark them). Then they can improve or adapt them to meet their unique mix of customers and resources. Thus, you may look around one day and find that your best ideas have been improved on, taking away your best customers.

Of course, you can return the favor by doing what we reviewed above: observing, listening to your customers, and providing the best mix of responses to their wants that you can.

Your competition is watching, experimenting, and trying new things. You need to as well. The market's gumbo of ideas, wants, and products and services is never static, never a sludge. Stay flexible and pay attention.

Setting Your Price

You've already heard me say that price is not the issue, that value is. That doesn't mean that your competitors won't try to attract customers from you by lowering prices, offering introductory discounts or coupons, or even *low-balling*—offering prices below cost to get customers to try them (and theoretically to be impressed enough to return).

The danger here for most nonprofits is that a for-profit competitor probably has deeper pockets, and thus a much greater ability to price lower and for longer than the nonprofit does. However, a nonprofit competitor may underprice out of lack of business savvy (not understanding that the issue is value and not cost). In either situation, the temptation is to try to match price for price, and that can be deadly. If your competition offers a low price, evaluate it carefully. Does their price include everything that your price does? For example, does an introductory assessment at a competing mental health center for $49 include the same array of services, tests, and record review as yours? Does the lower-cost day-care center have the same staff-to-child ratio as yours? Does the "cheaper" tuition at a competing school include all student fees?

Most organizations don't compete solely on price—they compete on a mix of price, quality, availability, service, speed, and comfort. This mix is known as *value*, as we have already discussed. If your service is truly more valuable to the customers (which you can find out by asking them), they will be willing to pay somewhat more. Don't get sucked into a price war that you can't win, especially if you can give more value to your customer.

Promotion and Distribution

Here is another part of the mix where you can learn from observation: advertising. Watch what your competition does. Particularly if you are being targeted by a for-profit, look at how they let people know that they are there. Do they truly advertise (billboards, online, in paper publications)? Do they have handouts, posters in grocery stores, or targeted ads on the radio or television? Think about what kind of customer they are trying to appeal to with such advertisements. It may give you a clue about their marketing and business plans. If, for example, the ads for a mental health center note "day care on site," it is pretty clear that they are interested in parents, and more probably in single moms, who may be most in need of such a service while they are using mental health counseling or group therapy services.

As in the caution I included in the "Market Inquiry" section, don't always assume that every kind of advertising and promotion that your competition uses is automatically for you. It probably isn't. And, with perhaps deeper pockets than yours, they can probably chew you up in a competitive paid advertising campaign. So pick and choose your places to promote carefully, and don't let your competition draw you into a fight you can't win.

Then there is distribution. Again, this is the *how, where,* and *by whom* part of the equation. Your competitors will, undoubtedly, try new things. They will need to so as to draw your customers away from you. Don't be too inflexible to try new things yourself. If what your competition is doing is working, consider whether it will work for you. This area, more than any other, goes to the core of becoming and remaining responsive. Watch your competition (they are watching you) and learn from what you see.

As I said earlier, Chapter 7 will be entirely on your competition, and many of these subjects will come up again in more detail. But suffice it to say here that your competition is doing the same basic things that you are. Be observant, open-minded, flexible, and prudent in your responses to their innovations, and you will improve your own set of services, benefit from your competitors' marketing expenses, and perhaps remain competitive yourself.

Recap

In this chapter, we have had our first exposure to the classic marketing cycle. You need to chisel this sequence into your brain, as you will need it over and over as you go through the endless circle of asking, listening, and adjusting, asking, listening, and adjusting.

Let's review it one more time. The marketing cycle is:

1. Market definition and redefinition
2. Market inquiry
3. Service design and innovation
4. Setting your price
5. Promotion and distribution
6. Evaluation, evaluation, evaluation

We next looked at the marketing disability of most nonprofits. Remember that you are trained to diagnose needs, not ask for wants. You need to get over this disability if you are to succeed, and you need to warn your staff about their disability as well. Remember, everyone is on the marketing team, and everyone needs to ask, ask, ask, and then *listen.*

Finally, we looked at the marketing cycle through the filter of your competition, exploring what your competition does at each stage of the cycle and how you can and should react to it. Remember that you can easily get drawn into an escalating promotion or pricing war.

The marketing cycle will work if you follow it consistently. But it is not an event; it is a constant, endless process that will constantly and endlessly result in your improving your services and increasing the satisfaction of your customers. In short, your organization will do more and better mission. So use the process!

Discussion Questions

1. Do we really know who our markets are? For all services and all funders?
2. How do we know what our markets want? When was the last time we asked funders, for example?
3. Do we recover all our costs in our pricing? Plus a profit? Is there a mission reason not to? When?
4. Does our promotion just scatter-shoot, or is it aimed at a target market?
5. Do we succumb to the marketing disability? How can we get staff and board past it?

CHAPTER 6

Who Are Your Markets?

Chapter Thumbnail

➤ Market Identification and Quantification

➤ Market Segmenting

➤ Focusing on Target Markets

➤ Treating All Your Markets Like Customers

Overview

In Chapter 5, I showed you the marketing cycle that works, and works well, in a wide variety of situations, allowing you to improve your services, make the people whom you serve happier, and produce efficiencies and effectiveness that your organization has not seen before. What was the first step in the cycle? Right! *Define and redefine your market.* Good for you—you *were* paying attention! In this chapter we will go into that first step in detail.

In these pages, I'll show you how to define your markets, and who those markets *really* are. I suspect you will be a bit surprised at some of the markets we list.

Then, I'll show you how to segment your most important markets into smaller parts. This will prove very valuable as you try to focus your efforts on your truly critical markets, and as you differentiate between the markets your organization really wants to serve and those that you would rather not be involved in.

Next, I'll show you some objective and subjective ways to focus on your most important and most desired markets. One of the most important rules in business is the Pareto Principle, known commonly as the *80/20 Rule*; I'll explain what it is and how to take advantage of it. I'll also show you some ways to use your strategic plan to focus on the most important markets. By using both of these techniques you will be better prepared to make the most of your necessarily limited marketing funds and time; you can put your efforts where they will do the most good.

Finally, we'll get into detail on a crucial part of the marketing effort: treating each and every one of your markets (even those you may not especially care for) like a valued customer. If you, your staff, and all your volunteers learn this admittedly sometimes difficult skill, you will go a long way in both marketing and competitiveness. I'll show you some specific ideas on how to adapt to this new paradigm.

By the end of this chapter, you will have a thorough understanding of your markets, why they are all important to attend to, and how to sort through them and then focus on the most important.

Market Identification and Quantification

Who are these markets we keep referring to? Let's look at a form that will help you focus on the many, many markets you actually serve. As you look at Exhibit 6.1, note how many different markets there are and keep in mind that this form probably does not include all of *your* organization's markets!

When I first suggested that you examine your markets, you probably immediately thought of the different groups of people you help through your services. That's understandable, but only a part of the whole picture. You *really* have, as you can see, four different and distinct main categories of markets: internal, payer, referral, and service, and probably 10, 20, or even 40 different markets contained within those four categories. For example, in the category of "Donors," many nonprofits could subcategorize "Annual Fund Donors," "Special Event Contributors," "Online Donors," and so forth. Each category is important; you can't provide services without money, or without a staff or a board, and nearly all organizations depend on referrals—someone sending people to them—for a significant percentage of their work. Each category bears further analysis.

 NOTE: You can and should develop a form just like the one in Exhibit 6.1 for your organization. Draw one up on a flipchart, or

EXHIBIT 6.1 **The Markets of a Nonprofit**

INTERNAL	Board of Directors
	Staff Members
	Non-Governing Volunteers
PAYER	Government
	Membership
	Foundations
	United Way
	Donors
	Insurers
	User Fees
SERVICE	Service A
	• Client Type 1
	• Client Type 2
	• Client Type 3
	• Client Type 4
	Service B
	• Client Type 1
	• Client Type 2
	• Client Type 3
	• Client Type 4
REFERRAL SOURCES	Many different sources, all with different wants

have someone design one in your word processor. You'll have the same internal markets as here, but you need to be as specific as possible about the funders, services, and referral sources you have. I'd suggest drawing up the form now, and then having it with you as you read the remainder of the chapter so that you can pencil in your markets as you see examples from other nonprofits. ■

Internal Markets

There are three of these: your board, your staff, and your non-governing volunteers. All three are crucial, and all three deserve to be treated like valued markets, utilizing the same marketing process that we discussed in Chapter 5. All three groups deserve to have their diverse and often changing wants met, to the extent possible. Unfortunately, most nonprofits either ignore this issue, or drastically underestimate the importance of these markets. They treat their board as a necessary evil, their staff as a commodity, and their volunteers even worse. The management "knows" what the staff want (more money), so they never ask. The management doesn't really care what the board members want as long as they come to meetings, don't ask too many questions, and donate every year to the annual fund drive. Volunteers are to be put in whatever position is most in need, not matched with their skills, or oriented, supervised, or trained.

The downfall of these perceptions is that, in a competitive world, they don't equate to reality. You need excellent board members, and to get and keep them, you need to treat them as a valuable resource. Likewise, you are going to need to attract and retain good staff, and it will be tough: You need good staff more than they need you. For many nonprofits, volunteers are doing an increasing percentage of very high-end work, offering huge payroll savings while providing a network into the community that no other force can. And, in a competitive world, board members, volunteers, and staff have lots of choices of where to put in their hours. It doesn't have to be at your place.

So, make a big mental note: In the process of becoming market oriented and focusing on your external markets, don't forget your internal ones.

Payer Markets

These are the people who send you money for the services you provide. You may be offended that I consider these people a market. After all, you are here to do good works. Money is just a vehicle and an unseemly one at that. The people you really need to pay attention to are the people you serve, right? Partially. In the old days of having a monopoly, you could afford to do this. No more. If, in a competitive market, you ignore the payers and the internal markets and direct your attentions solely to the people you serve, you are on the short road to oblivion. Remember, there are two primary rules of nonprofits:

> **Rule One:** *Mission, mission, mission.*
> **Rule Two:** *No money, no mission.*

Ignore these at your peril, since money is the enabler of mission.

As you can see, there are many payers, and we should examine their different wants. I need to caution you here: Do *not* accept my listing of wants as gospel. Go ask them yourself. The following list generalizes the different wants of many payer markets, and almost certainly misses some important details of the wants of one of yours. *Ask them what they want!*

- *Government.* For many readers, the government (federal, state, county, or city) is a key customer, one that may even form the backbone of your income structure. Too often, unfortunately, nonprofit managers don't think of these important funders as *valued customers;* they consider them the *enemy*. While that attitude may have worked in the past, you can no longer afford to demonize government payers.

What do government purchasers want? Generally, they want a set of services (carefully defined) provided to a set of people (also carefully defined) in a set period of time, often in a set manner, with no audit exceptions and all paperwork in on time.

If you don't like having government agencies as key customers, develop a long-range marketing plan that reduces or eliminates them from your income stream. But while they are there, treat them with the respect that all your customers deserve. Ask them what they want and give it to them.

 HANDS-ON: If your organization has government income, consider this question carefully. When was the last time you asked your government project officer/funder, "How can I make your job easier?" Never? You are not alone, but that kind of question is essential to stabilize and improve relationships with all customers. When you read Chapter 11, "Incredible Customer Service," remember that it applies to this market as well. ■

Finally, don't fall into the trap of thinking of "government" as all one market, with identical and never-changing wants. You may well get funds from more than one government source, or even from different programs within a single agency or department. Each of these sources and programs has different legislation and regulations controlling it, and thus each has different wants from your organization. Each of them deserves your attention, at least if you want to continue to have them as a payment source.

■ *Membership.* Many nonprofits have a membership, which is an excellent way of developing important linkages with the community and a regular donation base—if, and only if, the membership benefits are worth the fee. Environmental groups, museums, zoos, symphonies, and public broadcasters are all examples of organizations that have built large, longstanding membership bases.

What do members want? It depends on the organization and the sales pitch that it uses to get the members. PBS members want quality programming, and often get a premium gift and a monthly program guide with their membership renewal. YMCA and YWCA members would not be satisfied just to know that the Y is open. For their fee, they want access to locker rooms, gyms, and pools, and reduced fees on Y programs. Museum members may get reduced admission fees or priority purchase on hard-to-get exhibit tickets.

You need to carefully and regularly assess the benefits that accrue to your members. You might want to make a list of the membership organizations in your community; that's the competition for these kinds of funds. Are your members satisfied? You don't know until you ask, and in a competitive world, you can't afford not to know.

- *Foundations.* Foundations come in all shapes and sizes. There are huge ones like Gates, Ford, or Robert Wood Johnson, and hundreds of small local community, corporate, or family foundations spread through nearly every city and town in the nation. Their interests and funding procedures vary widely, as do the amounts of money awarded each year.

    What do foundations want? While the breadth of interests is sweeping, within their areas of interest, most foundations want pretty much the same things: innovative projects that meet their criteria, organizations that can demonstrate strong community support, and projects that can be self-supporting, generally within three years.

    Foundation funding is *extremely* competitive and, if you don't carefully research the wants of the foundation, you are wasting your time and theirs. Most foundations give you a good list of their wants right in their funding requirements, which can nearly always be found on their web site. If you can, go beyond that and, if the foundation has a staff, talk to a project officer or, better yet, go to meet with them (if that is allowed and encouraged) and dig a little deeper into what their "hot buttons" are. Ask what they like to see most and what they like to see least on applications. Then listen and do what they ask!

- *United Way.* If you are interested in United Way dollars, or get them now, pay attention to changes in funding priorities and methodologies. United Ways are struggling with a new paradigm: People don't need them to give to individual organizations; they can go online and do it in two minutes. Talk about competition! That said, if you are receiving funds through United Way, talk to people (both staff and volunteers) involved with the organization in your community. Stay on top of any significant changes in wants. These funds are also increasingly competitive.

- *Donations.* Still the bedrock of many small, community-based organizations, and certainly the case for all places of worship, donations (including bequests and corporate funding) are also highly competitive. Notwithstanding that, organizations in the United States and elsewhere that demur from seeking donations ignore one of their key assets: the ability to take tax-deductible gifts.

What do donors want? Again, it depends, and lumping all donors together in one market basket is fraught with peril. The wants of annual givers vary widely. Some people might want to give you a bequest. Some people want to support one program. Others prioritize giving to an endowment. Some want credit and visibility; most don't. Don't assume. Ask. And, if you are really serious about maximizing your donations, consider obtaining the services of a reputable professional fund raiser. Why? Can't you just do this yourself? Not necessarily; way too many organizations try to do a little fund-raising, or a little fund-raising in a lot of areas (special events, direct mail, bequests), and wind up doing all of it badly. Here's the truth: *Fund-raising does no mission.* As a result, *it had better make money.* In a competitive environment, you have to establish and maintain a core competence in one or more areas of fund-raising before you start. That may mean training for your staff and volunteers, or it may mean hiring a professional, or both.

Finally, I need to underscore the necessity of having your organization be online for its donations. If you can't accept credit cards and/or PayPal online, you've lost money—period. No discussion. More and more people are more and more prone to doing their charitable donations online. A week after the 2010 earthquake in Haiti, National Public Radio reported that 80 percent of donations from Americans received by charities for earthquake relief had come online. That's *80 percent.*

■ *Insurers.* Some readers work for organizations that get funds through insurers. Insurers are, of course, financial intermediaries. As such, they are supposed to be obligated to pay for whatever condition or treatment is prescribed and covered through their policy. However, even though the insurer is supposed to be obligated by the policy of the insured to pay your organization, the speed and ease of that payment (and sometimes even whether the payment is ever received at all) depends in large part on your organization meeting the wants of the insurer. Whether your organization provides health care, home health services, mental health care, substance abuse treatment, orthopedic devices, long-term care, or preventive services, meeting the wants of the fiscal intermediary, the insurer, is essential.

What are the insurer's wants? Usually these are heavily centered on process and paperwork. In the past few years, those wants have expanded to include technological competence: Can you bill the insurer online? Can the insurer access your information online? More standard issues still are relevant, however. Was the insured medically required to seek services? Were they preapproved? Does your organization have the right licenses, certifications, and quality assurance? Do your staff? Are the forms complete? Are you part of the managed care contract? These questions are really wants.

If you are in any part of the human services field, you need to know how to "play the game," which is really just a cynical expression for meeting the markets' wants. Pay attention to the process, the paperwork, and the fine print. You'll get paid sooner, and more fully.

■ *User Fees.* These are admissions fees, ticket purchases, tuition, fees for counseling, or other payments received directly from the end user, the person whom you serve. Like donations and memberships, they represent a direct link between your organization and an individual payer who gets some benefit from the organization, either in service or self-esteem.

What do users want? They want what they pay for to be *high* quality, to have *high* value, and to meet their wants. Remember, price is not the issue—value is. If price were the only thing, no one would attend Harvard, Stanford, or the University of Chicago. They would all go to state colleges and universities. But all three of those institutions, like countless others of high cost, have thousands of applicants on their waiting list because of the value of the education and the name associated with it.

How do you find out what users want? Again, you ask. And, you try hard not to fall victim to your marketing disability. It is particularly easy here, since you are so often providing services for a fee, and so, this, of all areas, is a function for which you have training and experience. It is not difficult to fall into the trap of assuming that you know what the customers need (and you probably do) and ignoring what they want (which you don't know until you ask).

All of these markets are important, but later in this chapter I'll give you some ideas about how to focus on the most important—the ones that hold the key to your future.

Service Markets

Just as with the payer markets, there are many, many service markets. These are the people whom you serve, and they can be broken down by age, gender, education, income, zip code of residence, ethnicity, or the program or programs that they utilize. Most readers probably have thought that these were the people whom you worked for, and that this was the only market you were serving. It is key to mission, certainly, but the internal and payer markets are essential as well.

As with the payer markets, it is crucial that you avoid lumping the people you serve together. The more discrete groups that you can identify, the more you can focus your asking and responding to them.

 FOR EXAMPLE: A mental health center provided numerous services. As it went through its marketing planning and market identification, it noted many markets within each service. Let's look at just one—outpatient counseling. The staff and board identified the following markets within this service:

One-to-One Counseling:

Chronically mentally ill
Depression
Trauma victims
Veterans
Teens in the high school
Violent offenders

Small Support Groups:

Grief and mourning
Chronically mentally ill
Veterans with post-traumatic stress syndrome
Violent offenders
Alcoholics Anonymous
Veterans

Of course, each of these groups of people has different wants. To assume that all outpatient clients have the same wants would be ludicrous, but I see an awful lot of organizations that consider such lumping appropriate. Don't follow their lead. ■

Although I cannot do your market analysis for you, I urge you to break down your services by type of service and type of service consumer. Now, I want to focus on a critical service market that we haven't discussed yet.

Referrers

We've already noted that your organization, like all others, has a limit on how much time and money you can spend on marketing. Wouldn't it be great to have people (whom you don't pay) out there sending you members, clients, students, or parishioners? You can, and you may already. They are called *referral sources*. These may simply be informal recommendations from happy customers—someone who went to a play at your theater and was impressed, or a parent who loves how his or her child is developing in your preschool. Or they can be formal referrals from another professional, such as a surgeon referring a head trauma patient to a vocational rehabilitation facility, or a rabbi referring a troubled member of her congregation to a psychologist or psychiatrist.

What do these referrers want? Happy customers want to share their happiness, but it never hurts to thank them if you are aware of the recommendation. For the formal referral sources, though, it is a bit more complex. The first thing most referrers want is *capacity,* for you to have the ability to take the referral immediately and get it off of their desk. The second thing they want is *quality,* which is demonstrated by outcomes, by accreditation, or simply by having the same treatment philosophy that they have. The third thing most referrers want is to find out what happened. Most people want to know the outcomes, and more importantly, they are interested in the personal stories of success that come from interaction with your organization. Obviously, for some readers, privacy will be important (perhaps legally binding), but stories can be made anonymous with a little work—and it will be worth it.

These wants are the ones that I see from my travels around the country. But as I cautioned you earlier, don't depend on my observations. As with any other market, you don't know what they want until you ask. Do you need referrals and recommendations? Absolutely! Find out what your referrers want and give it to them. Remember that, in a very real sense, the happy customer recommendations are the result of giving those customers what they want. The more you ask, the more you know. The more you know, the more you can respond. The more you respond, the happier your customers will be. The happier they are, the more of these referrals you will get!

All of your markets—internal, payer, referral, and service—deserve attention. Paying close attention to so many diverse groups is not always easy, especially since your organization, like all others, has only so much money and staff time to throw at even this critical activity. So what do you do? There are two more steps to take control of all this marketing identification. The first is to learn about market segmenting, where you turn the tables and think through who it is you *want* to serve and compare that to who you currently serve. The second is to focus on your targets. I'll show you how to do both, and we'll start with segmenting.

Market Segmenting

We've already begun our discussion of market segmentation in the earlier example of the mental health center that identified in great detail all the different service markets it served. While this kind of differentiation is important, market segmenting in today's environment is more complex, and more potentially rewarding than simply breaking down your current markets into the smallest possible divisions.

Market segmenting is the technique of looking at your larger markets in more finite parts, and then deciding which ones of those parts your organization can, should, and wants to serve. It is a technique that should really focus you on what you do best, and it is one that is relatively easy to learn.

You can view segmenting your markets from several angles. Perhaps you want to look at all the different kinds of people you provide with a particular service. By itself, this listing gives you the ability to focus on different wants, but it also arms you to make some important decisions about the people you serve. Do we want to continue to focus on this group? Does serving this constituency mesh with our strategic plan, our vision for our future? Is this market segment growing or shrinking—likely to buy more or less of what we are selling? Nonprofit managers who are responsive to markets and their constant changes are asking these questions. Unfortunately, many nonprofit managers balk at such tough decisions because they are afraid of offending a traditional constituency by cutting back on a longstanding program, or because staff (or more often board) members resist abandoning a pet program.

 HANDS ON: As you make lists of your markets and their segments, ask yourself, "Why are we providing this service?" and "Why are we serving this population?" If your immediate answer is solely, "Because we always have," you should stop and assess whether you should continue to. Think through issues such as: Do you have true expertise in the service or population? Is the service provided elsewhere as, or more, efficient? Is this a core constituency for your organization? Is your organization identified primarily with this program or service population? Would reducing or ending this service dramatically affect your fund-raising? And, of course, a crucial but not stand-alone indicator: Are you making or losing money in this area or with this group? Answers to these and many other questions will combine to help you make your decision, but never just continue to provide a service out of reverence for tradition. Make sure that it makes good mission sense today, not just in 1983.

Another way to use segmenting would be to look at a potential market for a new product or service and to see which areas, which segments, you want to pursue. With this use of segmenting

(continued)

(*continued*)

you can pick and choose your target markets more efficiently and effectively. ■

FOR EXAMPLE: An organization in the Pacific Northwest works with individuals with disabilities, finding and creating employment opportunities. The organization was presented with the chance to purchase a car wash, which potentially could provide excellent and steady jobs for its clientele. As it looked at the markets, it didn't fall into the census trap I discussed earlier, and understood that its market was not the population that lived within 15 miles, but the people *with cars and trucks* that drove by regularly, whether they lived close by or not. After making this initial cut, the organization looked at some segments that needed clean vehicles. These can be summarized as follows:

- *Retail:* People coming in to wash vehicles that they personally own. While this had advantages in terms of community visibility for people with disabilities, it also had the disadvantage of being seasonal, and very dependent on weather and day of the week. Thus, the likelihood of steady employment was low.
- *Pre-Sale Cleaning for Auto Dealers:* Dealers need to clean cars prior to showing them. The organization looked at this as a real possibility for steadier work, but found that the liability of having to drive the cars and trucks to their site and the cyclical nature of auto and truck sales were two large barriers.
- *Cleaning of Fleets:* This market (which can consist of utility, postal, realtor, college and university, government, and other fleets) was a legitimate contender. The contracts would be large, steady, wholesale, and the drivers of the vehicles could simply stop in on a scheduled basis to have their vehicle cleaned.

The result was that the organization moved toward fleet cleaning, but only after trying retail. The initial try at retail was a mission consideration—more positive visibility in the community—but it was overwhelmed by the up-and-down nature of the business, resulting in long idle times for the staff. After this, they moved to the fleet cleaning. ■

You can use segmenting to affirmatively decide which markets you want to pursue, rather than simply reacting to all comers. But even with segmenting, you will still have many, many markets to monitor, and, as we have already said, only so much time and money to spend. You need to focus.

Focusing on Target Markets

Now you know who your markets are, and you have segmented them to show where market opportunities may lie. But where do you focus your efforts? This is important to get the most out of your marketing, and there are two methods to utilize as you try to decide where your target markets lie. The first is empirical while the second is more subjective. Using both is recommended, because by blending the results, you will make the best decisions on which markets to target.

Eighty Percent: The Pareto Principle

The first assessment method you need to apply comes from the business canon called the *Pareto Principle*, commonly known as the *80/20 Rule*. This tried-and-true maxim says that "80 percent of your income comes from 20 percent of your customers." When I first heard this spouted off at a business meeting 20 years ago, I thought to myself, "What drivel! How could something so pat and simplistic hold true across industries and businesses that vary so widely?" Perhaps you share my cynicism. Try it. I did, and the rule worked. I regularly apply it for clients that are in the depths of marketing planning to help them focus their efforts on the most financially important of their customers.

 HANDS ON: Try this: Take out your income and expense statement for last month. Look at the income side of the ledger for the year to date. Take the total income and multiply it by 0.8 (80%). Then start with your largest customer, and add their income to that of the second largest customer, then the third, and so on, until your running income total reaches the 80 percent threshold. Now go back and count how many customers that took. If you now look at your entire customer base, you will find that the number of customers it took to reach 80 percent is *very* close to one-fifth, or 20 percent. ■

Using this method for your service markets is sometimes tougher, because of the difficulty of coming up with a common denominator of units of service, but it can be applied for most organizations with a little work.

What is the point of this methodology? Go with the flow. Focus on the largest one-fifth of your customers. I did not say, however, to ignore the smallest four-fifths. In a competitive environment, customers who get ignored tend to vote with their feet. And I don't think you would like to have 20 percent of your income stream vanish. But this methodology does help you rationalize spending the most time talking to, visiting, and asking your largest customers, both payer and service.

The Strategic Plan Method

Now that you have done the empirical approach, look at these same markets from a different point of view, through the lens of your strategic plan and your market research. Ask the questions: "Which of these markets do I want to grow?" "Which parts of my community are the most important in terms of my mission?"

If, for example, you get only $5,000 a year in donations out of $750,000 total income, but your strategic plan calls for raising $200,000 per year in five years, you had better focus immediately on figuring out this market, asking its wants, and attending to them. If you had looked at the empirical analysis based only on percentage of income, you wouldn't spend much time in this area, since it represents only six-tenths of 1 percent of your total income.

Another example of this has to do not with increasing the income from a certain market, but with decreasing your dependence on a current large customer. Many nonprofits are intent on reducing their dependence on a traditionally large purchaser, such as the government, United Way, or private donations. In this case, it may make sense to lessen what may have been a day-to-day focus on these markets to a reduced priority. But don't ignore them! They are still large payers and, for the time during which they remain large payers, treat them well.

Once you have done both of these assessments, pick your target markets and focus on them. And here is where you may have the most trouble, at least if your assessment results in a change in priorities. People, following the laws of physics, tend to move to the path of least resistance. In marketing, that may mean talking to, helping, selling to, and asking only the people you already know, are already familiar with, and are already comfortable with—at the cost of starting cold in a new but high-priority market. Watch yourself to ensure that you are paying attention, and dividing your time appropriately, according to both your empirical and subjective analyses.

Treating All Your Markets Like Customers

In Chapter 2, we touched for the first time on this issue. Now that you have seen all the various markets you need to serve, perhaps this issue takes on a slightly different look. Let's go into this a bit more deeply.

Customers, Customers Everywhere

I hope that you and your staff already treat your service recipients as valued customers, greeting them warmly, offering assistance, solving their problems, and listening to their concerns. While you may not do this personally, it is critical that you and your senior management team both lead in this area and supervise closely, by regularly (and unpredictably) wandering around, watching and listening to the interactions of staff and your customers. Unfortunately, just as in the for-profit world, the nonprofit world is divided into organizations that understand this and organizations that don't.

I am sure that if you and I met and I asked you to give me examples of businesses in your community that were committed to customer service and those that didn't have a clue, you could give me a list of both types immediately. People pay attention and remember when they are treated well and when they are not. And while your nonprofit, like others, may have been given a break in the past by customers due to your status (and the perception that you weren't really a business), that slack has been tightened up, and you are now being held to the standard of a proprietary business.

In fact, customer service is an important enough issue for you in your quest for competitiveness that the entire Chapter 11 will detail methods for providing "Incredible Customer Service," a level of attention that is rapidly becoming the benchmark for customer interaction throughout the nation. Here, I just want to continue the assault on the first obstacle to overcome: the idea that everyone—funder, staff, board, service consumer—is a customer.

Barriers to the Customer Service Mentality

There are a number of issues that get in most nonprofit staff's way, and most of them we have already touched on. But I want to reiterate them in a slightly different light here to provide you with additional insight to persuade you, and then give you ammunition to convince staff and board members. First, if people are not treated well, most will vote with their feet. Although you have traditionally had total or virtual monopolies on your kind of work and funding in your community, the coming wave of competition does not stop with your funders. Don't let your former status get in the way of dealing with your current condition.

Another barrier to developing a customer mentality has to do with the marketing disability we discussed earlier. If I know so much more than the people I serve, shouldn't they be simply grateful for my wisdom, my help, my beneficence? *Hmmm.* This sounds like some doctors I know—doctors who don't get the fact that *I* am paying *them,* who make me sit on my heels for hours without apology, who treat me like a kindergartener, who always seem in a rush and don't see the person behind the patient. These are doctors that I no longer, and will *never* again, consult. Remember, there are customers everywhere, and there are competitors everywhere. Don't send your customers to your competitors.

Internal Customers

One result of competition is that your community has or will have more organizations that do what your organization does, in part or in whole. A result of this is that your staff will have new options for their employment. They no longer have only one place in a community to ply their trade. There are multiple opportunities. And to reinforce what I have said for years, you need your good staff more than they need you. Without good staff it is difficult to do good work. Put another way, good staff are the enabler of good mission.

I don't think anyone can argue with the fact that there are a fixed (and limited) number of qualified and engaged board members in any given community, and every organization would like to have them. Thus, if I as a board member want to serve, and I am not getting my wants met with you, I can easily resign and go help some other, more customer-oriented organization. An aside here is that many board members want to be associated with "quality" (also called *businesslike, customer-oriented*) organizations, and this means the nonprofits that market constantly and serve *all* of their customers well.

Funder Customers

Now to those pesky funders. This will be the longest stretch for many readers, as an awful lot of you have spent most, if not all, of your careers fighting with your funders rather than thinking of them as customers. Years of this kind of training and the resulting prejudice and difficult interpersonal relationships will be hard to overcome, what with our egos and pride getting in the way. And, even if you are the first one to stop fighting and start being attentive, the funder will (quite naturally) not trust you or even initially be nice to you, for some time. Turning relationships around takes time, and you don't have much left, so start now.

Many readers are thinking, "But my funders are so unfair! They ask us to do more and more without an increase in funding. They want more paperwork done to account for every nickel, and they want it all done on unreasonable schedules when they themselves are virtually never on time. They are customers from hell, and they really act more like they *own* us than like *customers*." I've heard this basic set of sentiments thousands of times. Here are two points: First, all businesses have customers from hell. Go to any airport during bad weather, and watch the gate agents deal with angry, irrational folks who are mad at the gate agent *personally* because it is snowing. These agents don't yell back. They have learned how to deal with their brand of the customer from hell. You need to as well. Here is a preview of a key customer service rule we'll cover in Chapter 11:

The customer is not always right. But the customer is always the customer.

All of us, including customers, are wrong now and then. But that does not mean that the relationship changes because of the error. You are still selling something, and they are still buying. Act that way.

Here are a couple of other notes on the new paradigm of funders as customers. First, if one or more of your funders are from state or local government, and if you are active in your state trade association, you may well be interacting with the same people in two roles: vendor and lobbyist/activist/advocate. Thus, one day you work with the state department, wearing the hat of executive director/CEO, and ask, "How can I make your job easier?" and the next day you come in the same door as a member of the state association and object to a new regulation, rate, oversight clause, or piece of legislation. This perennial schizophrenia can be trouble. One way to reduce the problem is to clearly and repeatedly identify yourself as a representative of the *XYZ Association,* perhaps going to the level of even wearing a name tag with the association's logo on it when you are doing its business. However, even that does not guarantee that the state or local agency staff will differentiate between your differing hats. I am not suggesting that you need to give up lobbying. Just be aware of, and try to minimize, the potential cost.

Second, in many cases, I have seen organizations start to treat their funders like customers and, over the succeeding months, the funders have begun to respond by treating the organization more like a vendor, and less like a slave. In three cases, the funders started to let the nonprofit be accountable for outcomes, not for process, reducing their paperwork load. In two other cases, the funder changed its funding method to allow the organizations to keep what they earned—the ultimate indicator of the vendor-customer relationship. Here is a case yet again of leading by example, and having people follow your lead.

Service Customers

Finally, consider your service recipients. Why wouldn't you treat them like customers? It's because of the nonprofit marketing disability. You know what they need. It is not a big leap from there to think that you know more than they do and thus devalue them, their ideas, their suggestions, their complaints, and their wants. Don't do it. Each and every person you serve is ultimately a customer, and more and more a customer who can choose not to return. Here, as with the funders, your customers are not always right or reasonable or polite. But they are always customers.

I don't want you to think that I think this is easy. It's not, particularly at first. But you need to start now to think of all your customers as customers. In Chapter 11, I'll show you a number of tried-and-true techniques to empower your staff to fix problems, deal with complaints, and meet customers' wants. But for now, just start thinking of everyone as a customer and start practicing your refrain: "What more can I (we) do for you?"

Recap

In this chapter, you have, perhaps for the first time, looked at your organization's many and diverse markets. You saw that you have *income markets, service markets,* and even *internal markets* of board and staff members. Next, we looked at those markets and I gave you some broad generalizations about what each market wants, with the caution that you don't really know what any market wants until you ask. We moved on to market segmentation, and I showed you how to accomplish this task and how to use it to take a more assertive stance in choosing who it is you want to work for.

With so many markets identified, you needed a way to focus your efforts and to target the most important markets. I showed you how to do this important task, both empirically, with the 80/20 Rule, and subjectively, by integrating your strategic plan into the marketing mix.

Finally, we turned to the difficult and controversial subject of treating everyone (payers, board, staff, and service recipients) like customers. We covered each group and I hope that I convinced you of the problems you will face if you don't jump on this competitive bandwagon.

In a competitive environment, you have to be aware of who your markets are and focus on the most important ones. You have to treat each like a customer. You have to ask their wants. Asking and customer service will be the subject of later chapters, but now it is time to move on to the other group identification process that is integral to successful marketing: identifying your competition.

Discussion Questions

1. Let's make a list of all of our markets in each of the following categories: funders, internal, service, and referrer.

2. Do we *want* to be in all of these markets, or are we just here because we always have been?
3. Are there markets that we want to prioritize, to target? What are they by the 80/20 Rule? Or, based on our strategic plan?
4. Do we treat everyone like a customer? How can we be better at it?

CHAPTER 7

Who Are Your Competitors?

Chapter Thumbnail

➤ Identifying Your Competition

➤ Studying the Competition

➤ Focusing on Your Core Competencies

Overview

I have said over and over that you are in an increasingly competitive and always-online world, and the facts surrounding that statement are irrefutable. Areas where you didn't compete five years or even five months ago are now open arenas. Things that you feel are secure from outside pressures will not be next year or perhaps even next month. Competition has become more and more the norm and less and less the remarkable exception. And everything you do is available for everyone to see instantly online. There is no place to hide.

Thus, it is important to think of some people and some organizations as competitors. For many readers, anyone outside your own organization has always been "the community"—usually a friendly, welcoming term. In many, even most, cases this will still be true. But, as a mission-based manager, you need to learn the often obscure difference between a community member and a competitor, between a colleague and a competitor, between a peer and a partisan. Not an easy, or, for many readers, particularly pleasant task. But it is an essential skill to learn if your organization is to compete at all. And, in some cases, the same person will be a colleague one day, a competitor the next, and a colleague the day after. Complicated.

This chapter will show you first how to identify who your competitors are and what they want that you have. We'll look at organizations that are after your clientele, your staff, your funding, and your donated dollar. We'll review this competition from the perspectives of funders, the services you provide, the people you serve, and your referral sources.

Then, once we have identified who your competition is, we'll look into what they are doing. I'll show you a number of tried-and-true methods of finding out your competitors' marketing methods, prices, and array of services. You will learn how to learn more about the competition and what makes it different, better, and often worse than your organization in the eyes of your clientele.

Once these two areas are covered, we'll look at your organization again and review the things that you have learned about yourself by learning about the competition: your core competencies. These core components of your identity are crucial to list and strengthen as you become more competitive. I'll show you how.

By the end of the chapter, you will know who your competitors are, how to find out what they are doing, and which areas are your strengths and which are your weaknesses.

Identifying Your Competition

Who are those pesky competitors anyway? To figure out who they are, let's review the array of markets that we covered in Chapter 6 and then compare those to your possible competition. You will see that you have competitors for each market, even those you may feel are sacrosanct. We'll start with your internal markets, and then move to payer, service, and referral markets (see Exhibit 7.1). Remember that the categories that I have included are both general and broad—that is, some of the categories that are listed may not be pertinent to your organization, and those that are pertinent are undoubtedly broken into many smaller components by market type and by individual competitor.

As you can see, the *internal* markets are just as susceptible as the external markets to competition. You may consider the issue of someone from the outside competing for staff to be a nonstarter for your organization, particularly if you are in a rural area or in a geographic area with no other organization doing what you do. For example, if you are a children's museum and the only one for 100 miles in any direction, you cannot assume that no one else will come after your management or line staff: They may

EXHIBIT 7.1 **Internal Assessment**

Internal Markets	Possible Competitors	How Do You Compete?
Board members	Other not-for-profits with board and volunteer positions available. One voracious competitor for the limited not-for-profit board "capital" in many communities is the United Way, which is structured to use up thousands upon thousands of volunteer hours each year. Good organizations want good board members. Don't lose yours.	You ask the board members what they want, treat them as a valued resource, and give them important things to do.
Staff members	Other organizations (both for-profit and not-for-profit) that are hiring people with the same skills as your staff.	You treat the staff with dignity and respect, involving them in management, budgeting, marketing, and planning. Like any other market, ask them what they want and give it to them when possible. Don't assume that just because you were once a staff person you know what today's staff want. You don't, so ask.

very well do so. Note that in Exhibit 7.1, I say that the possible competitors for staff are "organizations . . . hiring people with the same skills as your staff," not "organizations providing the same services as yours." There is a big difference.

And, while many people who work in the not-for-profit environment want to stay there and not jump to the for-profit world, there are undoubtedly numerous organizations in your community that are not-for-profit and do good works. As the entire sector becomes more competitive, don't count on your friend from the United Way board not raiding your staff (or your board, for that matter).

One note on staff competition: There is a very positive trend in this area—people from the for-profit sector, government, and the military, mostly in their fifties and early sixties, are moving to the not-for-profit sector. These Baby Boomers have, in many cases, done their 20 to 25 years at their employer, and qualify for retirement. They are at the age where many reassess their life and remember the altruism of their youth. And then they act, by changing jobs and doing "something that matters." Don't forget to look in the for-profit arena for good staff, and also don't forget to emphasize what they want—that you do "something that matters." These sector-switchers are a huge trend, one that you need to be on top of if you want the best people.

Finally, on the subject of staff, while I have long contended that money is not *the* issue for most staff in most organizations, it certainly is *an* issue for all staff in every organization. If your organization is like most not-for-profits, you don't pay your staff what they could get elsewhere in the community, and there may not be a reasonable chance that you can in the near future. But you do need to try to pay a competitive wage, and to do other things that you can to be competitive. Some of those are listed in Exhibit 7.1. More are detailed in the staff management chapter in *Mission-Based Management*. It isn't always about money.

 FOR EXAMPLE: Consider this question: Have you ever met an *unhappy* Federal Express delivery person? Neither have I. Second question: Have you ever met an unhappy United States Postal Service worker? Me too. Who gets the higher starting salary and benefits? The USPS worker. Similar to Federal Express are Cisco, Disney, Marriott, Lands' End, and many other superb firms that, like all of us, lead with their line staff. Their compensation is fine, but not the best in the industry. To paraphrase J. W. Marriott, Jr., they take care of their people, and their people take care of them. ■

To be competitive for staff you need to take care of them, and that is not, repeat, *not,* always represented by dollar signs.

Now let's look at your external markets, starting with the *Payer* market (see Exhibit 7.2). The people that send you money are *certainly* subjects of your competitor's interest. As you review the payer assessment chart, remember that your organization will have its own unique set of payers, and the ones you need to pay attention to will be the largest, the ones that have priority in your long-term plan, and the ones that are under the most competitive pressures, *in that order.* Don't wait to treat your target payer markets well until *after* there are competitors in the picture. Start now.

EXHIBIT 7.2 Payer Assessment

Payer Market	Possible Competitors	How Do You Compete?
Government	Any organization or individual who can qualify for the funding under the government's regulations. More and more government agencies are going to true bidding for all services, and including for-profits in their vendor pool.	Know your funders' regulations cold. Make sure you meet all their "silly" regulatory and bureaucratic wants. Ask in advance what they want, and be consistent in keeping your promises.
Membership	All other not-for-profits that offer memberships are potential competitors, but mostly within certain fields, such as mental health, environment, the arts, animal rights, and so on.	Make sure the benefits of membership are clear and tangible. Ask your members regularly what they want for their membership dollar. Add value—from the perspective of the member.
Foundations	Foundation funding is extremely competitive, and the competition comes more and more from organizations that have hired help to appeal to the foundations. Almost all of this competition is not-for-profit organizations; it may or may not be from your town, state, or area of service.	If you are planning to spend a lot of time in the foundation world, read the foundation press, get help from an experienced, successful grantwriter, and stick to the foundations that have an interest in what you do. Use the Internet to quickly learn what any particular foundation's expectations of you are.
United Way	Every other not-for-profit in your community that participates in the United Way, and many new not-for-profits that are starting up and applying to the United Way for funding.	Meet the United Way guidelines for funding precisely. If your United Way does community needs assessments, make sure that you participate so that you can ensure that your service area needs are included fairly and accurately.
Donations	Any and all not-for-profits that seek and accept charitable contributions. This broad category can be divided into corporate and individual, large and small, and regular and bequest.	Focus on the kind of donor most likely to be interested in what you do. State who you are (your mission and values) clearly. Get professional training if you plan to be competitive. And, get online: You need the ability to take donations (easily) through your web site.

(continued)

EXHIBIT 7.2 (*continued*)

Payer Market	Possible Competitors	How Do You Compete?
Insurers	Insurers, mostly as a result of managed care pressures, are looking for low-cost, high-quality providers of services. No longer limited to just health care, this can include any and all services covered under Medicaid.	Play by all the insurers' rules, including their forms, any preadmission certifications, and any licenses and accreditation you may need. Work with the people that you serve to meet the insurers' requirements as well.
User fees	Any not-for-profit that provides the same type of services that you do and makes the user directly pay through tuition, ticket fees, admission charges, office visit fees, and so on.	You need to ask your users what they want, how happy they are with your services, and where you can improve—constantly.

As you can see, you have a lot of potential competitors, and in each case I have suggested one or more of the basic components of our marketing cycle: Select the target market, find out what they want, and modify (or create) a service to meet the wants.

Next is the set of external markets that you are probably most concerned about, the *service* markets. These, most importantly, are subject to competition. And, since the number of people you serve is very often closely tied to the funding you receive, you need to attract and retain your clientele over a long period of time. But beware that your competition is doing the same thing. Let's examine how and why, and start with you doing a little homework.

 HANDS ON: Make a copy of the table in Exhibit 7.3. If you can enlarge the copy to fill an 8-1/2 by 11 sheet of paper, so much the better. Then, fill in the table as best you can, either alone or with a team of management and line staff. Exhibit 7.4 is an example of a filled-in table.

As you do this, remember to be a*s specific as possible.* ■

EXHIBIT 7.3 **Self-Assessment**

The Services We Provide	Competitors	Where They Excel	Where We Excel

The People We Serve	Competitors	Where They Excel	Where We Excel

Fill in the self-assessment table, making multiple copies of the blank table if you need to. If your copier has an enlargement capability, use it! The essential part of using this table is to begin the process of identifying who the competition is, and learning what you do well in that particular market. Additionally, I've divided the chart into two parts: The Services We Provide, and The People We Serve. This division is intended to focus you on the fact that competitors may come after people first (AARP goes after people over 50 and then focuses on the services that they need) or the service first (an arts organization advertising summer classes). Be thorough, and remember to look at the sample in Exhibit 7.4.

EXHIBIT 7.4 **Example of Self-Assessment**

The Services We Provide	Competitors	Where They Excel	Where We Excel
Short-term residential shelter	1. Salvation Army	Capacity	Friendly, accommodating staff
Job readiness training	1. Helping Hands 2. Veterans Administration 3. Local Job Corps 4. Welfare to Work providers	? ? ? ?	Staff with job experience
Counseling	1. Local mental health association 2. Private psychologists	? ?	Experienced counselors

The People We Serve	Competitors	Where They Excel	Where We Excel
People who are homeless	1. Salvation Army 2. Helping Hands Homeless Shelter	1. Capacity 2. Capacity, counseling	Sympathetic, nonjudgmental
People with autism	1. St. Mary's Hospital 2. County Developmental Disabilities Association	1. Marketing 2. Array of services	High level of training of staff

As you can see, the agency in Exhibit 7.4 is just starting its internal analysis, and is unsure of where its competition excels. Thus they definitely need to do more research. The things that they feel they excel at are mostly "friendly, experienced staff, sympathy, and training." That may be nice, but is it what people want? They need to carefully review and make sure that what they excel at is what people *want*.

Last, but definitely not least, let's examine your all-important *referral* market and see who is competing with you there. Remember that your referral sources are the people who send you clients, students, parishioners, and members. For some readers, you may get referrals solely through word of mouth from currently happy customers. For many, particularly those in human services provision, referrals are a much more formalized part of your organization: A physician refers a patient to your organization for occupational therapy, a social worker refers a teenager to your program for counseling. In these cases, it is important to find out the perception of the referral source about your organization and your competition.

If you don't have referral sources in the formal sense, remember this: A happy customer will sing your praises to 10 to 20 people over the next year. An unhappy customer will complain about you to 100 people within the next two weeks. Thus, you *do* have referrers, and when we cover customer service (Chapter 11), you will learn how to keep those referrers happy.

In Exhibit 7.5, you'll see a sample of a referral listing for an organization that provides rehabilitation services to persons with spinal cord and head trauma injuries. It includes headings: Our Referrers, What Do Our Referrers Want?, and Whom Do They Refer to Us? This categorization allows the

EXHIBIT 7.5 **What Do Our Referrers Want?**

Our Referrers	What Do Our Referrers Want?	Whom Do They Refer to Us?/Comments	Who Is Our Competition?
PHYSICIANS			
Dr. Jones	Quick acceptance of patient, insurance coverage, accredited facility	Head injuries (two 70-day patients last year).	St. Jude's Hanneman Rehab
Dr. Majeski	Insurance coverage, accredited facility specializing in spinal cord	25 occupational rehab patients last year—mostly spinal.	Unknown
Dr. Wheeler	Insurance coverage, Medicaid certified, accredited facility	Various patients —mostly inpatient (40 last year).	Unknown
Dr. Foresta	Quick acceptance of patient, insurance coverage—all types, accredited facility	Only two patients two years ago but 20 last year. Mostly short-term assessment patients.	On staff at St. Jude's?
INSURERS			
Company A	Quick acceptance of patient, Medicare/ Medicaid certified, accredited facility	20 patients each year for the past 5 years.	Unknown

(continued)

EXHIBIT 7.5 (*continued*)

Our Referrers	What Do Our Referrers Want?	Whom Do They Refer to Us?/Comments	Who Is Our Competition?
Company B	Quick acceptance of patient, Medicare/ Medicaid certified, accredited facility	Just starting to send us longer term. Only reimburse 80% of normal charges. Five patients last year.	Unknown
Company C	Quick acceptance of patient, Medicare/ Medicaid certified, accredited facility, managed care capacity	Leader in managed care. Short stays mandatory. Fifty patients last year.	Unknown, but talking with three rehab centers about inclusion in managed care network.
Company D	Quick acceptance of patient, Medicare/ Medicaid certified, accredited facility, managed care capacity	No history. A new player in the community. But covers almost 20% of the community due to three large employers.	Unknown
Company E	Quick acceptance of patient, Medicare/ Medicaid certified, accredited facility	Heinous oversight and paperwork. Only 10 patients per year.	Part of new managed care network?
EMPLOYERS			
Meltdown Utilities	Lowest possible Workman's Comp results, deal directly with insurer, managed care capacity	Board President is on the board at Hanneman?!	
Ace Manu- facturing	Lowest possible Workman's Comp results, deal directly with insurer, managed care capacity	Five or so injuries per year. Ace is working on risk avoidance, and thus will be sending us fewer people in the future.	Unknown
Acme Auto- mobiles	Lowest possible Workman's Comp results, deal directly with insurer, managed care capacity	Rapidly growing. Unionized. Sends us 20–30 people per year, but automating quickly.	No preferential arrangement yet.

EXHIBIT 7.5 (*continued*)

Our Referrers	What Do Our Referrers Want?	Whom Do They Refer to Us?/Comments	Who Is Our Competition?
Cellular Four	Lowest possible Workman's Comp results, deal directly with insurer, managed care capacity	Doubling the size of the workforce every three years. Sent us 10 people last year, but all long-term patients.	Unknown.
Microhard Group	Lowest possible Workman's Comp results, deal directly with insurer, managed care capacity	Low accident rate for population.	No admissions in past two years.

organization to identify groups as well as individuals and focus on both the referrer and the market that they provide. For instance, if Dr. Jones sends only two patients per year, that may not make her a priority for the organization. But, if both of those patients are long-term, high-income patients, perhaps spending some time with Dr. Jones is advisable.

Looking at insurers, you will see that there are significant differences in what the referrers want, and thus in which referrers this organization should actively pursue. The same is true for the employers.

Notice that in this last analysis regarding the employers, the organization doing the analysis has not yet figured out who their competition is to any great extent. They obviously need to complete their inquiries. By using a chart such as this, the organization can be an aggressive market segmenter and choose the markets in which they want to compete, reducing their emphasis on other markets, and focusing their limited time and dollars on the market segments that best fit with their strategic plans.

You need to know who your competitors are, but this does not mean simply making a list. You need to look at them through various lenses: your funders, the people you serve, the services you provide, and the people who refer to you. Only by doing these different analyses can you hope to really get a good grasp of where to focus your greatest competitive efforts.

Studying the Competition

By applying the tools in the previous section, you can develop a list of your competitors and then prioritize the market segments to focus your efforts. Even with that focusing, you still have a list of priority competitors, ones that you need to find out more about. In using the tools I just provided, you were asked to fill in what the competition does well and compare it to what you do well. I assume that your input on those charts was preliminary and based on word of mouth, or assumptions. If you are like most readers, it was probably not based on careful analysis.

What You Need to Know about Your Competition

With your competitors, you need to find out important information that you can use to become a better competitor yourself. You need to learn the following four core things about your competitors:

1. *What services do they provide?* Do they compete with you across the board, or only in certain areas? If they are a full-spectrum competitor, you probably need to investigate them more carefully than if they are only competing with you in one area, unless they are providing only your most profitable service.

2. *What clientele are they seeking?* Do they target the same population that you do? Or, do they just take the most lucrative segment of your population (a technique known as *creaming*)? However, if your target markets and theirs do not really overlap, this is also important. If you are targeting people over 60, for example, and the competitor has that age cohort as a secondary or tertiary market, you may not have to worry as much.

3. *What value do they give to the customer?* Remember, price is not the issue, value is. What does your competitor do that provides value to the customer? An added value at a museum might be a well-designed map, or a number of easily accessible benches or rest rooms. An added value for a counseling center might be a particularly friendly receptionist and free coffee in the receptionist area. Whatever the competition is doing, is it something that you can also provide well, and that is within your mission statement?

4. *What are their prices?* Is the price truly comparable to yours, or do you (or they) offer more service for the same price? Whereas price is not the *main* issue (value always is), it is an important one for many customers. Make doubly sure you do your best to compare apples to apples when looking at price. Otherwise, you may make bad decisions based on the assumption that your price is lower (or higher) than the competition's.

 FOR EXAMPLE: A few years back, I was working with two competing not-for-profit organizations that were considering a merger. These organizations provided sheltered employment to people with disabilities. They were reviewing each others' "daily rates"

(prices) and one saw that their own rate was nearly twice that of their potential partner. They came to me upset, because they feared that this low rate indicated poor quality of service and they did not want to even consider joining up with a "poor-quality organization." I asked them why they felt the service was poor, and their answer was, "Look, our daily rate is $140 and theirs is only $82. They can't give good service for $82." "No," I agreed, "not unless they don't include the same costs in their rate as you do in yours."

In the end, we found out that that was the case. One daily rate included transportation, meals, and supervision after work. The other organization offered all of these same services, but billed them separately. Thus the comparison of prices with the name "daily rate" was invalid and misleading. ■

You need to find out about services, target markets, value, and prices—at a minimum. It would also be nice to know about other things, but these are the core issues to look at first. How do you find out? You do a little market research—aimed at your competition.

Where Do You Look?

Where do you start? What resources do you have? How much time do you spend on this? The answer to all three of these questions is the same: It depends. It depends on how actively you are competing. It depends on whether the competitor is retail (where a lot of information is in the public domain) or wholesale (where prices and services are more difficult to research) and whether they get government funds, when everything is public. It depends on how much time and money you have to spend.

However, you need to start somewhere, so here's a list of resources that you can use to learn about your competition:

- *Online.* There is, of course, an enormous amount of information on the Internet. Here are some great places to start:
  - Go to the competitor's web site. There is often a large amount of data on the firm, their services, and even their prices right online. You may also see their marketing strategy, be able to note what they are promoting, watch for sales or price discounts, and even get bids directly online. If they have a newsletter or an RSS feed, subscribe.
  - Look in the online public record. If a competitor has bid for any public dollars, particularly against your organization, that bid is

public information, and so is the background information on the firm that goes with it. Go to the funding source's web site and poke around, and if you can't find what you are looking for, ask for it by e-mail.

- If the competing firm is a not-for-profit, you can learn more about it at Guidestar, or Charity Navigator, and other online watchdogs. Pay particular attention to how current their data is. Make sure you're not looking at a 5-year-old IRS 990.
- If the firm is a for-profit, go to www.ceoexpress.com and look for the research area. There you will find the best and most up-to-date research sites and tools on the Web. Use them.

 HANDS ON: While you are at it, check your own records. You can enter and edit information on Guidestar.com. You can edit and update information at the Secretary of State and IRS. Make sure your information is up-to-date and accurate. When you run a search on a competitor, always run one on yourself—to find out what your competitor, and potential customers, are finding out about you. ■

If your competitor is a for-profit, you may be able to get information on them through a national database such as Dun & Bradstreet or a local information source, such as the Chamber of Commerce or the Better Business Bureau.

In either case, one of the first steps I would take is to check online, then call or e-mail the competitor, and ask for information on services and fees sent to you. There is no need to lie and pretend that you are a service recipient. Just ask for written material and have it sent to your home. If you think that they will recognize your name and not send it to you, ask one of your staff to make the same call.

Your referrers also usually have sets of information at their offices or on their web site to provide to their clientele. For example, a social worker usually will keep information on all the programs he or she may suggest to a client; a minister may have materials from many resources in the community; a teacher may have materials on the many available tutoring organizations. (*Note:* They should have current copies of your marketing information as well.)

- *Customers.* Your customer base is an excellent source of information. When you do customer surveys, add in some questions on your competition. Ask such questions as: "Have you received this service from other organizations in the community? When? From whom? What did you like best about them? Worst? Why do you utilize our services rather than theirs?"

Between surveys, you can ask customers informally when you see them in your organization. By doing this you will not only often learn important competitive information, but your customers will also feel that you care about their opinion of what is important. Never discount the value of informal, regular asking. Your organization needs to have a culture of constantly asking.

- *Your state trade association, state association of non-profits, community foundation, or local management services organization.* These groups all should be tracking at least the issue of not-for-profit activity in their respective areas. Your state trade association (for whatever you do) is the best place to start, but the state nonprofit association that deals with all not-for-profits in your state is also a good statewide resource. For a listing of state associations, go to www.ncna.org. Community foundations and management services organizations (MSOs, which are nonprofits set up to help other nonprofits manage better) are more local in interest and influence. For a list of MSOs, go to www.allianceonline.org. For a listing of community foundations, go to www.tgci.com/resources/foundations/community.
- *Board, staff, and volunteers.* The more ears and eyes out there, the better. After you make a list of your competitors and prioritize that list for the most pressing investigation, make copies and provide them to your board, staff, and volunteers to let them know what kind of information you need, what questions you want answered, and that you would appreciate any help that they can give you in gathering the information. Now, suddenly, instead of just you and your circle of friends, acquaintances, and interactions, you have 20, 30, 50, or more people doing the same thing. The likelihood of getting information increases dramatically. One important side benefit of asking these people for help is that it reinforces the issue that competition is real and not just some figment of your imagination. Use your resources—in this case, that means all of the other people inside your organization.

What Your Competition Is After

With these four important sources in mind, let's turn our examination of your competition to the people or things that your competition is trying to take away from you. Each group on the list that follows will have its own sources of information that may be of help to you. Opening up channels of communication early is important, so that you have established trust and access to information. Thus, even though not every one of the six items or people on the following list will be a priority for you today, you may need access to information about that area in the future. I am not contending that you should give each area equal priority; just don't completely ignore any of them.

Remember, as you read the list, these six categories are those in which competitors are trying to compete with you—for good board members, excellent staff, donations, bid work, volunteers, and direct services. In each, you need to find out how they are competing with you and try, if you can, to beat them.

 HANDS ON: Think about the following six issues related to your competition:

1. *Board members.* Ask board members (and friends and neighbors) who are serving or have served on other boards what they like most and least about their board *service.* Don't ask detailed and pointed questions about the other organization—you may not get good information. Focus your questions on the functions of the board that they liked and disliked. If there are board workshops run through your United Way, community foundation, local MSO, or local college or university nonprofit program, go to them and learn about the state of the art. You need to make your board service desirable.

2. *Staff.* When staff come aboard, ask them what they liked most and least about their previous job. When they leave, ask them in an exit interview what attracted them to their new job (or drove them away from your organization). Read the want ads to check salaries and benefits. Take part in salary surveys run by local or state trade associations, or your state nonprofit association, to get a handle on competitiveness.

3. *Donations.* Be a constant observer of how you personally are asked for money, and urge your board and staff to do the same. Do you like being "hit up" in the supermarket parking lot? By snail mail? By e-mail? By phone? In person? Within these groupings, what approaches do you like and dislike? Do you give online? Does your staff or board? Look at the printed materials other organizations are handing out, and how they pitch for donations on their web site. What appeals to you and what doesn't? The field of donations is incredibly competitive and sophisticated, and new innovations pop up all the time. Pay attention!

FOR EXAMPLE: In 2005, I received a letter from our mayor (on her letterhead) announcing that I had been selected for an annual honor associated with one of our human services not-for-profits. The mayor noted that I had been selected for my "numerous achievements," and that I would be feted at an awards dinner about six weeks later. I was a bit dubious at this point, since the letter said that my achievements were in the area of "financial consulting," which is not what I do.

But then the other shoe dropped. The mayor was sure that I would appreciate the honor and that I would agree to commit to raise $1,000 for the not-for-profit! I've heard of a $1,000-a-plate dinner, but never a $1,000-a-plaque award! My reaction was, shall we say, not happy, but in a small town like ours, you really don't want to unnecessarily irritate the mayor. Fortunately, I had a conflict to be doing training out of town on the night of the awards banquet and sent my regrets.

Overall, I give the organization an A for innovation, but the bait-and-switch approach really turned me off. ■

4. *Bid services.* When you participate in a bidding process, are the other bids, particularly the winning bid, made public? Can you find out who the other bidders were? As I mentioned above, if the bid was for public dollars, the information is public. Go get it. Find out what the winning bid offered (assuming that it wasn't your organization). Try to find out as much about the competition here as you can. I am involved in bidding for a project probably twice a year, and I always ask who else bid, what they offered that was different, and (if I didn't get the work) what was the deciding factor in selecting the other consultant. Sometimes it is something I can't control, such as that the other consultant was from the local community; sometimes it is something I could have done differently, such as the array or sequence of services offered. Sometimes, of course, it comes down to price. But each time I learn, and so can you. Never just walk away from a bidding process. Get as much information as you can.

5. *Volunteers.* If your organization uses volunteers (other than the board of directors), then you know how important they are. As with board members and staff, ask your volunteers if they have done similar work in other not-for-profits, what they liked and disliked about their time there, and why they now help you.

(*continued*)

(*continued*)

When you talk to your volunteers, use a group session rather than individual meetings. Volunteers tend, for the most part, to be a bit awed by the senior management staff, and putting them in a peer group will not only make them more at ease, but also generate more ideas and reactions for you. In addition, it saves you time.

6. *Direct service ideas.* Here, your antennae need to be out for new services, service innovations, and ways that your competitors are adding value. Keep checking web sites, but remember my caution about assuming the currency of information. It may well be incomplete or out of date. Your other sources are the customers we discussed earlier, your staff (again, the more ears the better), and, in many cases, the people from whom you buy specialty products or services. Ask these vendors who else is buying products from them, and learn what you can from them about those organizations. For example, if you buy physical therapy (PT) equipment from a large vendor, ask them who else in the area is buying similar equipment. They will give you a list of your potential competitors. Don't stop there. When the salesperson comes in, ask, "How's business? Any big sales lately?" Suddenly, you find that your most important competitor is replacing all its PT equipment in the next three months. This is important information if you also know that customers value new equipment, or, as in the story in Chapter 2, your staff members want to work with the newest equipment. Ask your vendors as well as your customers. ■

In all of these cases, you are asking, asking, asking, and then trying to fit the often fragmented pieces of the puzzle together. The culture of asking is the root of your information, and you need to have a lot of people asking as well as a system to get the information back to you promptly. History is full of examples of organizations that had critical information but didn't communicate it to the person who most needed it at the crucial moment. Don't follow their path. If you just gather information but don't communicate it, you aren't doing your organization any good.

I'm sure that you have noticed that I did not give you any one source or even a set of sources that will necessarily meet all your information needs. Finding out about competitors is often a haphazard quest, with incremental progress in some cases, and huge gains made in others. It will depend on the competitor, the situation, and your resources. But just because you don't think that you can get all the information you want immediately doesn't mean that what you *can* gather isn't important. It is. For your core competition, go after the information, keep it up to date, and use what you can to improve your own services and products.

Focusing on Your Core Competencies

By using the techniques discussed in this chapter, you now know how to identify your competitors, how to find out information about them, and how to focus on the most important of your competitors. Now, what do you do? Do you try to compete on all fronts, with all types of organizations, in all services and for all groups of people?

Of course not; you don't have the resources, energy, or time to do all of that. What you need to do now is the third step in a three-part analysis. Let's review what you have done in the first two steps and then examine the third.

Review the Markets

You have done this (as described in Chapter 6) already. You should know who your markets are, how many there are, which are your focus for the future, and which aren't. You have applied the 80/20 Rule and know its implications.

Evaluate the Competition

You should have done this as well, as described earlier in this chapter. You know as much as you can gather about your competition, including an analysis of the competitor's strengths and weaknesses compared to yours.

Look at Your Core Competencies

It is time for this third, crucial step. Since you can't compete on all fronts, where do you focus your actions? One place to do that is where you are already strong. Remember the SWOT (Strengths, Weaknesses, Opportunities, Threats) analysis that you used to run when doing a plan? Do it again now with your board and staff, but stop after the Strengths and Weaknesses parts. Identify the things you do well and the things you could work on. (*Note:* If you have never done a SWOT analysis, they are terrific and worthwhile exercises. A good place to start on the Web is www.mindtools.com/swot.html.) Now, compare those two lists to the things your markets want. Are the things they want the things that you do well? If so, fine; if not, do you need to invest in improvements? Or, should you focus on a market segment that wants the things that you do well?

FOR EXAMPLE: A sheltered workshop in western New York State recently told me of a decision to get out of the business of packaging as a way of employing people with disabilities. The packaging industry had become too price-competitive, and too oriented to Just-In-Time, both areas where this organization did not feel it could compete well. Instead, it looked at what it *did* do well, and found that service—*high-quality* service—was its strength. Over a three-year period it changed its focus to work with customers who valued high levels of service. ■

FOR EXAMPLE: A client organization of mine in Missouri decided that it could no longer provide residential services to mentally ill people because the regulations and expectations of their funder—the state of Missouri—were too high compared to the amount the state paid. This was a change in market wants that the agency could not meet; it could not do the service well for the amount it was being paid, and was dragging down other services by subsidizing the residential area of the organization. After a very difficult and emotional decision process, the board cut the residential services loose to a group of staff who left to form their own nonprofit. ■

Now, look at the list of strengths and weaknesses again, in light of your competition's strengths and weaknesses. Do you compete strength-to-strength or weakness-to-strength? Do you need to bolster some areas to meet a competitor's strength, or should you compete in an area where they are weaker? Remember, the key here is to consistently find ways to add value to your services, value from the perspective of your customer.

When you are done with this analysis, you should have a defined list of the things you, your staff, and your board feel that you do well, your core competencies. Focus on those; invest in keeping them state of the art. Buy the training, equipment, and staff that you need to keep these areas a focus on excellence for years to come.

Remember that you are not your competition, and that you don't want to be. Your organization is unique in its own right. Certainly, study and learn from your competition. But don't try to copy them in everything. Be yourself—focus on the markets you want using your own core strengths.

Recap

In this chapter, we have covered the important points that will help you identify and learn more about your competition. We looked at how to analyze your competitors through the lens of your services, the people you serve, your referrers, and your funders. I then showed you how to use staff, board, volunteers and friends, and even vendors to continually gather information on the four key questions you need to answer about your competition:

1. What services do they provide?
2. What clientele are they seeking?
3. What value do they give to the customer?
4. What are their prices?

We then turned to the issue of finding out about how the competition is coming at your board, staff, and volunteers, and in direct bidding. Finally, I showed you how to analyze all of this information in light of your organization's core competencies. Focus on the things that you do well, and match those with what your target markets want.

One final word about the competition: Respect them, but don't fear them. They are organizations made up of people just like you, trying their best to provide a product or service in a chaotic and often confusing world. Never assume that they can automatically do things better than you. Find out where they are good, and find out where they are weak. All organizations have some of both. The biggest mistake I see as not-for-profits realize that they are entering a competitive arena is fear. Fear closes your ears and eyes to information about your competitors. Fear incapacitates you, making you incapable of innovation and flexibility. Fear makes it impossible for you to take a risk on behalf of the people you serve. It will eat you up.

Embrace competition as a way of forcing you to do more mission, sooner and better. Respect your competition, and pay attention to them. Respect yourself as well, and be proud and at the same time realistic about your organization's capabilities. Compete head-to-head when you have to and when you can. Focus on your core strengths, build customer loyalty by giving them what they want, and you will be successful.

In order to give your customers what they want, I have told you that you need to ask, ask, and ask. That is the subject of our next chapter.

Discussion Questions

1. Do we really know who our competitors are? How can we keep better track of them? Should we focus on the top 10 or on the competition that is in our 80/20 markets?

2. Who competes for our referrers now? Are we doing enough for our referral sources? Can we do more?
3. What are our core competencies? Are we excellent in these? How can we maintain that excellence (improve our status)?
4. How can we keep up to date on all the techniques and knowledge that we need to maintain excellence?
5. In our target markets, do we need to worry about competition, or is there enough market for all of us?

CHAPTER 8

Asking Your Markets What They Want

Chapter Thumbnail

➤ Surveys

➤ Focus Groups

➤ Informal Asking

➤ Asking (and Listening) Online

➤ Asking Mistakes

➤ After Asking

Overview

Ask, ask, ask, and then listen! I hope you are beginning to repeat that as a marketing maxim, because it is the best one I know. Only by asking *regularly*, and asking the correct people the correct questions, can you find out that all-important piece of information: what your markets want. Only by asking regularly can you keep track of how those wants change with time. Only by asking and listening can you overcome the marketing disability that I described to you earlier. You need to ask.

But how do you ask? Whom do you ask? How often, and in what format do you ask? What kind of outside help do you need? How much will it cost? Where do you start? Does the Pareto Principle apply to asking? All of those questions will be covered in this important chapter.

First, we'll look at the most common way of asking: *surveys*. We'll go over survey methods, how to develop a survey, where to get help, and how many people you need to survey to be sure that your answers have meaning. We'll look at a couple of sample formats, review how many identifiers you should use, and examine ways to make tabulation and analysis easier.

Then, we'll turn to *focus groups,* a favorite method of many market analysts. We will cover how to plan and run a focus group, what to ask, what not to ask, whom to invite, and where to get help. We'll look at how to analyze the data gathered and what to do after the focus group meets.

Next, we'll talk about informal interaction as an asking tool. We'll cover ways to ask, what to ask, training your staff to be constant askers, and some problems that other organizations have had with regular asking. Then, we'll look at some fatal mistakes people make when they ask—ones that you want to avoid.

Then, we'll examine the increasingly popular area of asking online. I'll show you some benefits and things to avoid, as well as ways to watch out for your nonprofit's online reputation.

Finally, we'll cover what you should do *after* you ask. This will include tabulating, analyzing and sharing the information, getting back to the people you asked, and integrating the information into your marketing plans. By the end of the chapter you should have a number of hands-on tools and ideas on how to proceed with this crucial part of the marketing cycle.

Surveys

We all know about surveys: They are expensive and complex and get very little response. Right? Wrong, at least as a rule. Surveys *can* be expensive and complex and have undependable results. They can also be inexpensive, simple, and can garner a near 100 percent return. In this section we'll look at what surveys are and some rules for keeping them affordable, useful, and easy to add to your marketing efforts.

Surveys, when done properly, gather *objective* or *quantitative* data, that is, data that can have statistical significance and be statistically defended. You can analyze this data over time by asking the same questions every 6 or 12 months. For example, if you survey your staff, you can analyze the percentage who respond that they are "very satisfied" with their job, and see whether that number goes up or down each year. This is called *trend analysis.*

Alternatively, you can look at the same data and analyze it between groups in the same survey. Going back to our staff survey, you could examine whether the job satisfaction was higher in administration or in direct service, in one of your locations or another. This is called *cohort analysis.*

Another benefit of surveys is that, if done correctly, you can survey a small group of people and accurately transfer the findings of the small group to a much larger one.

 FOR EXAMPLE: I am sure that you see the results of survey data on television or in advertisements regularly.

"Our most recent poll shows that Candidate X is ahead of Candidate Y by a 53 percent to 41 percent margin with 6 percent of the population undecided." *Then the announcer (or the graphic) adds,* "Survey of 2,045 American adults conducted June 15 to 16. Survey results accurate within three percentage points." ■

The surveyors looked at a tiny slice of all Americans and then made an extrapolation of those results to the population as a whole. This ability to survey a small group is very, very cost-effective if you need to know what a large group thinks of your organization, but only if the survey is done properly. You can't just ask 15 people on your block a question and have any confidence that the results represent your community as a whole (unless the block *is* the entire community!).

Thus, surveys have benefits that can really help your marketing. You can see how you are doing now, as opposed to last month. You can see which market segment is most in want of your services. You can find out who is happy and who is not. You can survey the *who,* the *what,* the *where,* the *when,* and the *how much.* What most surveys are not particularly good at is finding out the *why,* at least in any depth. For the *why,* you have to use a different set of tools, including focus groups, interviews, and informal asking. More on these later.

We will define a survey as a standardized, written sequence of questions given to a group of people to elicit information on a particular subject. The most important adjective here is *standardized.* You want to ask everyone the same questions, with the same tone, in the same sequence. Standardization is a crucial part of getting statistically reliable information from the survey.

Whom could you survey? In theory, any market that you currently serve or desire to serve and in which you want to become or remain competitive. In practice, you would probably survey only your largest, your target, or your most crucial markets. You could survey consumers, donors, funders, staff, referral sources, and even (though I don't suggest it) the community as a whole. You could focus your questions on need, on your competition, or on the satisfaction of the survey group with your organization.

As you can see, there are a lot of people whom you can survey, and a lot of information that you can get out of them. However, you have only so much money and time, so let's look at 10 suggestions for getting more out of your surveying. I want to ensure that all of your surveying dollars are well spent.

1. Have Instructions

At the beginning of the survey, have instructions for the reader. Keep them *simple* and *short*. Include the reason for the survey, any special instructions for how to fill it out, where to send it when it is completed, and the deadline for submission to have input considered. Also name a contact person for any questions that may arise.

2. Be Brief

You need to be as brief as you can be. When people fill in a survey, they are doing you a favor; giving you some of their time as well as their opinions. Help them by keeping the survey as short as possible. I see a lot of people who think that they are being smart by asking everything they possibly can on one survey to "save money on mailing." What happens is that the longer the survey, the less likely people are to fill it in. Thus the "savings" get eliminated since the return diminishes.

3. Be Focused

This is one way to accomplish point 2. Focus each survey on a particular issue: customer satisfaction, needs analysis, product testing, and so on. Don't mix the questions; you will mix up the survey and its resulting data. Be focused, be brief.

 HANDS ON: *Warning, warning, warning!* Your CEO or board president may very well come to you and ask you to make your survey longer, saying something like this: "Since we're sending out the survey anyway, let's save some money and throw in a few questions on one or two other subjects." Resist! Blame me! Why? Because not only does this soak up the limited time people will give you to fill out the survey, but it causes you to lose the focus you have worked so hard to acquire in the survey. Fewer people will return the survey, and it is now less focused. Thus, you don't save money—you waste it. ■

4. Don't Ask Too Often

If you send a board member or a staff member or a donor a questionnaire every week, how many do you think they will fill out? I have already told you that you need to ask regularly to track trends and keep up on new customer wants, but *regularly* does not mean *daily*. Again, value the time of the people you are surveying. Ask them, but only as often as you absolutely need to. Remember, there is a thin line between being curious and inquiring and being a pest. Don't cross it.

5. Ask the Questions in the Correct Sequence and Wording

You can really mess up the data you get by asking questions in the wrong fashion, the wrong way, or even in the wrong order.

 FOR EXAMPLE: There is a wonderful story that I have heard repeated for years (and that I suspect is apocryphal) about graduate students in marketing who each year go down a busy street at noon, holding up an 8-by-10-inch glossy photograph of the current president of the United States. They ask the first 100 people they see the following question: "You know who this is, don't you?" and get a 95 percent correct response rate. Then they ask the next 100 persons, "Who is this person?" and get only a 79 percent correct response rate. According to the story, this experiment is repeated annually by each class to make the point: Be careful how you ask—it skews the answers. ■

You can really get valueless information by asking the wrong question the wrong way. My suggestion is that you should make a list of the information you want and then follow the suggestion in point 10.

6. Limit Your Identifiers

Identifiers are the things you usually fill out at the beginning of a survey. Are you male or female? What age group are you in? Are you married, single, divorced, or widowed? What is your income bracket? These are all identifiers. You will almost certainly want to have these in your surveys, since it is the one way you can analyze the data by groups of people (called *cohorts*). For example, if you do a consumer satisfaction survey, you probably would like to identify people with the different programs you provide, or the different demographic categories you serve, or even the county (city, Zip Code) where they live. This lets you look at your data in more depth.

Identifiers are terrific, but they have a big drawback. The more you put on your survey, the fewer people will fill it in, for two reasons. First, it makes the survey longer, cutting down on the response level simply because the form looks too long to some people. Second, remember that most of the surveys you will do will deal with the happiness or satisfaction of your various customers. In these kinds of surveys what you really want is to find out all the bad news: You want to find out what's wrong so you can fix it and improve your services. But, the more identifiers you have, the more people feel that they will, indeed, be identified as an individual. Thus they will either not fill in the survey, or worse, they will fill it in but pull their punches, not being as frank with you as you would like. Then you have bad data, which is worse than no data. This second caution is, of course, moot in cases where you have people fill in their name. I suggest that for any survey where you ask for satisfaction levels, you keep the survey anonymous. My experience is that you will get much more useful information.

 HANDS ON: When making a list of what you need to know on a survey, particularly in the area of identifiers, make a list of the breakouts you would like to see. This might be by gender, age group, ethnicity, location of service, or countless other "slices" of information. Then look at the list and for each item on it ask the question, "What am I going to do with this information? Am I collecting it from curiosity or need? Will I be able to use the information I collect?" Be brutal with yourself in this area. There is a strong tendency for people to ask for too much information. I have read countless survey reports that are demographically loaded but light on real information. The reports nearly go into the shoe size of the respondents, but don't have much hard, useful information. Make a list and ask "Why? Why? Why?" before including each identifier in the final survey. ■

This is not to say that identifiers are not important. Some are crucial analytical items for statistical significance; others speak to important program and service needs or concerns. For example, if 90 percent of your program recipients are women, but 55 percent of your consumer survey recipients are men, you have learned that extrapolating the survey data for all consumers may be problematic. Thus having a gender identifier on that particular survey form is valuable. Similarly, for surveys that have questions that seek concerns with program hours, services, and other indicators of satisfaction, knowing which services the survey respondent uses most, or their location of service, may be very important. But their Zip Code may not be.

Be selective. Ask for some identifiers, but only as many as you *absolutely* need. Your outside help (see point 10) can give you some assistance in this area.

7. For Trend Data, Be Consistent

Trend data, as I mentioned earlier, looks at information over time: For example, how many of your staff are "very satisfied" with their job this year as opposed to last year and the year before? That is trend data, and watching the trends is a crucial part of good management, good marketing, and being competitive. I have long said that, while data in isolation is *interesting,* data in context (compared to something) is *valuable.* The context here is the context of time. Are the trends positive or negative? Are you gaining ground or losing ground?

 FOR EXAMPLE: Let's look at a list of information gathered from surveys that you might be interested in tracking over time. Note that this is a generic list for nonprofits and that you should add to (or delete from) this list to make it fit your unique circumstances.

- Customer/client satisfaction (may be more than one survey depending on the breadth of customers you serve)
- Staff job satisfaction
- Staff benefits preferences
- Community needs assessment
- Funder satisfaction
- Donor satisfaction
- Referrer awareness and satisfaction ■

Each item on the list could be a repeated survey (usually every 12 to 18 months) whose data could be compared with previous surveys. The trick in collecting trend data is avoiding the common pitfall of constantly amending (offenders in this area call it "fine-tuning") the questions so that the data is skewed, making it, at best, less accurate and, at worst, worthless. You need to ask exactly the same questions over and over. So get the help you need (see point 10) *before* you distribute your first survey.

Having said that, if you have a question that is not giving you valuable information, *drop it.* You save yourself and the survey respondent time. And, as circumstances change, you will need to add questions to accommodate those changes. But such amendments should be few and far between, and the wording of the questions that are repeated from survey to survey should hardly ever change at all.

 HANDS ON: When you do change parts of your surveys, make sure that you note it in the report. For example, let's assume that your previous consumer surveys had only four choices in a question that asked, "Which of our programs do you use the most?" and that your current survey gives six choices, as you have added two new services since your last survey. This change, while valid and

(continued)

(continued)

worthwhile, will skew the comparative data, and thus the change deserves a notation in the report. Always make such notations to be fair to the reader. And, if the only reader is going to be you, *still make* the notations, so that in future years you can remember what changed and why. ■

Work for consistency in your data gathering. It allows the greater utilization of the information that you have spent so much time and money gathering.

 NOTE: There are numerous other trends that you should be tracking within your management team, including financial ratios, donated dollars, days payable, staff turnover, customer complaints, salary comparisons, administrative percentages, and so forth. The list could take three pages, and, like any other, would need to be customized for your organization. Don't look only at survey trend data. There is a lot of information already inside your organization that you should be monitoring. ■

8. Include Closing Instructions

At the end of the survey, tell people what to do with the survey once it is completed. Even if you included instructions about where to send the survey and by when in the introductory page, do it again here, in large, bold typeface. If the survey is online, just make sure they know which button to click to send you the results. If you are asking people to mail the survey to you, include a stamped, preaddressed envelope. If you want them to deliver the survey to you in another form, make sure to specify how, to whom, and by when.

9. Say "Thank You"

At the end of your survey, thank people for their time and effort in giving you information. It seems like a small thing. It's not. Let them know you appreciate their time and also tell them what will happen to their survey, when they might expect to see results, how the information will be used, by whom, and by when.

10. Get Help

As you have probably gathered, surveying is not just something you wake up one day and start doing. It takes time, financial commitment, and a fair amount of expertise. It is easy to do poorly, and a challenge to do well. Doing it poorly results in that most dangerous of products: inaccurate and therefore misleading information. Doing it well can give your organization a true mission advantage: good, accurate information on which you can set policy, develop programs, improve services, and do more effective mission.

All of this is to say you probably need help, at least to develop your initial surveys and learn the ropes. There is a lot of help out there. There are professional marketing and surveying organizations, including a growing number that work solely in the nonprofit sector. There are instructors and professors at your local colleges and universities who teach marketing, surveying, and similar courses. There are professionals who work for large corporations whose job it is to develop their internal and external surveying. There are staff at regional planning commissions, agricultural extension offices, economic development agencies, and in your local mayor's or county/parish commissioner's office who develop surveys. As I mentioned earlier, make sure you check your local MSO, your state association of nonprofits, your state trade association, and your local United Way and community foundation. All of these are resources you can tap.

What can this professional help you with? There are a number of things. You should make sure that you get assistance in at least the following areas:

- *Selection of survey sample.* What is the best set of people to survey to get the information you want that is accurate while being affordable? This is a technical and statistically challenging area.
- *To pilot-test or not to pilot-test?.* If you are surveying a huge group, or making a multiyear commitment to a survey instrument, it may be smart to pilot-test the survey with a small group to make sure that it is working the way you want it to.
- *Question development.* While you should absolutely be in charge of what information is sought, the *way* that it is asked is crucial. Should particular questions be open-ended or "forced choice"? If forced choice, how many options should there be and what wording should be used? In what sequence should the questions be placed? Should there be confirming questions included?
- *Survey administration.* Your survey consultant can help you with administering the survey. Should you mail or hand out the survey? Should it be online or off? Should it be anonymous? Should it be done in person? The consultant may even mail out, collect, and analyze the data for you.
- *Online asking.* Get some help in designing your online questions and response methods. Talk to the expert about what online survey provider she prefers, and ask for any shortcuts or tricks that she uses to make her surveys (or survey reports) more useful and appealing.

Don't scrimp here. If you go the cheap route, you may have correspondingly less-than-valuable data. Remember: You get what you pay for.

If you plan to do surveying, I would strongly urge you to order a copy of an excellent basic surveying text. One I really like is titled: *Designing and Conducting Survey Research: A Comprehensive Guide* (Jossey-Bass Public Administration Series, 2005) by Louis M. Rhea and Richard A. Parker. It is excellent and will arm you with the basic information you need to work with your outside expert.

Focus Groups

Focus groups are great. They allow you to easily do what surveys do not: to follow up on initial responses, accessing feelings, reactions, and emotions at a much deeper and more personal level. Focus groups at their core are facilitated sessions of 8 to 15 people that focus on a particular issue. They are often used to test people's reactions to a new product, or to a potential advertisement, or to compare reactions to two or three different potential advertising slogans or campaigns. Speaking of campaigns, politicians use focus groups regularly to test their messages prior to general distribution.

As a mission-based manager, you have a number of potential uses for focus groups. These could include:

- Testing a potential new service with consumers, referrers, and funders
- Following up on survey results that revealed a problem (or an opportunity)
- Testing various themes and slogans for a capital campaign

There are, of course, dozens of other uses for focus groups.

Focus groups gather what is called *subjective* information. They elicit immediate reactions, in-depth commentary, and emotive responses in ways that surveys cannot.

 FOR EXAMPLE: Let's say that you are surveying a core constituency and on one question you ask, "Overall, how would you rate your satisfaction with the services you receive from our organization?" You give the respondent a scale of 1 to 7 with a 7 being equivalent to "Terrific!" and a 1 being equal to "Awful." The responses are consistently 4s and 5s, where in previous years they have been mostly 6s and 7s. What's going on? Surveys are not the best way to find the answer. By the time you receive the data and analyze it, the respondents are on to other things. But you can ask these questions in a focus group: "How do you like our services? Why? Is your level of satisfaction lower, higher, or about the same as last year? Why?" And, when someone in the group says something like, "Well, I'm not as happy because the staff just aren't as friendly," a set of follow-up questions can be asked right on the spot by the facilitator, honing in on what the problem may be. None of that can be done efficiently by survey. ▪

I have six suggestions for making your focus groups more valuable, less expensive, and more productive:

1. Get a Facilitator

This is *absolutely* crucial. You need to have a person *from outside your organization* who can plan and run your focus group. Focus group facilitation is a real skill, and it is much more important that your facilitator be strong in facilitation than an expert in your area of service. You can teach her or him about what you do.

Why have an outsider? Because the people in the focus group will be more frank with an outsider, and an outsider will be more objective about what she or he hears than you or anyone in your organization can be. Thus you get better, and more objectively viewed, information. Even if you are the best facilitator on the planet, the participants will see you as biased if you are a paid staff or even a board member. Don't try to save money by doing the facilitation yourself. Find an outsider.

Facilitators are available in a number of places. Ask your Chamber. Call a marketing organization. Call or e-mail your MSO or community foundation. Check with your state association of nonprofits. Call your local college or university's program on nonprofit management. Talk to the marketing department of a large company or bank in your community. Get references, and check them. You want someone skilled in facilitation who is willing to work with you in eliciting the information you need.

2. Focus Your Questions

After all, it is called a *focus* group. You need to focus your questions on a few key subjects. Your facilitator should help you with this, by turning your information needs into open-ended questions that lead people to open up and share their opinions, reactions, and emotions. You have only a limited amount of time (see point 4), and so you want to have your issues focused and in a priority order. Don't ask a group that is supposed to focus on a new service how they like your existing ones. It will get them off track and use up valuable time.

3. Have a Homogeneous Group

Here's another key ingredient to a focus group that succeeds: Put people with similar characteristics around the table. For example, if your organization is a science museum, and you want to study the reactions of all your consumers to a potential new exhibit, don't have a group that includes high school students, post-doctoral scientists, and senior citizens. Inevitably, one portion of that group will dominate the discussion and the others will feel disenfranchised and not participate. Again, focus your efforts, in this case on one type of person, and you will have more responses, better information, and an increased value from your investment.

4. Don't Wear Out the Group

You have between 90 minutes and two hours, and then people's creative brains turn to mush. A good facilitator will keep track of the time and ask questions in priority order, but will also tell you that within the 90-minute to two-hour time range you should dismiss the group. No sense in keeping people when they are not going to be productive. This underscores your need to focus your questions; you have only so much time.

5. Compensate the Group

In the commercial world, people are often offered between $100 and $250 to participate in a two-hour focus group. You probably can't afford that, and in fact may insult people who are associated with your organization by offering them money. But do offer them something: coffee and doughnuts, lunch, transportation, a parking voucher. Get a restaurant in your community to donate gift certificates that you can hand out. Hold the group in a safe, comfortable space. After the session, thank each participant by letter, perhaps accompanied by a token of appreciation like a coffee mug, attractive paperweight, or other premium. Talk to your facilitator about what the community standard is for compensation, and don't be stingy. These people are providing you with literally invaluable information.

6. Analyze the Results between Groups

After each session (which should be audiotaped), analyze the results. Are you hearing similar issues? Are there enough issues left incomplete that more sessions are warranted? Do you want to add another group made up of the same type of people, or an additional one made up of a different category of people? Have your facilitator tell you about body language, inflections, and other things that she may have picked up. Have the facilitator give you her overall impressions of the group, and list where she thinks you have opportunities to improve.

How many groups should you run? Like any other question of this sort, the answer is: It depends. Focus groups are expensive to administer, but many experts suggest that you run enough so that you begin to hear the same information repeated. Thus, if you are a school, you may run groups of parents, students, faculty, and alumni. You might run only two of all the types at first, and hear the same thing in each group except for the parents, who might have so many different issues that you want to run three or four sessions. Again, you don't want to mix groups, and you don't want to work them to death, so plan your strategy carefully.

If you want to pursue focus groups, I again have a resource for you to read before you hire your facilitator. It is another good, basic guide to the subject: *The Wilder Nonprofit Field Guide to Conducting Successful Focus Groups*, by Judith Simon (Fieldstone Alliance, 1999).

Informal Asking

Here we confront a major cultural change for many organizations. Developing the regular "culture of asking" that I have referred to earlier takes time and the belief of everyone in the organization that they are on the marketing team. Only a total team effort will gather all the information, elicit all the wants, and pick up on all the problems and opportunities that are out there. Your staff and volunteers need to be urged, cajoled, and led to ask *regularly*. They also need to be trained to ask, because there is a lot of "bad asking" going on out there.

 FOR EXAMPLE: Here is an experience that most readers have shared. You go to a restaurant, eat, and then get your check. You approach the cash register to pay, and you are asked by the clerk behind the register about your meal. This can happen in two ways:

> **Option One:** The clerk looks down at the register, and, while keying in your bill, asks, "Was everything okay?," to which most of us answer, "Yes." This clerk was told to ask every customer how things were, and is complying with the letter of the training, but not the spirit. The question suggests that everything *was* okay. The clerk is on what I call *asking autopilot*. Recently, I had someone ask me whether "everything was okay" and I said "No." He finished up printing

> *(continued)*

(continued)

out the receipt, gave me my change, and said, "Well, that's great. Have a nice day and come back soon!" That's asking on autopilot.

Option Two: The clerk behind the register stops, looks you in the eye, and says, "How was everything tonight?" Then he or she waits for your answer, and responds appropriately. This person was trained to ask the open-ended question that forces the customer to come up with his or her own answer. Even if most of us respond with the stock "Just fine," we still are more likely to let the clerk or the manager know about problems with this question than with the question posed in Option One. ■

Train your people that asking is important and then give them the tools to ask correctly, and without skewing the answers.

Informal asking comes in many shapes and sizes. Different staff will be affected differently. Here are four ideas of where to start in developing some informal asking:

1. Have your staff trained to ask new customers where they heard about your organization. This might mean a receptionist, intake worker, someone sitting at an information booth, or any other person who would be the first point of entry.
2. When you interact in the community, try to ask people regularly, "What do you hear about our organization? Do you know anyone who uses us? If you do, how have your experiences been? If it's a friend or family member, how have their experiences been?"
3. When you see your key vendors—your banker, insurance agent, auditor, office supply company, printer, and the like—ask them: "What do you hear about us on the street?" "Do you have ideas about things that are not being done now that we could do?"
4. Most importantly, whenever anyone in your organization interacts with anyone you serve, who donates or contracts for services, who is a member, or who in any way can be considered a market, the final interaction should be this question: "Is there anything else we can do for you today?" This question, consistently and politely asked, will generate a constant stream of opportunities for service and improvement.

One danger in informal asking is that, since it is just that, informal, you don't have a formal path for the gathered information to flow to the correct place. For example, if a caseworker asks someone how his visit was, and the client answers, "Great, except the toilets really smell—that's a big turnoff to me," the information has *got* to get to the maintenance or janitorial staff. Otherwise, even though your people asked, the information was not put to good use. Make sure you train staff in *what to do with what they learn.*

More than any other kind of asking, consistent informal asking shows that you and your staff and volunteers care about the kind, quality, and level of service that your organization provides. It forces you to interact one-on-one, taking the chance of getting criticism or complaints face-to-face. People take note of that kind of risk-taking and appreciate it. Unless, of course, you don't follow up on the asking and make one or more of the mistakes listed in the "Asking Mistakes" section.

Asking (and Listening) Online

This is an area that has progressed dramatically in just the past three years. There are two ways to use the Net to ask, and one other critical online marketing opportunity: *listening.* We'll examine all three, but remember that using online data focuses on the rapidly growing part of every society that is primarily and often solely online. Thus, it's essential to ask in this manner. That said, you automatically eliminate responses from those people who don't like to be online or can't access the Internet. That number is waning, but it underscores the need to target your asking market by market.

With that warning, let's look at *active asking, passive asking,* and *online listening.*

Active Asking

Use one of the many online survey providers to create, distribute, and collect your surveys, and then to analyze the results. Providers like SurveyMonkey.com (my personal favorite for many years) are very inexpensive, even free for small surveys. And, they offer some key benefits that paper surveys don't. These include:

- *Ease of survey development.* It's very easy to choose the kinds of questions and methods of responses for your survey. You'll still need your survey expert to help you shape the questions, but the online part is quick and intuitive.
- *Speed of response.* Mailing out and getting a return on a paper survey can take weeks, and the response rate is low. E-mailing out a notice of your survey with the appropriate URL embedded is quick and the responses, in many cases, come back in minutes or hours, rather than days or weeks.
- *No need for data reentry.* Data from surveys that are taken in the field or mailed and returned always have to be rekeyed into a database, which is

time consuming and creates the opportunity for data entry error. That's eliminated with online surveys.

- *Real-time review.* You can watch the data come in and analyze it in real time.
- *Good analytics and reporting tools.* Your data can be graphed and analyzed quickly, or exported to a spreadsheet for further analysis or to your word processing software for inclusion in a report.
- *Transparency of results.* You can link your survey results directly to your web site so everyone can see them. I do this on my site with my training satisfaction survey. As a result, potential customers can see what others have said about my services.

When all is said and done, asking through an online survey provider is very cost-beneficial. If you haven't tried it, give it a shot.

Passive Asking

This involves using your web site to encourage comments and input on everything related to your organization, whether it be services, volunteering, or donating. Using a blog, or having part of your web site formatted to allow for online commenting offers you a great opportunity to get immediate feedback from people who are (usually) *very* happy or *very* unhappy with your nonprofit. The key is letting them let you know their feelings immediately.

I often get questions on this kind of feedback, usually resistance from executive directors and CEOs who fear bad press on their site. My feeling is that as long as you make it a policy to have someone checking these pages constantly and resolving any and all complaints immediately, you're better off knowing than not knowing.

Online Listening

This is related to passive asking, but extends to the entire Net. You want to make sure that you know when anyone says anything online about your organization, and while that may sound like a daunting task, it's not, thanks to Google. Go to www.google.com and search for Google Alerts. When you get there, you'll find a variety of ways to get notices from Google for free when any search string you want is found online.

 HANDS ON: Make sure you list a number of search strings that cover all the ways your organization is referred to. For example, The Springfield Association of Retarded Citizens could be searched as the organization's entire name, as its acronym (SPARC), or just

Springfield ARC, among others. Remember to put your strings in quotes to get an exact match. ■

I use Google Alerts to let me know when any of my books have been listed or reviewed, and when my name (both properly spelled and with common misspellings) has shown up somewhere. It's a great way to stay ahead of the online curve, to thank people who are complimenting you, and to deal with any complaints quickly.

Asking Mistakes

Of course, things can go wrong. You can ask and ask and ask, and have problems. Let's review the common mistakes that other organizations have made in the hopes that you can avoid them.

Not Expecting Criticism

If you ask, people will tell you their answers—even if they are the answers you think you don't want to hear. And it is naive to think that no one will ever have any problems with the way that you do your mission. They will. But I regularly see staff people wailing and gnashing their teeth about whatever, often tiny, criticism that their organization has received. I have literally seen organizations who send staff members to counseling to get over the shock of reading the survey responses that they have gathered.

Come *on*—no organization is perfect. People like to gripe. And, most importantly, you asked. What did you really expect?

The key here is to expect and even welcome criticism. I tell my clients all the time: "Praise feeds the ego, and we all need to be told, 'Good job' when we deserve it. But, while praise feeds the ego, *criticism feeds improvement.*" If your organization is dedicated to continuous improvement, you need to ask and have problems pointed out to be able to make those improvements.

Don't get gun-shy. If people take a shot at you, analyze what they said. Was it fair? Was it accurate? What want of theirs did it show you? Can you accommodate them? If the complaint was regularly repeated (in other words, not an aberration), then fix the problem!

Not Listening

This mistake is the logical endpoint of the marketing disability that I discussed earlier. You know it all, so why listen to what people want? You are the expert, so let's just appease people's sense of involvement by asking them, and then go on about our business. Far too many for-profits and non-profits fall victim to this tempting habit. After all, you're the expert, right? Sounds like the marketing disability to me; I know what these people need, so why really bother to change to meet what they want?

You *must* listen to what people tell you. That is not to say that you need to knee-jerk your responses and change your entire organization because 2 out of every 1,000 people are unhappy or that you should accommodate every suggestion. But you do need to give each comment, each criticism, and each idea a fair hearing. Otherwise, you are wasting your asking dollars and missing significant competitive opportunities. Remember, too, that many great ideas for service improvement come first as complaints, and come not fully formed. You need to listen carefully to concerns and suggestions and then take those seeds of improvement and nourish them.

Not Responding

So, you asked, and you listened, but, heck, it's too much trouble to change, to respond. You don't have the time or the money, and, anyway, you can't make all the people happy all the time. This is all true, but you'd darn well better work to make your target markets happy nearly all the time. And you'll do that by being responsive to their wants.

 FOR EXAMPLE: Imagine that I come out to your organization to do a speech for your board and staff. I start off and am really moving along. At the intermission, I ask you how you think that things are going. You tell me, "You are going too fast for some of our board members. Can you slow down and take some more time for questions? What you are saying is really good, and I want everyone to get a good grasp of it. We're in no hurry. Take your time."

What is my response? Do I tell you that I need to get through because your staff and board showed up half an hour late and I have a plane to catch? (The customer is not always right, but the customer is always the customer!) No, I tell you: "Thanks for the input, I'll pay more attention and take some time for questions. Let's get the people back in their seats and try to get back on schedule." When we reconvene, I ask for questions on the previous material and then proceed at a more leisurely pace, still paying attention to the clock.

Here, I made a reasonable response to a reasonable request. I asked, I got an answer that I really didn't want to hear, but, if I had just gone on, my customer would have been justifiably upset. ∎

You need to respond as well as you can, as promptly as you can, and as reasonably as you can. And you need to empower your staff to do the same.

After Asking

Now that you have asked, what comes next—asking again? Well, of course, but there are some things you should do after you have gathered the data. These include the following:

Analyze the Data

Look at your information critically and soon. Make sure that an interdisciplinary group of staff and board give the data close scrutiny. Was the survey sample significant? Are the results valid? If so, what did we learn? What can we apply? What trends pop out? What follow-up inquiries should we do?

You have taken time and paid good money to gather the information. Now, examine it carefully. I see too many groups that do a survey and either ignore what they learned or don't examine it until the information is so out of date that it no longer is relevant.

Close the Information Loop

You have just imposed on the people who gave you valuable information. Do the right thing. Tell *all the people whom you asked* what you learned. Send an e-mail out, or put a report in your newsletter, or just make an announcement at a staff meeting, but let all the people whom you asked (not just the people who responded) know that you listened and appreciated their input. Be sure to list the key things that you learned and the status of action on each.

 HANDS ON: Make a list of what you learned and then tell people what you are doing about it. It may look something like Exhibit 8.1. ■

EXHIBIT 8.1 Asking Feedback

We learned the following things and have taken the following actions:

Items A, B, C, D	We have already implemented changes to respond to these excellent ideas.
Items E, F, H, J	We are budgeting these for the next fiscal year.
Items G, I, L	We cannot accommodate these suggestions because of regulatory restraints.
Items K, M	The board will discuss these policy change ideas at their next meeting.

By doing this, you not only allow people to learn from each other, you acknowledge their input and take credit for taking action—something that most people are pretty cynical about. They often assume that their ideas go into a large trash barrel. Don't let that happen. Instead, tell every person you asked what you heard and, equally importantly, what you have done about it. Show them that you are responsive.

Accommodate the Wants of Your Markets

If you ask, people will tell you what they want. Now that you know what they want, make whatever changes you can to accommodate those wants. This, of course, is the opposite of two of the errors people make that we reviewed in the previous section: not listening and not responding. While you should never make promises you cannot keep, you should always try to accommodate your markets as best you can. This means that you should review your survey or focus group information with the people who provide your services, and try to come up with ways to accommodate what your customers have told you. Don't just tell staff what to do. Have them become part of the marketing team by learning how to use the information that you are gathering to do a better job.

Incorporate Your Information into Your Marketing Plans

In Chapter 12, I will show you how to put all of your marketing information into a cohesive plan. It suffices here to say, don't ignore the data that you gather as you go about putting together your initial plan and, more importantly, in adapting your marketing methods to changing circumstances. It is very easy to say, "Well, we've decided our goals for this year, and we'll review this new information that we've just gathered next year during our annual review." Next year may be too late. If you are confident of your data, use it. Good planning takes into account changes in the situation. If you have new information, even if it conflicts with the course you are on, use it! Imagine a ship's captain whose vessel is set on a particular compass heading. He gets information from a satellite that there is a huge ice pack ahead. Does he stay on course (going with the plan), or does he use the new information, go around the danger, and eventually achieve his goal—reaching his destination safely?

Recap

In this chapter, we have covered the crucial function of asking your markets what they want. You need to develop a culture as well as a system of asking to maintain your competitive edge. If you don't ask, how are you ever going to keep pace with the constantly changing wants of your target markets? Answer: You aren't.

First, we looked at surveys, and discussed ways to and ways *not* to survey. I made 10 suggestions for surveying:

1. Have instructions.
2. Be brief.
3. Be focused.
4. Don't ask too often.
5. Ask the questions in the correct sequence and wording.
6. Limit your identifiers.
7. For trend data, be consistent.
8. Include closing instructions.
9. Say "thank you."
10. Get help.

We then moved on to focus groups, noting how they obtain qualitative data rather than the quantitative data that surveys can gather. We went over the following six suggestions:

1. Get a facilitator.
2. Focus your questions.
3. Have a homogeneous group.
4. Don't wear out the group.
5. Compensate the group.
6. Analyze the results between groups.

We then turned our attention to how to get the most out of informal asking, noting that this kind of constant attention to customers really pays off in a variety of ways, but that it takes training and motivation, and everyone in the organization, to do it well.

We looked into the area of online asking, and discussed three ways to ask online.

We next reviewed what *not* to do, by looking at some common mistakes people make in their asking. These included not anticipating criticism, not listening, and not responding to what you have learned.

Finally, you were shown what to do after you ask, including analyzing your data, closing the loop, and making sure that you take appropriate actions to respond to your new knowledge base.

Asking, listening, and responding are parts of a constant cycle, a vital part of the marketing process. Now that you know how to ask, we can turn our attention to the next issue: letting people know what you do—making better marketing materials.

Discussion Questions

1. How often do we formally survey our target markets? Is this often enough? How recently have we updated the surveys that we do? Do we look at trend analysis now?
2. What about focus groups? They are expensive! Are they a good tool for us? For what kind of customer?
3. Can we get survey data from our competition? Is any of it public information?
4. Do we close the loop after we survey now? Should we? How?
5. How can we get better at both asking and listening? What about making sure that ideas from the line staff get to us?
6. Which of our markets would use online inquiry best? How do we best make use of this?
7. Do we have a good method of encouraging feedback and inquiry on our web site? How can we improve this?
8. How much of our surveying should we move online? Which of our markets is best suited to this method?

CHAPTER 9

Better Marketing Materials

Chapter Thumbnail

➤ The Problems with Most Nonprofits' Marketing Materials

➤ Solving Customers' Problems

➤ Things to Include in Your Marketing Materials

➤ Things to Avoid in Your Marketing Materials

➤ Developing Different Materials for Different Markets

Overview

It's time to look at your marketing materials. You now know who you are trying to serve (your markets) and what their wants and needs are. You know about your competition and what they are offering to your markets. Now comes a critical part of *both* your marketing and competitive cycle: getting the word out. In Chapter 5, I referred to this step as *promotion and distribution*. In this chapter, I'll show you how to do the promotion part of that step.

The term *marketing materials* covers a lot of ground. It can mean the traditional three-fold brochure, or stacked handouts that come in a larger folder. It can be your web site, a video on YouTube, an ad in a local newspaper or magazine, or a flyer that is placed under a windshield wiper. It can be your business card or your e-mail signature. It can be your promotional spot on local television or radio, the notices you send out in direct mail, or the educational materials you give free of charge to the people you serve, either in person or online. It can be information on memberships, donations, or even a promotional trinket such as a key chain, calendar, or coffee mug. For most readers, your organization will be promoted through a mix of these vehicles in addition to word of mouth, referrals, and straight sales.

But whatever it is, the mix has to address some similar issues. Many nonprofits, like their for-profit peers, do a great job at developing and appropriately using their marketing materials. Many, however, do not. And, many nonprofits are still doing that job as if they were living in the old, less competitive economy. They focus on *public relations* and *promotion* rather than *marketing*. There is an enormous difference.

Furthermore, there is an overarching rule for marketing materials: They must connect with the targeted market, from the customer's point of view. This means that good marketing materials grab the customers and show them that you understand their wants and who they are, and that you can solve their problems. By visiting your web site, reading your brochure, or listening to your radio spot, can customers quickly understand the benefits of using your organization's services? If not, you have not made the necessary connection.

In this chapter, we'll talk about *marketing* materials as opposed to *promotional* tools. First, we'll cover this problem as well as a number of others that I regularly see in nonprofit marketing materials. Then, we'll focus on the key issue: solving customers' problems. I'll show you how to tell whether your current marketing materials do this and, if not, how to improve them so that they do. Next we'll turn to the seven things that you should *include* in your materials, and another seven things to *avoid*. Finally, I'll give you some ideas on developing different materials for different markets, which sounds like a very straightforward and no-brainer idea, but apparently isn't, because a lot of organizations ignore it.

By the end of the chapter you should be much better able to analyze your existing marketing materials and to create new ones that really speak to and excite your many markets. Remember, your marketing materials are out there speaking for you every day. If they are speaking in some unknown tongue, you are losing opportunities to connect with people whom you could serve.

The Problems with Most Nonprofits' Marketing Materials

You have already read that the critical sequence in marketing is identifying your markets, asking those markets what they want, and then developing or amending services to meet those wants. This is called being *market oriented,* and it is far preferable to being *service oriented,* where an organization just pushes its available services with little regard to what the market wants.

Here is the problem. Most of the marketing materials that I see are *service oriented,* pushing the existing service array, usually in jargon, and hardly ever in a way that really appeals to the wants of the markets. The materials are dull, dense, and not of interest to very many people beyond the individual who wrote it. They are also often poorly written, unprofessional-looking, and out of date. They don't spell out the benefits of using the organization and make no attempt to connect with the customer.

Why, in an era of dirt-cheap, easy-to-use software and excellent low-cost color printers, do nonprofits scrimp on marketing materials? Why shoot yourself in the foot every time a potential customer, donor, referral source, banker, or board member sees your web site or promotional piece? The answer is multifaceted, and it has to do with (1) the marketing disability, (2) tradition, (3) being penny-wise, and (4) a misunderstanding of the true nature of marketing. Let's briefly consider each of these four issues.

1. The Marketing Disability

In Chapter 5, I exhorted you to overcome the marketing disability of non-profits. Remember that the disability springs from most nonprofit staff's professional training in diagnostics, which results in an attitude of "We know what you need" and the corollary (but unspoken) attitude of "We don't care what you want." This shows up in marketing materials that contain:

- A history of the organization (a self-congratulatory one at that)
- A list of services (usually in jargon)
- A description of hours and locations available
- A generic phone number and e-mail address

What have we here? Otherwise-useful space taken up with old news (the history that no one outside the organization really cares about), a cold, jargon-filled list of services that anyone without a master's degree *in your discipline* has trouble understanding, a "come-and-get-it" listing of times and locations, and impersonal contact information.

That's a *great* first impression—push your services, make no personal connection, confuse them with jargon. Often the marketing piece will add insult to injury by including a request for money!

 FOR EXAMPLE: I see marketing materials like the one described above in all parts of the nonprofit sector. In my work with organizations that provide vocational services to persons with

(continued)

(*continued*)

disabilities, I often see brochures or pamphlets that list the services that the organization can provide to such persons and their families. Here is a sample list, taken from a real (unfortunately typical) brochure that came across my desk recently:

- Employment assessment
- Job placement
- Family respite
- Vocational transportation
- Work supports
- Work hardening
- Supported employment
- Employee enclaves
- Occupational therapy

All of these terms are legitimate technical descriptions of services in the field. But to anyone outside (like parents, funders, donors, and anyone else who is not intimately involved in the field), most of them are Greek. I once asked a group of management staff from an organization that provides services such as these what the term *work hardening* meant, and whether they really expected people outside their organization to grasp its meaning. "Heck," said one, "ninety percent *of our staff* don't know what it means, and I'm not sure that I could give you an accurate definition." I then asked why they included it in their marketing materials. "Sounds impressive," was the answer. That's the marketing disability in full swing. ■

 HANDS ON: Try this jargon test: Hand your marketing materials to a couple of neighbors or friends who know *nothing* about your services. Ask them to read them carefully, circling every word that they do not *fully* understand. Make sure that they know that this is not a test of their knowledge, but a way of helping you make your materials more understandable. Include your newsletters, if you print those. Don't overload individuals; just give them each one or two things to review. You will learn a lot about what is jargon and what isn't. ■

2. Tradition

"We have a grand tradition here at our organization. We have a great reputation. We want to build on that." I hear this regularly but, interestingly enough, most often from organizations that have really lousy marketing materials. They are so focused on their past that they can't even see their present, to say nothing of their future. Good, *competitive* marketing is interested in what the markets want *today*, and in predicting what they will want *tomorrow*. As for yesterday, well, as the character Rafiki said in *The Lion King*, "Don't worry about it—it's in the past!" If your marketing materials or web site are focused on the past and look like they were designed in 1995 (perhaps because they were?), you are not going to be appealing to today's markets.

Let's look at the quote at the top of this section: first, the term *tradition*. As I said in the previous chapter, traditions are great, as long as you build on them. When traditions actually appeal to an important market, they can really help an organization. An induction ceremony for a club, fraternity, or sorority; a dress code at a restaurant; a particular emphasis on customer service at a hotel—these are all traditions that *could* really appeal to customers. My family and I go to a family camp in New Hampshire every summer, and at that camp, the Fourth of July is celebrated with the tradition of a parade, picnic, and games. We return every summer in part because we enjoy this tradition.

But traditions can also be customer aversive. Let's look at the same set I listed in the previous paragraph: an induction ceremony ("demeaning"), a dress code ("stuffy"), or customer service ("they weren't *that* nice"). So, you need to build on your positive traditions and get over your negative ones, remembering that it is not your opinion that counts, it is that of your markets. If your marketing materials are lost in the past, you will look like you are out of date, which is right up there with out of touch.

3. Penny-Wise and Pound-Foolish

This problem is a holdover from 10 years ago, and can be summed up in the statement, "We can't afford nice-looking materials or, heaven forbid, spend serious money on our web site. Good marketing is too expensive, and high quality is unseemly for a charity." That is wrong on two counts:

> **COUNT ONE:** These days, pretty much anyone with a mouse can use his or her computer and printer to quickly develop very high-quality marketing materials that can be updated easily, quickly, and inexpensively. Ten years ago, you might have spent $2,500 to $5,000 to design a brochure, letterhead, and business cards and get them printed. Today, you already have the computer and printer you need, and the software may also be in hand (Microsoft Office and OpenOffice both have tons of predesigned templates included). Then, you go to the local office store and pick one of the dozens of predesigned stationery sets, and you're in business.

COUNT TWO: Your web site (which we'll talk about at length in Chapter 10) is more expensive than your printed materials, but also more essential. And, while you want your webmaster to design the site so that your staff can update it without the webmaster's involvement (and billing), you do need the initial design to be done by professionals or at least by college students.

Spend a little money for a lot of return. For both your printed and electronic materials, raise the bar here within reason. Look at what your competition is doing. Look at what your markets want. Show that you know their wants in the quality of the marketing materials.

HANDS ON: When were your marketing materials last revised? Your web site? Your logo, slogan, letterhead, and other items? If you can't remember, or can't find the documents, it was too long ago. Refresh your materials now! As I said earlier, it's cheap, and we'll spend part of the next chapter giving you lots of specifics on how to take advantage of the benefits of low-cost technology in this area. ■

4. Public Relations or Marketing?

I've lost track of the nonprofit marketing materials I have seen that try to cover all the bases on one or two sides of an 8 1/2-by-11 sheet of paper or on one single web site window. When this happens, what you see included is all the things I listed earlier (history, jargon, money requests, etc.), but you never see a focus on the core marketing sequence of targeting a market, asking that market what they want, and then providing it. Instead, the organization has hired a public relations staff person whose training is really in dealing with the media and giving your organization a good image in the community, but not in marketing.

I don't intend to denigrate public relations. A lot of organizations that I know could use some talented PR help. But PR alone is *not* marketing. Good public relations can supplement a marketing effort, raise positive image, let large numbers of people know that your organization is there, and give a positive opinion about you. But that alone does not necessarily mean much to the marketing effort.

FOR EXAMPLE: A few years ago, I was assisting an organization that provides rehabilitation to people with spinal cord injuries in the Northwest with the development of their marketing plan.

During my first visit, the planning committee told me that they were going to spend $15,000 on a public relations firm to raise the image of the organization in the community.

"Why?" I asked.

"We did a survey, and only two percent of the community knows what we do. So we need to raise our visibility," they replied.

"Why?" I repeated.

"Because people need to know about us."

"Do you get a substantial amount in small donations, or are you planning on expanding your grassroots development efforts?"

"No."

"Do you get referrals from the general public?"

"No, from physicians, insurers, and hospital patient advocates."

"How many of them know about you?"

"We don't know."

"That is the group where your visibility needs to be highest."

The group had fallen prey to the PR ego bug. "*Everyone* needs to know about us!" But *everyone* wasn't their market, and the best way to focus your limited marketing resources is on the target markets that you have chosen. ■

Make sure that your board and staff understand the differences between marketing and public relations.

These four all-too-common problems lead to unfocused, service-based, poor-quality materials and web sites. Now that we know the reasons for an ineffective approach to this, let's look at what your marketing materials *should* be doing and then at checklists of things to include and things to avoid.

Solving Customers' Problems

All successful salespeople know that you develop a long-term relationship with a customer by repeatedly being there to connect with the customer and then solve his or her problems. As you watch television over the next few weeks, notice how many advertisements talk about (or demonstrate) a problem first, and then state that their product has the solutions. Do you have a backed-up toilet? Hemorrhoids? Poor cell phone reception? A flabby stomach? Do you need to get a package absolutely, positively, there overnight? All of these are the problems displayed in one five-minute stretch of commercials I saw recently.

Note that I am focusing on the problems, *not* the solutions. That is because selling solutions without a problem is being service based. Selling a solution *to* a market problem (want) is being market based. Thus, your marketing materials should demonstrate that you understand what your market wants, what their problems are, and that you can solve them.

 FOR EXAMPLE: I recently saw a brochure for an art museum that gave a great deal of information, but never really connected with me (or apparently many other people, as attendance was down). On the cover, you had the name of the museum, a picture of the building, and a lost-in-the-past slogan ("Providing Access to the Arts for Adams County since 1910"). Inside was a breathless description of the museum in very dry terms ("250,000 square feet of exhibit space, a permanent and rotating collection, lecture hall that is also used for small music performances and poetry readings, etc.). Then there was a listing of some of the artists whose work was displayed and a list of the collections on display. The back cover was a map, hours, a number to call for more information, and a web site URL.

All of this information (with the exception of the slogan) was factual and, to some people, important. But was it to a potential visitor? What about statements such as these:

> *Art comes alive at the Adams County Museum! If you are an art enthusiast, come see a local collection of the masters close to your own home. If you are an art teacher in need of exhibits to view and discuss, the Adams County Museum is a great field trip. If you are a parent who wants to expose their child to art, bring your child for a visit and then return for one of our art classes.*

Each of these statements connects with a target market that the museum had identified but not addressed in the marketing information. They had assumed that parents, patrons, and teachers could glean what they needed from a generic brochure. In fact, what they needed was *four* brochures: one general one, one for art patrons, one for art teachers, and one for parents. Each of these *focused* brochures could be headlined in a defined manner:

> "Free Resources for Art Teachers from the Adams County Museum." (Teachers are attracted to the words "free resources" like bees are to honey. Their problem is that

there are never enough resources to meet the needs of their students.)

"Art Activities for Kids at the Adams County Museum." (Parents have a problem: bored children. The word "activities" addresses that issue.)

I'm sure you get the idea. Figure out who your target markets are and write your materials to speak to them. ■

 HANDS ON: Never assume that markets will make the connection between your resources and their problems. They won't. And, in fairness, it's not their job. It's yours. In asking the markets about their wants, you should be asking about their problems. This information comes best through the focus groups and informal asking that we discussed in Chapter 8, but also it comes through reading the general and business press. You will read, for example, about the problems of Americans feeling that their days are too short. What is the lesson here? If you can *save them time*, you can attract them. You will read about their concerns about education and the breakup of the family. Can your organization make a connection here? Do you provide some kind of educational experience? Do you focus on the family unit in a definable way? If you do, these buzzwords should show up in your marketing materials. ■

Solving people's problems puts the focus on them, not on you. It develops empathy for them, not emphasis on your services. It makes a connection, and avoids the hard sell. And it works. I should also point out that solving people's problems should be the process by which your staff connect with individuals in person or by phone. Your staff and board, in their informal asking, should be willing to listen to problems, and then be thinking of how your organization can solve those problems.

Things to Include in Your Marketing Materials

Let's turn to a list of things that you should make sure are included in your marketing materials. (We'll look in more depth at your web site in the next chapter, although many of these admonitions will transfer online pretty well.) I would suggest that your marketing committee review all of your materials, commercials, handouts, and presentations for the following seven components. Remember, you have to *connect with your customer*, showing him or her the benefits of using your services.

1. Your Mission

If your mission statement (or charitable purpose) is succinct and not full of jargon, it is an excellent thing to include in most of your marketing materials. If it is so long that it will take up 90 percent of your space, forget it. But your mission is the defining statement of what and who your organization is, and you should be able to lead with it.

2. Focus

Each piece of marketing material should be focused on a target market or a service component. The art museum in the earlier example could develop a piece for art lovers, another for parents, and one for art teachers. That would be an example of focus on a target market. A YMCA might have a piece on summer camp, one on its aerobics classes, and one on its basketball and soccer leagues. That would be an example of focus on a service. But, and this is very important, even within the "service pieces," it is critical that you use terms that connect to the market wants. If you just focus on the service, you are back to that service-oriented rather than market-oriented mentality. (We'll look at different materials for different markets later in the chapter.)

3. Brevity

Blessed is the person who can say it in the fewest and clearest words. Remember that no one is forcing readers to spend the time reading your materials. They need to be *brief,* or your readers will get bored and stop reading. No run-on sentences or minute detail—give just the essential information. With apologies to the English majors reading this, your role model for your printed materials (not your web site, which can be much more detailed) should be *USA Today,* which is heavy on bullets and light on sentences with commas! Keep it short, and keep people's attention.

4. Connection

Do the materials clearly show that your organization understands the problems of the target market(s)? And, do they clearly state that you can help solve those problems? If not, you are trusting the reader to make those connections, and that is a mistake.

5. Appearance

As I mentioned earlier, there is no excuse for sloppy materials, poor writing, and cheap-looking paper or graphics. Your materials speak volumes about your organization. Designing and printing are so inexpensive that there is little impediment to developing professional-looking materials at a very reasonable cost. But, make sure someone actually proofreads the materials before they get distributed.

 HANDS ON: A spell-checker program is a wonderful tool, but imperfect. *To, too,* and *two* are three different words that will all slide by pretty much any spell-checker. Make sure you have any piece that is in the final stages of approval *read aloud* by at least two people before it goes out. Hearing what you are saying is much different from just silently reading it. You will dramatically reduce errors that a spell-checker can't find. ■

6. References

In certain materials, it will be important to list well-known customers. For example, if you are a health-care organization, it may be important to list the large employers with whose employee health plans you qualify, or the managed care plans. Other organizations need to make connections to state and national associations to show a level of quality ("Certified by the National Association of XYZ"), or to a community standard ("A United Way Agency"). As with your other text, be brief and include only those references that mean something to the target market for that particular marketing piece. For example, being accredited by the Joint Commission on the Accreditation of Hospitals may be important to a referring physician, but meaningless to a patient. Be selective and focused.

7. A Specific Source for More Information

Always include contact information that's specific, not general, where people can get more information. A specific contact person's phone number and e-mail address and the organization's web site URL are the minimum. You might consider adding a street address as well. Make sure that the e-mail address is a personal one, not just info@yourorg.org. Keep it personal and welcoming. Remember: When the person named changes jobs, you must reprint—and you shouldn't have printed 10,000 brochures in the first place!

All of these things should show up in some fashion in your materials. Now, let's look at the other side of the coin.

Things to Avoid in Your Marketing Materials

I assume that you have now gone through your materials to make sure that the seven items in my previous list are included. But there may well be things that are in your materials that you should pull out. There are certainly things to avoid. The following is a list of seven common items to keep out of your materials:

1. Jargon

The worst offense in marketing materials is to speak in a language people don't understand. You don't impress people by confusing them. Using jargon puts a big barrier between you and most audiences. I have long contended that if you can't explain or describe what you do in words that a sixth-grader can understand, you don't really understand what you do. Simplify. Clarify. And, U.S. readers should remember that the average American adult reads on a seventh-grade level.

Having said that, there is a time for jargon. If your marketing materials are aimed at professionals in the field, the jargon is the language of the profession, and thus appropriate. If, for example, you were developing a brochure to advertise a continuing education program in computers, the terms *ASCII*, *PC*, *icons*, *Java*, *Python*, and *troubleshooting* would probably be appropriate. If you were training on labor law, citing of the laws and using common labor law terms and issues would be important. Write for your audience.

2. Inappropriate Photos

Here is the sad truth: Most people don't care what your building looks like. You do, because you probably have put a great deal of blood, sweat, tears, energy, and money into the property. But most pictures of buildings are a waste of precious space in a marketing brochure. Pictures of people are usually much more effective, but even those can be counterproductive if they are grainy, unfocused, or so small as to be unrecognizable. Make sure each and every photo (or graphic) that you include is valuable and, like the text, simple, focused, and understandable. Also make sure that for any image of any person you use in any media (print or online) you have a valid, current, signed photo release.

3. Lack of Focus

There is nothing wrong with a general-purpose brochure, but there is something definitely wrong with having *just* a general-purpose piece, or with having a general-purpose brochure that tries to do everything for everyone. *Focus* is the heart of good marketing materials. Ask yourself, "What is the purpose of this piece of paper?" If the piece goes much beyond that central purpose, it is almost certainly unfocused and too long.

4. Asking for Time or Treasure

With the exception of fund-raising letters and brochures whose focus is explaining the various ways to give to your organization, asking for money or volunteers is outside of the core purpose of the marketing material and thus out of focus. I know that it is tempting to just throw in a sentence or two about donations and how readers can improve their lives through volunteering, particularly if you are desperate for that treasure or that time, but that desperation will come through, and some markets may well be turned off. Stick with your focus on core purpose.

5. A History Lesson

Very few people care about your organization's history, or even how long you have been in existence. Having said that, some organizations need to validate their experience and stability by saying things like, "Serving the Finger Lakes region since 1965." But more often I see brochures that use 400 words to explain the origins of the organization in great (and agonizing) detail. They list the initial incorporators, the first few office addresses, and even give pictures of some of the sites that the organization has occupied, noting additional important dates in history.

There is nothing wrong with history, and we certainly can learn from it. But is a recitation of your organization's past (however laudable) "on-message" for the marketing piece you are developing? Probably not; but if it is, is your recounting of the development of your organization brief and readable? Stay focused.

6. Out of Date

I really love pictures of staff, board, and service recipients in bell-bottoms, with shag haircuts, or wearing leisure suits. They make me want to run right down to the disco. The problem is the disco is closed, a part of the past. Pictures from a bygone era will set you up for ridicule, not respect. They will disenchant people, who will wonder whether it is just your photos or your programs that are outdated. Again, in this era of quick and easy software that includes photos at the click of a mouse, there is no excuse for having your brochure look like a retrospective work of art.

7. Boring

If you wrote the text in a particular piece, you probably won't be a good judge of this. Get it read by people inside and outside the organization. Ask hard questions: Is this boring? Does it run on? Can we say more in fewer words? Are we "on-message," focused, and keeping connected with the intended audience? Don't trust your own instincts here. Get a few outside opinions. I usually am pretty happy with my own writing, but it is *always* improved by the friends, coworkers, and (in the case of my books) the editors who read it. Get two or three outside opinions. It will help you avoid the dreaded *B*-word.

 HANDS ON: I have the best way to get a real-world, inexpensive read on two issues: *boring* and *jargon*. Do this: Get a group of five to seven high school sophomores (not juniors, not seniors, not freshmen), sit them down with a pizza, some soda, and your printed marketing materials. Ask them to read through your materials, to circle any words that they don't understand, and to tell you in no uncertain terms what they feel is boring about your materials. Trust me; they will. Sophomores are 15 or 16 years old; they are not worldly enough to have heard most of your jargon, but they are old enough to *love* telling adults when they are wrong. Try this; lots of my clients have, and it *really* works. ∎

Developing Different Materials for Different Markets

I noted earlier the need to focus on different markets. Look now at the different markets that we discussed in Chapter 5. You may have donors, staff, volunteers, referrers, and board members, United Way, government users, insurers, members, or other markets and you can't just get away (or adequately address all these wants) with one threefold brochure. You need different materials for different markets. But you probably don't need 12,402 different pieces. Nor do you have unlimited resources or time to develop lots of materials, even accounting for the low cost of hardware, software, and color printers.

You want to have a focused set of materials, and you probably will have to develop them over time. Here are some tips for developing the best materials for the least money.

Plan Using a Committee

Don't try this alone. Get a group together and then plan your materials. Which markets are big enough and important enough to merit an individual piece or pieces? What are their wants? What should each piece address? What kind of look should it have? Should it be a brochure, an 8-1/2 by 11 sheet, or a booklet? How much money do you want to spend and when?

Get a Uniform "Look"

You probably have a logo of some kind. If you haven't updated it since the previous millennium, now might be a good time to think about it. Whether you develop a new logo or keep your existing one, get a scanned, digitized version of it. You'll need that for your remaining work. Have a consistent paper color, typeface (font), and setup to your materials. One excellent way to jump-start this is to look through catalogs that sell paper in "look" sets. You can get 8-1/2 by 11 sheets, brochures, cards, even announcements all in the same look, and just add your text and graphics to them. But, however you approach this, you want to have an identifiable and consistent set of colors, text, and graphics in all your materials.

Meet the Wants of the Different Target Markets

"Well," you say, "I have identified 100 different markets. Do I need 100 different brochures?" Probably not, but you do you need to focus your marketing materials on your target markets. Let's look at the types of materials that you might develop, and the target markets that they might address. Remember as you read Exhibit 9.1 to focus on your target markets.

These are just a quick set of ideas. You will undoubtedly have many more. The bottom line in this area is to remember to meet the wants of the markets, and to recognize the virtually impossible task of doing that in a single, general brochure. Focusing your materials on your target markets is the key.

Recap

Now you know the way to improve your current marketing materials, and to develop new or modified materials as you enter new markets. You should realize that marketing materials need to solve problems and identify with their target audience, and not sell products and services. You should be able to recite the seven things to include in your marketing materials:

1. Your mission
2. Focus
3. Brevity
4. Connection of problems and solutions

EXHIBIT 9.1 Target Markets and Associated Materials

Market	Want	Possible Marketing Materials
Board	Initial information, ongoing information.	Board orientation manual, newsletter. Online newsletter. A special section of your web site.
Staff	Initial information, ongoing information about the organization.	Staff orientation materials. Online newsletter. A special section of your web site.
Donors	Information on ways to give and what happens to the donation. A number to call or e-mail to write (with a name).	Specific piece designed for donors. Online newsletter.
Government	Information on program quality, program availability, meeting of regulations.	Specific piece designed with needs and keywords of government—emphasizing outcomes, quality, and certification levels. Online newsletter.
Foundations	Demonstration of expertise and experience in the field of the foundation's interest.	Probably a general informational piece, with a specific application for funds. Perhaps a piece on the mission statement, endorsements. Online newsletter.
Membership	Information on the benefits and costs of membership. A number to call or e-mail to write (with a name).	Specific piece on the value of becoming a member—from the member's perspective. Online newsletter.
Service recipients	Information on services and outcomes. A number to call or e-mail to write (with a name).	Pieces designed with target groups in mind (parents, teens, seniors) or regarding specific services for larger groups (camps, congregations, tours). Online newsletter. Special section of your web site.
Referral sources	Information about the quality of the program and its array of services.	A piece that might be filled with jargon if designed for a professional referrer. Online newsletter. Special section of your web site.

5. Appearance
6. References
7. A specific source for more information

You should also know the list of things to avoid, including jargon, inappropriate or unnecessary photos, a lack of focus, asking for money, including a history lesson, being out of date, and being boring. Finally, you learned about how to create different materials for your different markets, and how to remain focused within those materials on the markets' problems (their wants) rather than on your services, no matter how wonderful they are.

Remember, your marketing materials speak for you when you are not there. In a very real sense, they are delegated the responsibility to be your salesperson, to answer questions, to promote your services, and to establish a rapport with a potential customer—all without any supervision, and often without the opportunity for follow-up or evaluation.

If your marketing materials are good, then you have hundreds or even thousands of "spokespersons" out in the community that are helping interest people in your organization. If your materials are not good, at best you have simply wasted some time, money, and paper. At worst, you are hurting your organization every time someone looks at your brochure, sees your web site or your ad, or hears your piece on the radio. Speaking of web sites, they are an integral part of the marketing mix, and we'll discuss them at some length in the next chapter, "Technology and Marketing."

Spend the time and the money to get it right. Follow the list of things to include, and remember, you aren't just in the promotional business any more. Otherwise, if you build it, not only will they *not* automatically come, but they won't even care. But if you build what the market wants, and then show them how it solves their problems, they will come in droves.

Discussion Questions

1. Do our materials include jargon? How do we know?
2. Is there a good flow from our paper materials to our web site?
3. Have we figured out which markets want paper and which don't?
4. Do our marketing materials sell services or solve problems?
5. How do we measure up to the list of things to include in our materials?
6. How do we do on the list of things to avoid?
7. Let's look at our target markets. Do we have marketing pieces that are developed specifically for them? How can we improve in this area?

CHAPTER 10

Technology and Marketing

Chapter Thumbnail

➤ Tech Is an Accelerator of Good Marketing

➤ (Your Web Site Is) Your First Chance to Make a Good Impression

➤ Asking and Listening

➤ Beware the Digital Divide

➤ Social Networking/Social Media

➤ What's Next?

Overview

So far, you've seen the keys to marketing—identifying your markets, asking them what they want, accommodating those wants as much as you can, involving everyone on your marketing team, and remembering that your job is to get people the services they need in the ways that they want. This is all good marketing practice, and applicable to services, development, and employee and volunteer recruitment.

What we haven't talked much about is technology, or *tech*, as I call it. Now we will, and in depth. For many marketers, tech is seen as a cheap way to communicate and sell. Inexpensive it is; cheap it is not. For some marketers, tech offers the opportunity to inundate their customers with their brand. Not so smart. For others, it's a cost-efficient way of keeping in touch. True, but only with certain markets. Are web sites *the answer*, or a terrific marketing tool? The latter.

We'll look at all of these issues and many more in this chapter. The thing to remember, whether you were born after 1980 and thus "born digital," or born before 1950 and perhaps a bit sick of all the technology, is this: Technology is ubiquitous in our society, and in the nonprofit sector as well. I have long said that the future of philanthropy is with those nonprofits that successfully merge mission and technology. This does not mean that we won't feed people, or hug the grieving or sick, or read to second graders in person. But it does mean that if we don't figure out how to utilize this terrific tool, we won't be one of the nonprofits that survive over the next 10 to 15 years.

By the end of the chapter you should be much better able to look at how you are merging tech and marketing and ask some key questions that can help you improve your capabilities in this crucial area.

A note of caution: I will be providing some resources for you throughout the chapter, in the form of organizations and web sites. This is, as most readers know, fraught with danger given the pace of innovation in technology. Thus, by the time you read this, some of these resources will undoubtedly be outdated. But some will still be valid, and I want you to have as much of a head start as possible.

Tech Is an Accelerator of Good Marketing

It's right in Jim Collins's wonderful book, *Good to Great*: "Technology is an accelerator of a good idea, not a substitute for one." I could not agree more, nor could I start the chapter with a better and more applicable caution. You can't just count on technology to hide bad work, poor survey development, or inferior branding. If you do online surveys but don't ask the right questions, all you do is get poor information faster. If you don't target the portions of your web site to your particular high-priority markets, all you do is confuse and frustrate the people you want to please. If you don't listen and respond to the comments posted on your organization's blog, why did you ask in the first place?

That said, technology can really help your marketing efforts, no matter what part of the nonprofit sector you serve. You can reach out, ask, inform, schedule, accept donations, and communicate more efficiently than ever before. And that statement is becoming truer each day.

Here is one more reality check for you: If you don't use technology to the max, if you don't reach out online, if people can't find everything they need about your organization on your web site, you are going to lose two entire generations of adults now, and every generation that comes after. You may not be online, or tech savvy, but these people all are—as are an increasing number of your competitors. Tech is, in a very real sense, a market want for an increasing percentage of the population. Eschew it at your peril.

Let's look briefly at the things that tech can do well to support your marketing efforts.

First Impressions—Your Web Site

Think of pretty much anyone born after 1980. If they are told about your services and need them (or a family member does), or they hear that your nonprofit is a great place to volunteer, or they want to donate to your mission, or they are interested in a job, where will they look first? That's right, on your web site. Where will they go second? To some other web site of some other organization. Will they call you? No. Will they read your printed literature? Doubtful.

For these people, as well as for millions born before 1980, your web site is your first and last contact site. So, it better be good.

 FOR EXAMPLE: My middle son, Adam, is an aerospace engineer, and like most people of his age, an avid volunteer. After grad school, Adam and his wife Pam moved to Silver Spring, MD, and they began looking for volunteering opportunities. My wife and I visited them shortly after they moved, and the subject of their volunteering search came up at dinner. Of course, their search for places to volunteer started with the local nonprofits' web sites. That was no surprise. But during dinner Adam looked at me and said, "You know, Dad, if a nonprofit's web site is crappy, I don't look any further, since I figure if their web site is crappy, their services are, too." Pam nodded and added, "All our friends feel that way." ∎

Is that true? Are nonprofits with poor web sites also giving poor services? Of course not, at least not always. But if people assume that they are, the damage is the same—no volunteering from great young people like Adam and Pam.

Asking and Listening

The ability to get good information from clients, volunteers, donors, and community members quickly (often in real time) and efficiently is a key benefit that technology provides us. Whether from blogs, tweets, postings on Facebook, or other social media sites, we can see feedback on our services and organization and respond right away.

We can also solicit input by encouraging feedback on our web site, by electronically surveying key markets, and by researching and paying attention to our competition.

An Educational Tool

We want more people to know more about our organization and the issues we are concerned with. Distributing our brand and getting the word out about our mission and the way we address it are all things that technology can help us with, whether it be through our web site, video, or webinars. Remember, many of your markets want more information about you, or about your issues. They key word is *want*. Meet the want (at least in part) with technology.

A Conduit for Help

All nonprofits could use a little more help. The old adage is that all the easy problems have been solved and only the tough ones are left. I like to add that it seems that many of those problems have been left primarily to nonprofits. Do you have enough money or staff to do everything you want to do related to your mission? I didn't think so.

Tech can help us access people's time, talent, and treasure. You can ask for help and organize volunteers, take donations, and have people assist in problem solving, all online. Again, people want to help, but many only want to help online. Give them the chance.

That's just a brief look at the many ways tech can help us with our marketing and mission. For the remainder of the chapter, we'll drill down into a few key areas to get you going.

(Your Web Site Is) Your First Chance to Make a Good Impression

You learned, in my story about Adam and Pam, how important your web site is. You've read my question and answer about people born after 1980: They will always start on your web site, whether it be for information on services, to volunteer, to donate, or to seek a job. Your web site is your first (and often only) chance to make a good first impression.

I have visited literally thousands of nonprofit web sites, and many are good, and some are excellent, but some (to put it plainly) are simply awful—and worse than no web site at all. You need to make sure that your web site is both deeper and wider than just a repeat of your printed marketing material. And, you need to keep it up to date, not only in terms of content, but also in look and in use of reasonably current technology.

Here are some basic questions about your site. I hope this is a pleasant read for you, but let's see:

- Does your web site tell your story—or, more accurately, the story of how your mission helps? Does this include video?
- Can people find out about your locations, hours, and services *easily* (within two clicks of opening your home page)? Can they get directions and print a map?
- Can people sign up for appointments, purchase tickets, or check their grades (whatever is appropriate to your organization) online? Can they apply for a job, or sign up for a volunteer opportunity?
- Are there sources of information on your site for people to learn more about the issues that concern your organization? For instance, if your core service is foster care, is there a deep set of resources on becoming a foster parent, adoption, and so on?
- Is there transparency information on the site, including information about key staff and all of your board, your most recent IRS 990, audit, and strategic plan?
- Can volunteers and donors (current or potential) explore options of things that they can do to help your organization?
- Does your site look just as good on web-enabled phones as it does on a computer screen?
- Do you accept donations online by either credit card or PayPal? Can such donations be restricted by the donor?
- Can people see your current letters of accreditation, licenses, and any other quality assurance documents?

I'm sure as you read this you can think of many other things that could reach out to people who access you online, meet their wants, and impress them with your ability to solve their problems. And, of course, don't be afraid to ask people what they want from your web site. They'll give you great feedback and useful improvements to consider. As I've said repeatedly, ask, ask, ask, and then listen!

With that overview, let's drill down more deeply into a few more areas.

Board-Only and Staff-Only Areas

These parts of your web site offer immediate access for your board and staff as well as opportunities for them to learn more about what's going on in the organization. Here's what to do:

1. Set up the board site as a subarea of your web site. Make sure to secure it, so that only approved people can get in. For most organizations, a username and password are sufficient. One very useable format for this is to have a username that is the first letter of the first name and the full last name (for me, this would be pbrinckerhoff) and a password of the first name. That way, your web site administrator can set the access and, of course, remove access when a board or staff member leaves.
2. Set up an easily found link on the starting page of your web site for the board area and the staff area (I suggest two different areas, not one combined one—there will be overlap, but start with separate areas). Before you start, ask both groups what they'd like to see on their parts of the web site, and then listen to their ideas. After the sections are developed, hold an informational session for both board and staff, showing them the site, how to access it, and what is available for them to use.
3. On the site, you can include any of the following things that other non-profits have included: a list of staff (with pictures if possible), a list of board members (with pictures), board member e-mail addresses, a list of all committees with the times and locations of meetings, access to all committee meeting minutes as well as minutes of board meetings, scheduling information for upcoming meetings and training opportunities, copies of all policies, printable copies of forms that board or staff members use, explanations of all program functions, and other announcements for the organization. One organization I work with has an opening page for board members that lists all the meetings coming up for the next three months.

Consider doing the same thing for your other volunteers, particularly if your volunteers are mostly younger. This kind of deeper web site is exactly what the Web is for—a customized communication tool that can enhance your mission, internal communications, and board, staff, and volunteer satisfaction.

Public Education

One of the best things your web site can offer is public education on the issues that concern you. You can research and list books, CDs, videos, links to articles of interest or educational web sites, and other resources for further study by your web site visitors. This is a community service, and it keeps your site visitors coming back. It can also tie in nicely with our next topic: affiliations.

Affiliations

Not only should your site show your links to social networking sites that you are using, you can also affiliate with a commercial site as a way to raise funds. The easiest of these is Amazon.com. You can sign up as an affiliate at Amazon, post one of dozens of logos as a link on your web site, and, when people go to Amazon through your web site, you get 5 percent of whatever they purchase there. There are two major applications of this. First, if you do public education as noted above, you can list specific books, videotapes, and other resources on your web site, and have links directly to those items on Amazon (you can even download the book cover graphics from Amazon). This is a lower-impact way of affiliating. Or, you can note your affiliation to Amazon (or any other affiliation you have) and place a link on your opening page, then e-mail all your supporters (particularly during the holiday shopping season), asking them to purchase their online gifts through your affiliation link. Again, free money, but not without controversy.

 HANDS ON: This is, at its core, a political choice: Do you want to commercialize your web site? *Talk to your board* about this before you just up and do it. I have dozens of client organizations who use this as a low-cost revenue stream, and dozens of others who do not. It is your choice, but one you want to make in coordination with your board. ■

There are many affiliation sites as of this writing, including Amazon, Barnes & Noble, Lands' End, and Nordstrom. Check the site out, see what the deal is, and after you decide whether you want to affiliate at all, affiliate only on a site-by-site basis.

 HANDS ON: Remember that affiliation income will be treated by the IRS as unrelated business income, and you must report this in your annual 990-T filing. But, don't panic! You can offset the unrelated business income with some of your web site management and ISP costs. While I have dozens of client organizations that have affiliation income, I don't have any that have *net* unrelated business income (and thus pay taxes) after they deduct legitimate web site expenses. ■

Video

If a picture speaks a thousand words, what's the word count for a short video of someone who has benefited from your services, or who has had an awesome volunteer experience—a hundred thousand? I don't know, but I do know that video is becoming the best way to communicate the emotion of your organization's mission and story.

People love to look at short videos of all kinds of things, from learning a skill on HowCast to online learning at colleges and universities. And, YouTube has made this far cheaper for you. Not only has the quality standard of video dropped, every high-schooler for the past decade has had to work on a bunch of videos for school projects, so they would know how to help you. Thus, either people on your staff or the children of your staff can help you. The software to edit video is on most computers, and tons of people (staff, board, volunteers) have good digital video recorders. So, you have the tools and the skills—what's holding you back? I'll also give you a great resource for this at the end of the chapter.

I think you know how important your web site is. And, since the state of the art is changing all the time, you need some resources to keep up to date with the various components of your site. You'll find those at the end of the chapter. Just remember what your mother told you: You only get *one chance* to make a good first impression.

Asking and Listening

You've heard me say it probably two dozen times: ask, ask, ask, and then listen! Asking is an area where tech can help, supplementing your in-person and paper asking and giving people new ways to tell you about what they want. Let's look at surveying, your web site, and telephony as ways of asking for and getting feedback.

Surveying

Ten years ago, when people surveyed, the only way that tech could really help them was by putting the data into a database, analyzing the information, and developing reports with cool charts and graphs. You can still do that, and will have to for your paper or in-person surveys.

 HANDS ON: There are a variety of good database tools available, but if you don't have one, don't go out and buy one. Go online and look for open-source database applications, such as the one included with OpenOffice. I've used all the OpenOffice tools for a decade and they are bug-free and don't get hacked the way Microsoft products do. And, they're free—a good price! ■

But technology has really moved along in this area, and the most helpful is online surveying. Online survey sites, the most prominent of which, at this writing, is SurveyMonkey.com, allow you to easily develop a wide variety of surveys using different survey techniques. The survey is easily customized and edited, and then you distribute the survey either by e-mailing it or by posting the URL for the survey on your web site as a way of getting input.

As I said in Chapter 8, the key benefits of electronic surveying are that you eliminate the opportunity for data entry error, you can view the results in real time, and you can develop great analysis and reports easily, even posting them online if you choose to.

That said, remember the digital divide. More on this in the next section, but you can get online survey input only from those people who are online or who are comfortable in that environment. Many customers, donors, and volunteers will respond only to an online survey. Others never will. Therefore, there is a need to target your survey methods to the markets you are surveying.

 HANDS ON: Using high-tech surveying does *not* get you off the hook in regard to my rules on surveying, which we discussed in Chapter 8. You still need to focus, you still have only about four minutes, you still need to restrict the number of identifiers, and you still need to get some help in designing the survey questions. ■

Web Site

This is pretty straightforward: Make sure there is a place on every page of your web site for customer feedback. Usually, this is just a link that initiates an e-mail to your organization, but it could also include a blog or a link to your Facebook or social media site where people can post their reactions to what you are doing. You want to offer the opportunity for input in every way possible, so make sure your online visitors can tell you how you can improve.

Voice Mail

I know, I know—voice mail is *so* last century. But, a large portion of the population uses it every day—and there's the trap. Voice mail is so common that no one pays any attention to it; we all use it, so what's the big deal? The big deal comes in two ways: first, how customers get to your voice mail, and second, whether your people check and follow up on their voice mail. First, let me reassure you: I love voice mail as much as someone born in 1990 loves texting. Having the ability to quickly transmit my message, need, or complaint, to do it efficiently and with whatever emphasis or emotion is appropriate for the message, is terrific. It removes the potential for transcription error from a receptionist, and can be accessed 24 hours a day by both caller and recipient.

That having been said, there are pitfalls, and the biggest turnoff to a caller is a lengthy, confusing, or redundant system that takes too much time. Remember the four-minute rule in surveying? You've got about *40 seconds* via voice mail. We already know that you need to have a live person answer the phone during office hours, but let's look at some issues involved in your customers' access to your voice mail.

 FOR EXAMPLE: A friend of mine, who works for a national insurance company and travels all the time, lives on his phone. He has seven zillion minutes on his cell phone, and a topic that comes up regularly when we eat breakfast together is the latest cool phone. Of course, he was one of the first to get a pager, then a cell phone, then a PDA, then an iPhone. But whenever I call him to either change an appointment or set one up, I get this sequence:

1. A 10-second message from my friend, telling me to leave a message
2. A 20-second message from a computer telling me which button to push for various options—one I have to listen to *completely* before I can choose
3. A *second* 14-second message from my friend telling me to leave a message
4. A *second* 10-second message from the computer

It's a good thing we're friends. This drives me nuts every time I call, and I'm sure it does the same to his customers. And, yes, I've told him about it. ■

 HANDS ON: When was the last time you called in to your organization and tried to go through the entire process (no shortcuts—pretend you are a new caller)? Do this today. Time yourself: How long does it take until you actually can start talking and leaving your message? Now, do the same thing again acting as someone who knows your extension. How long is it now? For new callers, no more than 40 seconds is acceptable; for people who know your extension, 10 seconds max. This may well mean that you have to change the greeting, both at the agency entry level and at your own mailbox. Remember, always have a live person answer the phone during office hours, but make the recorded part as easy as possible. ■

The other issue is checking your voice mail—or people never checking it. Customers, funders, donors, and volunteers expect that, when they leave a message, they will get called back. Soon. Very soon. (In the next chapter, you'll learn that customers never have problems; they have *crises*.) Make sure to remind your very, very busy staff that part of their very, very busy jobs is checking and responding to their voice mail. How often that should be done depends on your organization. I have client organizations whose absolute rule on voice mail is four times every workday and at least once on weekends and holidays. It's the same for their e-mail. This is because they work with women in crisis, and people in crisis *cannot* wait. I've been in their staff meetings when everyone takes a voice mail break at once. What will work for you? It depends on how urgent your customer problems or service issues are. But err on the side of too often, and talk this through at a staff meeting.

 HANDS ON: The same can, of course, be said for text messages, and if the organization noted above was dealing with teens in crisis, the service staff would have had to distribute their cell phone numbers. Here's why: Teens won't call, but they will text. It's their default method of communication (again, as of this writing). ■

One more time: You have to be where your markets are—and they are online.

Beware the Digital Divide

We've all heard of the digital divide, and many people are concerned about it. I am, too. You may even have decided to skim this chapter because you've been thinking: "Yeah, yeah; I know tech is a big deal. But the people *we* serve don't have easy access to computers; they don't have e-mail. All this online stuff really doesn't affect us."

FOR EXAMPLE: The events in this story occurred in late 1999, which was the Dark Ages in terms of Internet access. A friend of mine who runs a huge homeless shelter on the East Coast and who, like me, is a bit of a tech-head, called me late one night to tell me about a person who had checked in earlier that evening. My friend does intake once a month to keep himself close to the people his organization serves, and a person who, according to my friend, "was a caricature of a homeless man, the person a group of fourth-graders would draw if asked to draw a homeless man," showed up at the intake desk. My friend checked him in and, since it was the first time this man had used this particular shelter, asked him how he heard about the shelter and why he had chosen to come in. The man looked at him for a second, and said, "Well, I was, y'know, surfing the Web, and I came across your web site, and it looked good, so I, like, came over."

Where does a homeless person surf the Web? You know, don't you? At the library. I've told that story a hundred times in training sessions, and when I tell it *everyone* laughs, I assume with surprise, and yet *everyone* knows the answer to the question of where the homeless man got online. Nevertheless, we continue to believe that the Net doesn't affect us. It does. (And don't forget, this story occurred way back in 1999.) ∎

In addition, remember that online access to your organization doesn't limit itself to just the people you serve. Go back to your list of markets. What about your funders, donors, volunteers, and staff? Most if not all of them have the ability, even the desire, to access you in a variety of right-now ways. The people you serve are a *vital* market. But they are not your *only* market.

One more thing about the divide—it's changed. Whereas availability of free computers at libraries, places of worship, and nonprofits like the YMCA and Boys Clubs/Girls Clubs has widened access for many people, the big jump has come away from desktops and laptops to web-enabled phones. These increasingly cheap tools are allowing people from nearly all parts of the economy to have online access 24/7/365, which is as it should be. But can the poorest of the poor afford them? No.

However, many of our most economically challenged neighbors do have cell phones, and the incremental cost of upgrading to a web-enabled phone is far less than the cost of a desktop or laptop and the monthly fees to be online, free wireless locations notwithstanding.

So, what is the digital divide I caution you about? It's the digital *comfort* divide. There are (and always will be) people who don't want to go online, who aren't ever going to be comfortable with putting their credit card number into a web site donation box, who don't have an e-mail address and don't want one. While the number of these people is waning every day, they still make up a significant portion of our population. Just as I admonished you to not go low tech and write off the people born after 1980, you can't afford to write off the people on the far side of the digital comfort divide, either.

What does this tell you? You have to *target* and provide for both groups' wants. In my book *Generations*, I call this *meeting techspectations*. Don't forget to do just that.

Social Networking/Social Media

As this is written, social media are all the rage in nonprofit circles. We've been late to the party, whether it's Facebook or Twitter, and the blogs and technical assistance sites are full of ways to use these terrific tools to further your nonprofit's cause. By the time you read this, some other application or tool will be hot, and Facebook and Twitter will have innovated as well, so I won't waste your time by telling you how to best use them. I will provide some resources for you in the next section, but first, here are some rules about this area:

- *Social networking is here to stay.* It is a terrific way to communicate, and increasingly an expectation of staff, volunteers, donors, and board members. I have clients who have set up social networking sites on Ning.com or Facebook for their younger board members and staff, and they are hugely popular. The technology works, and has enormous potential.
- *Social networks are where an increasing number of people reside online.* Again, this is all about meeting techspectations. If you want to get someone born after 1987 to come to your weekend volunteer activity, you'd better be on Facebook. For someone born between 1980 and 1985, you'd better be on Twitter. You get the idea.
- *You have the resources you need to figure this out.* They are called your *younger staff*. Talk to them (and high-schoolers) about what kind of media they like, where they spend their time, and how they use the technology. Then, and here is the key, delegate the responsibility to get your organization up to speed in this area to your younger employees or volunteers. They get it; they were born digital. All you need to do is understand that social networking is an essential part of your marketing portfolio and cut your staff loose to get you there.

What's Next?

I haven't a clue. You will, to a degree, but that's because you'll read this at least a year after I'm writing it. New ideas, applications, trends, fads, and great tools will be coming along at a rapid pace. It will be your job to sort out what fits with your mission and your goals in marketing and technology.

In some cases, it will be best to sit and wait and see what evolves. (Some readers will remember that MySpace was the "it" application for a while; then Facebook ate MySpace's lunch.) In other cases, the sooner you can adopt a new technology, the better. Twitter would be a great example of this. It's easy, cheap, and got incredibly popular, incredibly fast.

How to decide will be your job, and the job (I hope) of your younger staff and volunteers. But, no matter what comes along, there will be online help for you. I doubt whether most of the following resources will still be there when you read this, but there will be others. Consider this a starting list:

- **Techsoup.org.** This awesome resource is the place to start for technical assistance, low-cost (new) software, and a terrific weekly newsletter. It's also the place to get the best ideas for your web site. Go here first for all things nonprofit tech.
- **Nten.org.** Another great nonprofit tech resource, nTen tends to do more online and live training, but that may well change.
- **SurveyMonkey.com.** The best online surveying resource as of this writing. Inexpensive (free for small users) and flexible, it's the best way to reach people who are always online.
- **YouTube.com.** Yes, it's fun to look at, but don't forget that YouTube has brought the cost of video *way* down, and made our appetite for video pretty much insatiable. And, YouTube Charity helps you get going in this essential area. YouTube also has a volunteer cadre of videographers interested in helping charities.
- **Google.org.** As with YouTube, google.org helps nonprofits with online technical assistance and donations.
- **DesignOutpost.com.** One of a number of places you can get graphic arts assistance very cheaply and in a very cool way.
- **ConstantContact.com.** Need a good way to get your online newsletter distributed, or your charitable event out to your e-mail list? Constant Contact is the best way to do that as of this writing.

Recap

Technology can be a marketing accelerator, but I cannot emphasize enough (1) that it can never be a substitute for a marketing orientation among the staff, (2) my belief that asking and listening is a way to improve services, and (3) that there should be a commitment to overall customer satisfaction for all your varied customers. In this chapter, we've covered the ways tech can help you, with the caveat that those ways are always changing and always improving.

First, we briefly looked at a set of ways that tech can help your marketing, and then we drilled down into your web site, which I noted is increasingly the place where you make your first (and often last) impression.

We moved on to asking, and looked at the benefits of online surveying, and how to encourage people to give you input on your web site.

I cautioned you about the new digital comfort divide, and reminded you that every market is important, and that some have significantly different tech wants. Accommodating those tech wants is what I called *meeting techspectations.*

We turned to social media, a force in technology that is not going to do anything but grow. I gave you my three rules for social media and encouraged you to empower your younger staff and volunteers to get your nonprofit up to speed in this crucial area.

Finally we talked about what's next—and I told you I don't have a clue. But I did provide you with the best resources out there in the tech arena as of this writing.

So, now you know it all? You do know about the marketing cycle, about identifying markets, about asking and listening, and about great marketing materials. You are armed with tech ideas and applications to accelerate your great marketing ideas. Yet, there's one more area to cover, and it's the subject of our next chapter: customer satisfaction.

Discussion Questions

1. Do we use technology well in our pursuit of mission and in our marketing?
2. Have we delegated to our younger staff and volunteers enough in this area, particularly in social media, video, and emerging technologies?
3. What can we do better on our web site? Should we have dedicated areas of the site for staff, board, and volunteers?
4. Is our online donation area good enough? What about our employment area?
5. Can we reconsider our printed marketing materials given the improvements in technology that allow us to print our own stuff?
6. Are there better ways to survey and track the data we gather? Which online survey provider should we use?
7. What regular research do we do on our competition? Can we do more online?

CHAPTER 11

Incredible Customer Service

Chapter Thumbnail

➤ Three Customer Service Rules

➤ The Customer Is Not Always Right, but the Customer Is Always the Customer, so Fix the Problem

➤ Customers Never Have Problems; They Always Have Crises, so Fix the Problem *Now*

➤ Never Settle for Good Customer Service—Seek Total Customer *Satisfaction*

➤ The Unhappy Customer

➤ Regular Customer Contact

➤ Turning Customers into Referral Sources

Overview

In a monopoly, you can treat your customers in whatever way you want, and they will still stay as customers. Why? Because they don't have any choice. If you are the only game in town, they have to use you. But in today's competitive environment you must appeal to customer wants and give exceptional, even incredible, customer service to stand out from your competition.

We can all rattle off organizations that do this. Why? Because they give us, as customers, a positive experience that we don't soon forget. Nordstrom, Amazon, Lands' End, Dell, Marriott, and Federal Express are all examples of organizations where exceptional customer service is the *minimal* standard from day to day and from employee to employee.

In this chapter I will show you many examples of incredible service and some tangible ways to make your organization a place where customers are more than just pleased with you. First, we'll look at the issue we touched on in Chapter 6, how to treat everyone, even your funders, like a valued customer. The attitude in your organization from top to bottom, from staff to volunteer, has to be that the people outside the organization are always valued customers. I'll show you how to instill that philosophy and the things that result when you do.

To treat people well and to solve their problems, you need to solve them *quickly*. Since you cannot be everywhere at once, and since problems can and do occur at any time, you need to train and empower your staff to make any problem right. For some readers this is a really scary idea, and I'll show you how to implement it with the least pain and risk. We'll go over the rules of customer service, and look at ways to use marketing and customer service to do more mission, using a concept I call *compassionate urgency*.

Compassionate urgency helps us when we look at our next issue: solving customers' problems, solving them promptly, and showing we care. I'll also show you here why it is important not to settle for customer *service*, but to seek total customer *satisfaction*. And, I'll show you six rules for how to deal with the inevitable unhappy customers who, like it or not, will show up on your doorstep, on the other end of a phone, or on your web site comment section eventually—no matter how good your customer service is.

Next I'll show you how to make and maintain regular contact with your key markets and customers. These regular interactions are the foundation of the communications flow that you want to establish with your customers so that they will tell you their wants and problems.

Finally, I'll take you to the next level. Not only do I want you to provide incredible service, not only do I want you to solve customers' problems with an empowered staff, but I also want you to take your good customers and turn them into referral sources—ones that continually send you new customers. Sound like fun? I'll show you how to play the game.

By the end of this chapter you should have a very good idea of how to improve the standards of customer service in your organization, the reasons why it is so important, and some techniques to apply right away to empower your staff and work toward a new level of incredible results for your markets and, as a result, for your mission.

Three Customer Service Rules

I've said this only about 20 times so far, but it can't be said enough: Your environment today requires that you, your staff, and your volunteers treat everyone well, everyone like a customer, even though you may never have thought of them as anything but the enemy. You simply must treat everyone—staff, board, volunteers, service recipients, and funders—like a customer if you are going to succeed in today's economic and political reality.

We discussed treating everyone as a customer a bit in Chapter 2 and at more length in Chapter 6, but it is so important (and so often ignored by nonprofits) that I want to go through it again, this time with some ideas for how to bring your staff and board along for the ride. Let's review the three core rules of excellent service to all of your customers:

1. The customer is not always right, but the customer is always the customer, so fix the problem.
2. Customers never have problems; they always have *crises,* so fix the problem *now.*
3. Never settle for good customer service. You should always seek total customer *satisfaction.*

Success in the area of customer service (and customer satisfaction!) starts with those three statements. Not, of course, just with making the statements, but with believing them, and with structuring your organization to accommodate them.

First, of course, you must look at *everyone* as a customer. I know that this is a real stretch for many readers, and a nearly insurmountable one for certain staff and board. For you, it may be difficult to think of your board as customers, when they have always seemed like a group of nice, but sometime meddlesome, burdens. It may be tough to equate staff, whom you are supposed to monitor, supervise, and (sometimes) discipline, as customers. It may be a challenge to think of a funder as a customer at all, particularly if you have spent the past 15 years fighting with them over regulations, funding criteria, and oversight.

But they all *are* customers. That is why they made the list of key markets in Chapter 6. You can choose to treat them as such and have a much higher likelihood of success. Or, you can treat them like you always have and increase your troubles tenfold. I will assume for the rest of the chapter, in fact for the rest of the book, that you will make the effort to recognize everyone as a customer. Is the idea to make your job easier? No; it's really for the benefit of your mission and of the people you serve.

So, it's settled. Everyone is a valued customer, and the customer can make mistakes, but the customer is still and always the customer. Sometimes customers are happy, sometimes not.

Let's look at each of the rules in greater detail.

The Customer Is Not Always Right, but the Customer Is Always the Customer, so Fix the Problem

Really, we get back to good management here. After nearly three decades in nonprofit management and consulting, I know that the single most important thing managers need to do with their staff is to *always tell them the truth*. This does not mean that you need to tell your staff everything, but it does mean that *everything you tell them must be absolutely fact, no exceptions, no exaggerations, no talking the talk and then not walking the walk*. What does that have to do with marketing? Lots, and here it impacts the way we motivate our staff. The old adage that "the customer is always right" is patently false, and we all know it. All of us know that we are not perfect. We all make mistakes. We also know that we are customers for many organizations and businesses. Thus, as customers, we are fallible. Your customers are the same: imperfect. In organizations that continue to tell their staff the old fable that the customer is always right, I have seen tremendous resentment build up in employees against both management *and customers*. This, to say the least, is counterproductive. A much more sensible way to look at it is that even though they may be wrong at times, their perspective is what counts. They *are* the customer, so make it right.

Lead here, and by doing so in front of staff, it will encourage them to overcome their natural resentment toward a customer who whines or complains inappropriately. It also lets *the staff* know that *you* understand what they are going through and dealing with.

Customers Never Have Problems; They Always Have Crises, so Fix the Problem *Now*

This can be the most mission-driven part of the three-part customer service maxim. From the customers' perspective, if they have a problem, it is not mundane, it is not run-of-the-mill, it is one-of-a-kind, it is *theirs*. If you or your staff, simply because you see this certain kind of problem all the time, treat it as no big deal, you will not address it quickly enough or with the empathy it deserves. We have all experienced this personally from the point of view of the customer.

FOR EXAMPLE: You wake up feeling awful. You have a headache, fever, chills, achy joints, runny nose, and a cough. You make the decision to stay home, and then wait for 9 A.M., when your doctor's office staff gets in, to call a nurse. At 9:02 you talk to the receptionist, give her your symptoms and say that you want to talk to a nurse. The receptionist assures you that one will call you as soon as possible. You hang up . . . and wait, and wait, and *wait*.

The receptionist and the nurse have had 300 calls for this kind of ailment in the past two days, and yours is just number 301. Your illness is not life-threatening, the treatment is what you are already doing (rest, fluids, pain reliever), so from their perspective it is not critical to call back immediately. They have bigger problems, such as the 10 people who just showed up unannounced asking to be seen as soon as possible (probably suffering from the same bug as you). Your call can wait.

Back at home, you are still feeling awful. You look at the clock every five minutes wondering: "Where the heck is that nurse?" By noon you are really angry, and by 1:00 P.M. you call back to find that the nurse is on her lunch break. By now, you are both sick *and* really mad. It doesn't matter that the nurse is pleasant, sympathetic, and helpful when she does call at 4:30 P.M. You are too angry to appreciate it. ∎

FOR EXAMPLE: Once you get well, you decide it is time to get a new clock. (You got sick of looking at it when you were waiting for the nurse to call.) You go to a local department store, find one that will look great on your wall, and take it home. When you put the batteries in and hang it in the perfect spot, you find that it keeps double time, moving two hours for every 60 minutes. You take it down, get the receipt, box, and bag, and return to the store, going up to the Returns/Customer Service counter. There is one person behind the counter and two people ahead of you. You wait. The counter staff person is friendly and helpful, but the first person is simply angry and wants to spout off for 10 minutes or so. You wait. You see another staff person on break in back of the counter and wonder why he can't help you. You wait. You finally are next in line, and the person waiting on you pushes a form in front of you to fill out that takes 10 full minutes to complete and seems more like an inquisition than a request for simple information. You leave very frustrated at the 25-minute exchange. All you wanted was a working clock. ∎

FOR EXAMPLE: You pull in to a gas station with a car that is running rough. The service manager listens to the engine and says, "Yeah, you need a tune-up. Take about 45 minutes." Of course, it takes two hours, since they need a coffee break, there are customers in for fuel, and so on. ■

In all of these examples the problem (illness, a return, a broken car) was made worse by the attitude of the employee. In every case, his or her attitude was natural and understandable—and wrong. The nurse has heard dozens of such calls every day, knew that there was no life-threatening issue, and made a professional judgment that medical professionals call *triage*. She ignored (or had never been trained in dealing with) the fact that you, from your perspective, were *sick*. You don't do this dozens of times every day, and you wanted a little assurance that you weren't going to die.

The entire methodology of returns when the clock was brought back was a mess. Many customer service counters in "customer-friendly" stores are now intentionally *over* staffed, just so that people won't have to wait to get their refund or exchange. This is because someone finally figured out that these customers are already put out, so why make them madder by putting them through the third degree? I regularly go to customer service counters now to exchange something, and the service staff person will say, "Do you want another item like this? Do you want one of our people to get it, or do you want to select it yourself? Just bring it back up here, I'll stamp it and you will be on your way!" Or, if it is a return for cash, it takes 45 seconds. They recognize that I want to be on my way *now!*

The service station sees poorly tuned cars all the time. What the manager forgot was that not only is the customer's time important, so are promises. She promised 45 minutes and that became the "contract." Additionally, when our car is broken, or at least up on a lift, many of us feel truly stranded, thus aggravating the frustration and impotence that we feel in the situation.

In all of these cases, seeing the *perspective of the customer,* which we discussed earlier, had not been taught and regularly reinforced. You may see 50 sick people today, but *their illness is their only one.* You may have 150 irrational customers returning things, but what they want is to (1) gripe, and (2) get their money back, or a working product. Let them do both, and soon. You may see cars like this all the time, but we need to get the customers on their way as soon as possible.

And here is the mission-driven part of this: For all the people who seek services, we need to have that sense of *compassionate urgency* I talked about earlier. We can't let the fact that we've helped 500 or 50,000 people with the same problem before make us take any customer, patient, student, parent, parishioner, or other user of our services for granted.

FOR EXAMPLE: The single best illustration of this that I have ever seen is a television commercial for our local hospital-based cardiac unit. The commercial is pretty standard, with a physician telling you why the unit is so good, a few visuals of the high-tech environment, and so on. The cardiologist who does the commercial is a friend of mine and, after I saw the commercial the first time, I asked him whether the tag line I liked so much was his creation, or some marketing consultant's. "No," he said "that is something we say *every* day in our staff meeting." The line is: "We need to remember that *what we do every day* here is a *once-in-a-lifetime experience* for our patients."

I have never seen it put better. Good marketing *is* good mission when it's done right—when your customers know by your actions that you care, and that you care about *them, their* issue, *their* family, *their* problem. And if they do, they will return for more services, and send others as well. ■

Now you know that every customer problem is a crisis, not just a problem. You may feel that you solve customer concerns quickly and efficiently, but does everyone else? You may feel that they do, and here is the test. Ask yourself this: When I am out of town for two or three days, or on vacation for a week, things break, stuff goes wrong, customers have problems. What happens then? Do my staff fix the problems, or do they wait for me to come back?

If you have told staff to fix customers' problems in your absence, do you then upbraid them about their solution? If so, they won't take such a risk again, and your customers will be poorly served. Staff must be trained and empowered to fix customers' problems. They must be coached, encouraged, shown how, and then entrusted to fix things when Mr. Murphy arrives, because he will.

 FOR EXAMPLE: All staff of Ritz-Carlton Hotels have the authority to spend up to $3,000 (as of this writing) on the spot to fix any problem that a guest brings to their attention. That's *all* staff: housekeeping, maintenance, front office, and security. ■

 FOR EXAMPLE: Lands' End Catalog is a business where 95 percent of the customers are never met in person by the staff. There is no chance to smile, to shake a hand, to look concerned. Yet, whenever I call, I am always made to feel welcome, like an honored

(continued)

(*continued*)

guest or even an old friend. And the staff will fix *any* problem I have with clothing, even after I have worn it and washed it a few times. "Send it back, Mr. Brinckerhoff, and we'll send you a replacement, credit your account, and we'll also pay for the shipping." ■

 FOR EXAMPLE: I once arrived at a Marriott Hotel at 2 A.M. with the mistaken idea that I had a reservation. The hotel was sold out, and it turned out that my reservation was at a Marriott on the other side of the same city. What did the clerk do? He could have said to himself, "This guy is an idiot. We're full. Let him take a cab to the other hotel." But no, he saw a customer with a problem/crisis. It was 2 A.M. His hotel was full, but he did have the Presidential Suite available. The President hadn't shown up yet, so he let me use an exorbitantly expensive room for $139. He solved my problem. At other hotel chains, he probably would have been reprimanded, if not fired. At Marriott he got commended for helping a customer (who, by the way, has told that story to literally tens of thousands of people), since Marriott empowers its people. ■

The bottom-line question here is: Do you really *empower* your staff to fix problems or just tell them to and then not support them? Empowerment means to delegate *and* support staff in their customer relations. It means that customer satisfaction is an organizational priority for everyone, and that you, as a supervisor, will go just as far to support your staff people in their customer relations as you would to actually satisfy the customer.

Let's face it. This is risky. All delegation is. But you need to have the attitude that you, as well as everyone else, learn from trying, and often learn best by making mistakes. Just the way competition is risky, so is letting staff fix problems in your absence. But if you encourage innovation, encourage initiative, coach and support your staff, and train them in the outcomes you want, then most people will rise to the occasion. You will find that some, perhaps many, of your staff have different ways of solving a problem, of meeting a want than you do. Often you will find that those solutions are *better* than yours. And that's okay.

Begin or expand your delegation with the understanding that the alternative is far more dangerous. If you don't delegate customer service, if you don't make sure that everyone is empowered to fix customer problems, if you make every issue wait for you to intervene personally, you absolutely will be losing customers. A competitive environment doesn't wait for you to personally get involved in every decision. It moves on. Empower your people to fix problems (*oops*, crises!) and fix them *now*.

Never Settle for Good Customer Service—Seek Total Customer *Satisfaction*

If I come up to you to sell my kitchen widget, and I just say, "Look at this widget! It is great! It is cool! It can do anything you need done in the kitchen!" you may buy it, or you may not. In fact, I can probably be so obnoxious and persistent that you will give me money to go away. Now, how many times will you let me sell to you? That's right—just once.

But assume I come to you and ask you how you are doing, what's going on in your life, and you tell me you spend too much time in the kitchen. I then whip out my kitchen widget and show you how it saves you time. If you believe my demonstration, you may well buy it, if it shows you enough value. But more importantly, you will let me come back later and try to sell you something else. Why? Because I tried to *solve your problem.*

I've already told you (but we can't discuss it too many times) that one of the great secrets of successful marketing is that it is really about how to make people happy with you because you solve a problem that is not of your making. If you ask a lot, ask regularly, and *listen,* people will tell you their problems. And if you understand their problems, then you will be able to make the connection between your organization's services and those problems. You can solve those problems, or at least give it a good shot.

 HANDS ON: *Never, EVER, EVER* assume that customers—even those who have intimate knowledge of your organization, its core competencies, and all of its services—can or will connect their problem to your solution. They *may,* but more often, they won't. Don't sit back and wait for them to come to you. Go to them. Ask, listen, respond! This type of asking is best done informally or in focus groups, as we discussed in Chapter 8, and all of your staff need to be part of the culture of asking. I see too many organizations that are stunned when people go elsewhere for services, because "they know about us." Well, perhaps they do; but do they know (or remember) what you can do for them, for their problems? Obviously not. ■

Solving customer problems also means that you need to learn to look at things from your customers' perspective. How do they view you? How do they see your staff, your board, and your buildings? If you only assume what they are thinking, if you say "I know what they need, because I've been here 25 years," you are not going to be getting to the issue: What is the customers' perspective on this?

Paying attention to the customers' perspective is the corollary of listening to their wants. Incredible customer service starts with trying to be in the customers' shoes, showing that you pay attention to their wants, their issues, their problems. Not paying attention to their perspective is an outgrowth of the nonprofit marketing disability. Recognizing that the problem is *always* a crisis and attending to it accordingly is essential. Having compassionate urgency is crucial. But looking at things from the customers' eyes will provide you with incredible insights. If you solve problems from your perspective rather than from the customers' perspective, you will solve the wrong problem, or solve the problem in the wrong way.

 FOR EXAMPLE: In 1991, a good friend of mine became director of a large state child welfare agency, an agency that was under tremendous pressure to improve. Bad things were happening to the children in the agency's care regularly, it was in the paper every day, the federal courts demanded change, and morale was awful.

The new director asked a group of people, including me, to head out and see what was really happening in the field, and we took a number of trips to agency offices where we talked to line staff as well as the people the agency served. We found all kinds of things we could fix easily, and all kinds of problems that would take years to solve. On our first day on the road, we were in a large office in the state's largest city. We had seen staff for about an hour, and walked into the client waiting area. I was with the deputy director, Gary, a really great guy who became, and has remained, a good friend. As we walked into the waiting area, we saw that over the intake desk was a large set of numbers (think delicatessen) that changed as we approached from 234 to 235. A disembodied voice said "Number 235 . . . Number 235."

Gary went nuts, turned a bright shade of red, and said to me, "That is *awful!* We are *fixing that!* We are *not* calling people by number. How disrespectful. We are *fixing that!*" I told him to calm down, and that I agreed; we needed to fix the problem. We sat down, talked to some people for about an hour, and left.

The next day, the edict went out from the state capitol to all offices: *The numbers come down. Call people by their names. Treat them with respect.* What a good idea. What a great improvement. Or not.. .

Four weeks later, I was assigned to go around the state and do what is called "sweep-up" in such change situations. Briefly, you try to find out if the things you tried to change actually happened. I wound up back in the same office, and talked to the staff, finding out that some things had improved, and some had not. Then I walked out, sat down with the clients, and started to chat. Pretty soon a *huge* man (and I am not a small person) comes over, gets right up in my face, and says, "Are *you* the fool who took away the numbers?" I admitted as much, and the rest of the people in the waiting room then gathered around and piled on (verbally only, but I admit I wasn't sure that it was going to end there!), telling me that I was an idiot and worse. I told them that the idea was to call them by name to treat them with respect, and they got even more sarcastic about my intelligence. I finally got them calmed down and tried to get them to tell me what the real problem was. They said this:

"When we come in and the ticket we take says 278, and the sign at the end of the room says 134, we know we have time to leave and come back. And, we know that no one will jump the line in front of us. When you call us by name, we're stuck here, and have no assurance we'll be seen in order. Give us back our numbers."

Ooooh, that hurt. The change that we made—taking down the numbers—was the only one we instituted *without paying people the respect they deserved by asking them what they wanted*. We *knew* what they needed: the dignity of being called by name. What they *wanted* was freedom and fairness! By giving them what they "needed," *we reduced the value of the service*. You've got to ask, you've got to listen, and you've got to pay attention to the perspective of the customer! ■

Do you pay attention? I hope so. Let's look through some other areas of customer perspective. Do you think through the way you provide services from the customers' point of view? Let's look at just a few of those perspectives.

- *Safety.* Is the location that you ask a customer to come to safe? Can you make it more so? Do you provide adequate lighting, locks, security, escorts, supervision, or whatever else it takes to make your customers feel secure?

 FOR EXAMPLE: A number of years ago (under a previous director) my wife and I both had our lockers broken into and items stolen at our local YMCA. After these robberies, I discussed them with other members and found a widespread concern with security, at least

(*continued*)

(continued)

in the 20 or 30 people with whom I spoke. I took these concerns to the executive director, and offered to volunteer for any committee that might be reviewing security and suggesting improvements to the Board of Directors. I told him that other people were concerned, and that, if unresolved, the concerns might well affect his membership numbers. The executive director's response was, "We dealt with this issue two years ago. There are thieves everywhere. Whoever wants to leave can leave. They'll be back." That's not exactly a customer-based perspective.

- *Parking.* Is there low-cost (or, better yet, no-cost), easily accessible parking for patrons of your services? Ease of access is very important.
- *Cleanliness.* Are your facility and grounds cleaned regularly (and I don't mean annually)? Do they pass the white-glove test? Do the lights/HVAC/toilets/phones/vending machines all work? All of this weighs heavily on how people think of you and your organization. This is an investment and an obligation, but all it takes is one cockroach or one backed-up toilet to send some customers ballistic.
- *Ease of finding where to go.* Is your facility easy to find? Is it easy to navigate from one area to another? Are there clear signs, or helpful people nearby, or is a visit to your facility like a trek to darkest Africa without a compass?
- *Greetings.* Do all of your staff greet all of your customers in a friendly, helpful manner every time they meet them? Are friendly greetings exchanged in the halls, lobby, galleries, or wherever and whenever they interact?
- *Bathrooms.* Are they easy to find and easily accessible? Are they *clean*? Are they safe? ■

There are many other ways that customers look at your organization, but if they are unhappy with these (or other issues), they will not want to return, or they will tell others about their bad experience.

 FOR EXAMPLE: I was in Chicago making an all-day presentation at a large, well-known hotel. At the first break, I needed to use the restroom, and I went to the men's room near the conference rooms. I entered a toilet stall, did my business, and looked around for toilet paper. Not only was there no paper, there was no toilet paper *holder*. Nor was there any indication that there had ever *been* a toilet paper holder—not even holes from a torn-out holder—nothing.

Now what? I am in definite need (and severe want) of toilet paper. I decide to wait for everyone to leave and then scoot into the next stall. But, I guess that about this time another meeting took its break because about 30 men descended on this men's room. Now I'm really stuck, and to make matters worse, I have 75 people waiting for me to return to the podium!

Was I happy? No. Later that morning I went to the front desk to relate the problem, suggesting that they get it fixed immediately. They were, to say the least, unimpressed with my crisis, treating it like just another maintenance problem. This was a major mistake. Since that time, I have probably told 3,000 people that story. ■

Thus it is very, very important to look at your organization through the eyes of your markets—your customers. That is why you ask and ask and ask. But you also need to make sure here, as in other parts of your asking, that you are truly listening and not merely waiting your turn to talk. Listen, and give them what they *want!*

 HANDS ON: If you haven't yet used the hands-on suggestion I made earlier, now is a good time. Find a friend who is willing to come in to your organization as a potential customer. Ask her to come in at her convenience and to take notes of everything that she sees that she likes, and everything that she sees that she dislikes—even in the slightest way. Pick a friend who you feel will be tough on your organization, and emphasize to her that you want to improve things. After the visit, have your friend list the good and bad parts of the visit and, if she is willing, have her do the "debrief" with your marketing team or management team. It will be an eye-opener, I assure you. ■

The Unhappy Customer

Fortunately, for many of your customers, simply asking regularly will suffice in terms of customer satisfaction, and problem identification and resolution. If you are in regular contact with them, they will tell you about their small problems while they are still small, and not have major issues with you. But about 1 in 10 customers will have a beef with you. And dealing with them in a courteous, helpful, and ultimately successful manner is a skill that everyone on your staff needs to develop and to practice.

Let's look at how to deal with this unhappy, ticked-off customer. Sometimes he is ticked off for a valid reason (from your perspective), sometimes not. Remember, the customer is not *always* right. But the customer is *always* the customer. Thus, you and your staff need some guidance in how to deal with the customer who calls or presents himself at your office door with a head of steam up. As you read these ideas, think about the last time such a customer vented his or her wrath on you. How many of these techniques did you use? What happened?

 HANDS ON: When dealing with unhappy customers, follow this checklist:

1. *Listen to their whole complaint.* Do not interrupt, cut them off, or in any way impede them from venting. If they are mad enough to complain, they want their whole say. Don't make them madder by correcting, interrupting, or explaining, at least not until they are through. Let them finish, *then* ask your clarification questions.

2. *Acknowledge the customer's perspective.* There are two possibilities: The customer is correct, and you have messed up, or the customer is wrong, and you haven't. In either case it is crucial that you acknowledge the customer's perspective. First, if the customer is correct, say, "Mr. Jones, it sounds like our mistake. I apologize, and I really appreciate the fact that you took the time to call." Or, the customer is not right, and you say: "Mr. Jones, I understand your frustration and I'm sorry you feel that way. I appreciate your letting us know about the situation." Acknowledge that you heard his problem and sympathize with his feelings. Make sure he knows that you heard him.

3. *Ask customers what they want.* Here is the place most of us mess up. We offer a solution to an unhappy person without asking *what he wants.* Don't do this. Ask first, "Now, what can we do to make this right with you, Mr. Jones?," and if he doesn't know what he wants, then offer a suggestion. More often than not, he really doesn't want anything other than to feel better and for the problem not to recur. Ask first.

4. *Never make promises you cannot keep.* As people who help, we want to make our customers happy. One way we think we can do that is by promising them *anything* that they want. It makes them happy now, but really unhappy later when we can't deliver. When you say, "We'll have the material mailed

to you today," "We'll be able to make your first appointment in a week," or "Check-in for a first-time client takes only 30 minutes," are all of these absolutely true? Can you do what you say, and to the letter? If not, don't say it, and make sure that all of your staff understand this. Here is an area where the person on the line of service can really make headaches for you. Tell your staff: Make only promises you can keep.

And, here's a promise that's easy to make, but impossible to keep: "Mr. Jones, I promise this will *never happen again.*" Have you ever heard of Murphy's Law?

5. *Keep excellent notes.* Particularly if you have a customer problem, keep excellent notes about what was said, who promised whom what and by when, and so forth. Documentation like this not only protects you, it also *reminds* you of what your obligations are, making it more likely that you will keep your promises, and it provides a means by which you can share the complaint with other staff to ensure that the problem you just dealt with doesn't get repeated elsewhere.

6. *Never assume a customer is happy.* Ask, measure, and interview. If you do have complaints, call those who complain yourself. This action alone will defuse 90 percent of complaints. But don't wait for them to complain—only 10 percent of people do and the other 90 percent (that don't) tell 10 other people, and *exaggerate their problem.* So get out ahead of the customer problem—ask, ask, ask. ■

Regular Customer Contact

Another crucial part of customer service is regularly checking in with them. With regular contact, particularly for the target group of customers, you will not only learn more about them, but have the opportunity to see their problems, sometimes as they occur, allowing you to offer a solution, sometimes with just your presence.

 FOR EXAMPLE: I regularly touch base with my key customers, just to chat. I don't try to sell; I don't try to tell them about new training sessions I may have developed, or new publications that we may offer. I just call, drop them an e-mail, or drop in and chew the fat for 5 minutes, or sometimes 15. I ask them what is going on in their lives, in their industry, and at their workplace. If they bring up a problem in an area where I have expertise, I will offer some ideas and suggestions on potential solutions.

(continued)

(continued)

I *never* sell on these calls. But I get lots of work from them, often on the spot. The reason is that I am visible and available, and show that I care about them. Highly successful salespeople whom I talk to all say the same thing: You have to stay in touch, you have to be visible, and you have to be available, and that means personal interaction. ■

 FOR EXAMPLE: Why do you think your insurance agent calls you on or around your birthday each year? Is it to wish you a happy day, or to remind you that you are getting older? No; it's to check in, to remind you that they are there, and to ask if there are any insurance needs that you might want to discuss. ■

 FOR EXAMPLE: Why do ministers greet their parishioners after services? Why do many make house calls, sometimes unannounced? To catch you being bad? No, to get to know you better, and to be available to help you if they can. ■

There are a number of parts to keeping in touch with your key customers that I would like you to consider. These are listed in the following. I want to point out that I recognize that you don't have time to do all eight of these for every market, but you should focus on your most important markets, using the 80/20 Rule that we discussed in Chapter 6. Also, remember that a key customer group is your funders. Don't leave them out of your regular contact planning.

1. *All key markets (payers, board, staff, volunteers, clients, contractors) should be offered the opportunity to have input into the organization.* For example, you can include customers in strategic planning by letting them review a draft of the plan. When you drop by to talk, ask them occasionally for ideas on how to solve one of your problems. Increase their ownership in your organization.
2. *Keep up on customers' important issues.* Read widely, and make notes of things that may affect your customers, whether an industry or a family issue. Ask them about it the next time you see them and let them know you understand their issues and their experiences.
3. *Tell them to call you if things aren't fixed immediately.* When there is a problem, let them know that if the normal solutions are not satisfactory, they can come back to you personally. Then, take the initiative and call them yourself to make sure that they are happy.

4. *Send a note thanking them for each payment.* This is a small thing, but easily done. A small postcard can be preprinted to accomplish this, or a quick e-mail can do the trick.

5. *If you make guarantees, make sure you can live with them.* Enough said.

6. *Make intermittent quality checks.* Show up or call up and have just one issue: Is everything okay? Make sure that your staff know that you are doing this, and you will get two benefits: fewer mistakes, and a customer who knows you are committed to quality.

7. *Always follow up with a new customer.* For new large markets, a personal greeting and quality check is mandatory, and this is a senior manager's job.

8. *Be pleasant.* Even when you are down, tired, frustrated, or sick, work as hard as you can to always be pleasant to others. Remember, you are always a member of the marketing team, and therefore always "on." Smiles, courtesy, and a pleasant attitude will buy you a lot of goodwill—goodwill that you may well need later. Here again is a place for our concept of compassionate urgency.

All of this is a lot of work, but you want customers to be customers forever. Invest in them and they will repay you tenfold. One of the ways that they will do that is by sending new customers, new clients, or new students your way. That is the subject of our next section.

Turning Customers into Referral Sources

How would you like a "free" source of customers, a source where you don't have to sell, make cold calls, send written materials, or make a personal visit? Does this sound good? Well, you, too, can take advantage of this source: It is your current customer base.

In the previous sections I noted that unhappy customers go and tell people (a lot of people) how unhappy they are. The same is true for happy customers. And it is all the more true for customers who feel that you are giving them incredible customer service. Thus, if you implement the ideas in this chapter, you should wind up with customers who are happy enough to be willing to send you others. But do you just wait for it to happen, or are there some things you can and should do to move the process along? There are, and I have listed five of them here.

1. Referrals Are Not Truly "Free"

You need to work for them and work at them. But if you have done a good enough job at customer service, the happy customer is a resource whom you should not waste.

2. Don't Be Too Eager with New Customers

One of the most common mistakes I see is people who have a new customer, and they immediately make him or her uncomfortable by asking for references or other referrals. Give a new customer time to fully experience your organization. Additionally, if I call a reference, I usually ask, "How long have you been a customer?" If the answer is "a week," I know that the referral, while perhaps sincere, is not based on such crucial issues as how the vendor solves problems. Be patient.

3. *Always* Ask for Permission to Use a Name as a Reference

Never use someone's name, or the name of his or her organization, without permission. Ninety-nine percent of people will happily agree to be a reference, but about half of them will be really ticked if they hear you are spreading their name around without their knowledge or approval. Do you really want to make half of your happiest customers mad? I don't think so.

You can ask for a lot of things of your customers in this area, including:

- Other organizations that are potential customers
- Permission to use their name as a referral/reference
- Mentioning your organization to peers
- Names of trade associations that they belong to

All of these things will be useful to you as you expand your marketing effort.

4. Remember to Meet Referrers' Wants

Your customers are giving you help. Do they want anything in return? Find out. For most people it may just be thanks, but make sure. Some people want their *title* always put with their name; some don't. Ask them.

5. *Always* Call or Write a Note of Thanks

I assume that you are tracking where your customers come from. Whenever you find out that you received a referral, call or write a note of thanks. Every time.

Don't ignore the benefits of all the hard work you have put into improving your customer service. Ask for help from your customers in getting more work. Nearly all will be glad to help you. They want you to succeed so that you can be there to provide more services to them.

Recap

There's nothing really incredible about incredible customer service. It is an attitude and hard work, consistent application of a few basic rules, and a team effort. But incredible service is something that is achievable, and something that is very important to your marketing effort in a competitive economy. In this chapter I showed you why incredible service is the *minimum* standard to apply in a competitive environment, and that the customer-driven outcome you really want is *customer satisfaction*.

We discussed incredible service, and the issue of solving customers' problems. We reviewed the falsehood that the "customer is always right," but also reviewed the fact that "the customer is *always* the customer." Thus it is essential to fix the problem when it arises, but also to ascertain what the low-key problems in a customer's life are and try to make a connection with your services. We also talked about having all your staff take on an attitude of compassionate urgency when dealing with everyone who seeks services from your organization.

Next, I showed you why it is so essential to empower your staff and to have them able to fix what breaks immediately, not just when you are available to tell them what to do. Then, we looked at ways to make and then maintain regular customer contact as a means both of ferreting out small problems before they become big ones and, just as importantly, of learning about customers' wants on a regular basis so that you can propose solutions that you or your organization can provide. I noted that this is especially important to do with funders and gave you eight points to make your customer contact more fruitful.

Finally, we talked about how to reap the benefits of incredible customer service by turning your customers into referral sources. I walked you through five ideas on how to get more from your customers and encourage their sense of ownership in getting you additional work.

Incredible customer service is the way to keep your existing customer base in an ever-more competitive world. It is a standard that more and more nonprofits are aspiring to, and one that you need to strive for. It is a lot of work, and an investment, but one that will pay off *very* well.

Discussion Questions

1. Are our staff empowered to fix customers' problems, or do they always rely on us? Do we encourage creativity and reward attempts to make customers happy, or do we punish our staff for not asking us?
2. Do we exude an aura of compassionate urgency with everyone who seeks services? How can we do that even better?

3. Do we sell services, or solve problems? Do we ask and then listen, or start with our hand out?

4. Do we regularly see all of our top and targeted customers? How can we do better in this area? Are the right people visiting these markets in the right way at the best intervals?

5. How much of our work is referral? Do we know from whom we are getting referrals? Do we thank them every time? Who else can we encourage to refer to us?

6. Think about the most recent experience with a business (restaurant, service, product, store) you had that was exceptional. What was it? Why was it exceptional? Do you think people come away from our organization feeling that way, and if so, how often?

CHAPTER 12

A Marketing Planning Process

Chapter Thumbnail

➤ Developing Your Marketing Team

➤ An Asking Schedule

➤ Targeting Your Marketing Effort

➤ A Marketing Plan Outline

➤ Marketing Planning Software

Overview

Now we need to put it all together. You have all the philosophical and technical information you need to move your organization toward becoming market driven and mission based. But to get from where you are to where you want to go, you need a plan.

Recall that earlier I said that you needed to improve, to change incrementally—1 percent at a time. I also noted that if those 1 percent changes were not directed by a plan, they could just result in your going in circles. It has been said that, without a plan, the only way you get where you are going is by accident. I agree; you certainly don't want to have the results of all your marketing efforts be haphazard or accidental. You don't want to have one part of your organization target one group of people and ignore another, especially if that second group is the target market for a different part of your organization. You don't want to have multiple "identities" to the public, nor do you want to survey the same part of your market five times, and another not at all. Good marketing planning should allow you to do all the things that you need to in a coordinated, efficient, and effective manner.

This chapter will show you how to begin the planning process. We will start at the beginning, putting together a winning marketing team. I'll make some suggestions on whom to pick, how to put the group together, and what their job descriptions should be.

Next, we'll examine how to develop an asking schedule. Recall that in Chapter 8, on asking, I noted that among the mistakes people make is asking either too often or too infrequently. This schedule will help you avoid that. But how do you choose which market to ask and when? I'll show you. That will lead nicely into the third part of this chapter, which will be some practical applications of targeting your marketing. You have already heard me say how you need to focus on your markets and target your marketing efforts. Here, I'll show you how.

Finally, I'll provide you with a fairly detailed outline for a marketing plan, showing you the content areas that I think are essential, as well as an example from a real marketing plan. We will also review how you can integrate your marketing planning into your organizational strategic plan. By the time you are finished with this chapter, you will have a good handle on how to get started with a coordinated, planned marketing effort.

Developing Your Marketing Team

I said early in this book that marketing is everyone's job, not just the job of the CEO or the director of marketing. Everyone is part of the marketing effort, but not everyone can sit on the committee, or team, that develops and implements your marketing plan.

You do need a team, however, and you need it to be broad-based and have a variety of experience and perspectives. You need the team to develop the marketing plans, develop your asking, allocate the marketing portion of your budget, and do the lion's share of the regular customer contact. Let's look at the makeup of the marketing team, and then review its responsibilities. I think you will find that by developing such a team, you will greatly improve the results of your marketing efforts.

Who Should Be on the Marketing Team?

I always like teams or committees that are broadly based. Thus I do not think that this group should be just board members, nor do I support teams that are made up of only senior management staff. Think of your organizational chart. It has vertical levels (senior management, middle management,

line staff) and horizontal dimensions (varying programs or areas of service).
I have found that a wide representation of your organization both vertically
and horizontally benefits everyone the most. You get input from all areas,
and grow your future leaders. If you believe me when I tell you that marketing is a team effort, and that everyone is on the marketing team, make
sure you put those words into action when you develop the organization's
marketing team. The following people need to be involved:

- *CEO*. The top staff person in the organization needs to be involved,
  at least in the selection of target markets, marketing planning, and
  other strategic issues. She or he probably shouldn't chair the committee,
  though.
- *Board member*. You should ask one or two members of the board to be
  involved in this critical part of the organization, particularly if you have
  a board member who is involved in marketing in her regular job.
- *Marketing director*. Whoever on your staff has the core responsibility for
  marketing should not only be on the committee, but he or she should
  most likely chair it.
- *Director(s) of services*. Whether this is one or more staff, the people
  in charge of your core services need to be part of the asking and the
  listening!
- *Mid-level and line staff*. You need people from throughout the organization. Many of these people have more direct contact with your customers
  than senior management, and thus their input is critical. It is also a great
  staff development experience for them.
- *Outside expert*. Some organizations find it helpful to have one or two
  outsiders on the marketing team, almost always people who have specific expertise to offer.

The team should probably not be any larger than 10 to 12 people, nor
much smaller than 5 or 6 people. That is the best size for a working group
such as this.

What Are the Marketing Team's Responsibilities?

Once you gather your group, what do you have to do? The following is
a list of outcomes that the marketing team should consider to be their
responsibilities:

- Develop a marketing plan coordinated with the organization strategic plan. This plan should include strategic as well as one-year goals,
  objectives, and desired outcomes. Most importantly, identify your target
  markets.

- Develop and administer a marketing budget.
- Develop a schedule of organizational asking.
- Develop and keep up-to-date all organizational marketing materials and the organization's web site, making sure that they are constantly updated.
- Develop and keep up-to-date the organization's "look" and logo.
- Monitor marketing trends in your mission discipline and advise the board and management team as appropriate.
- Implement adequate surveying, focus groups, and interviewing to stay in constant touch with the wants of the markets.
- Sponsor in-house training as appropriate on customer service, marketing, asking, and other related subjects for all staff.
- Keep in regular personal contact with key market segments.
- The team should regularly train themselves to further their own marketing expertise. Get outside education for team members on surveying, interviewing, market analysis, and materials development. Develop internal expertise.

This sounds like a lot to do, and it is. But if the group meets every two weeks (for two to three hours) for the first six months, and then monthly on a permanent basis, there should be adequate time to get it all done. And, to get you jump started, I have broken out some crucial things you need to get accomplished in your first six months.

Outcomes for the First Six Months

The following are some suggestions of things that your marketing team can strive for in your first six months:

- *Attain common ground.* It is important that you come to common ground on definitions and methods on achieving common goals. I would suggest that you have all team members read this book.
- *Identify your target markets.* Go through the market identification process that you learned about in Chapter 6. Work toward a consensus on who your target markets are.
- *Identify a contact for each target market.* Where possible, identify an individual at each of your target markets with whom you will keep in regular contact. This is easier for a funder, and more difficult for a target market such as "teenagers" or "nursing home residents," but even within those broad markets there will be representatives, advocates, family members, or others who can fill that role.
- *Assign a team member to each target market segment.* Each member of the team will have at least one (and probably more than one) market

to focus on. This will develop into an expertise over time, something you will really want to have.

- *Develop benchmarks.* Where you can, look at the status of these markets now. In many cases you will already have internal data you can look at. How large is the market? How many customers return? Where are our referrals from? How happy are the markets with us? How many complaints do we get? What percentage of our donations is made online? How much staff or board turnover do we have? What are the levels of customer satisfaction now? All of this information goes into your benchmark setting. These benchmarks will be your starting point for improvement, because if you don't set them now, you won't be able to tell later how far you have come!

- *Develop an asking schedule.* See the section in this chapter on how and why to develop an asking schedule. You need to coordinate your asking *now,* not later.

- *Develop a rough draft marketing plan.* See the section describing the outline of a plan for more on this. Suffice it to say that in six months you will be pressed to do all of the items listed here *and* develop a plan, but right now you can develop some goals and outcomes.

Your marketing team is a crucial component of your overall marketing effort. Choose your people carefully; give them the support and resources (including time away from their other duties) and make marketing a priority for them. Don't try to do this with one or two already overworked staff people. Get a group, motivate it, support it, and have high expectations of it.

An Asking Schedule

In Chapter 8, I showed you how to ask your markets regularly what they want. You will remember that there were interviews, surveys, focus groups, and, of course, informal and constant asking. You know that asking is important, and you know how to do it. But asking, especially with focus groups (and to some extent in surveys), is expensive. How can you get the most out of limited dollars? Also, one of the mistakes some organizations make is asking too much, resulting in bothering (even pestering) their best customers for information that they could have gathered more efficiently in a planned, coordinated manner.

Thus, your marketing team needs to develop a well-coordinated asking schedule, one that includes the timing and content of all of your surveys, focus groups, interviews, and informal asking. It needs to reflect the market priorities established in the plan, as well as the budget realities that constrain you. Remember, you won't be able to ask everyone everything every year. Your budget won't let you, and you don't want to pester. Give your marketing team the authority to plan and approve all organizational asking and you will get more information for your money.

Remember to get information back to the people who need it most—direct providers of services.

 FOR EXAMPLE: A preschool for disadvantaged inner-city children had instituted a program where all staff (teachers, administrators, cafeteria staff, and receptionists) would constantly be asking everyone they could where they heard of the school and how they felt about the services and the education provided. In doing an assessment of their marketing efforts, I reviewed the data gathered by survey, focus group, and informal interviews. I noted that there was substantial and valuable information gathered by the surveys, the focus groups, and the interviews conducted by the administrators, but very little if any interview data from teachers or cafeteria staff. I asked the teachers whether they were doing the regular informal asking, and they said yes, and that they were taking parent suggestions and implementing them whenever they could. I asked if they were getting any complaints or suggestions about other parts of the organization. They said yes, but hadn't passed them on, since they assumed that the same information was gathered by the administration.

The same scenario was being played out by the receptionist and the foodservice staff. They all were asking and dealing with ideas, suggestions, or complaints in their work area. Each assumed that any problems brought up regarding other parts of the organization were being heard there as well. The information never was passed on, and it was critical that it should have been. Some serious concerns and some significant opportunities were missed because the information flow was not completed. ■

Make sure that the information you asked for gets to where it should go. This may mean that a copy of any and all information gathered should come to the marketing team. Or, you may be able to design a routing system that gets the ideas and concerns where they need to be. But, in any event, make sure that you are getting the information that you are paying for!

Now let me show you an example of an asking schedule that incorporates the key elements: whom you are asking, when, how often, and in what manner. The example in Exhibit 12.1 is for a church that has extensive outreach, singles, and youth programs, which are their target markets.

EXHIBIT 12.1 **An Asking Schedule**

Method	Market	Cycle	Deadline for This Year
Survey	*Youth*	Every 18 months	February
	New members	6 months after joining	As needed
	Singles	Every 18 months	June
	General congregation	Every 2 years	None
E-mail Input	*20–40 year olds*	Every 6 months	February and August
Focus Group	*Youth*	Annual	One after survey
	Youth parents	Annual	One after survey of youth
	New members	Annual	One per year
Interview (formal)			None this year
Interview (informal)	*All*	Ongoing	Ongoing

As you can see from the table, the church has decided to focus this year's work on youth and singles, with a second priority on new members. Even though the survey cycle for the general membership is two years, it won't even be done in the next 12 months. Note also the e-mail input: This is targeted at the parts of the church that are most likely to have and use e-mail. A simple online survey, such as the one we discussed in Chapter 8, would suffice here.

 HANDS ON: As I noted in Chapter 8, one of the advantages of asking regularly is that you can measure trends. But how often is often enough? There is a balance between surveying all the time and surveying once a millennium. My general guidelines are these:

- *Staff surveys:* Every 18 months—which gives you enough time to implement appropriate suggestions and have them take effect.
- *Consumer surveys:* Some people survey annually, some every six months. It will depend on your type of services. A school might formally survey the parents and students semiannually, whereas a symphony orchestra might ask its patrons only once in a strategic planning cycle. Generally, I would say annually.

(continued)

(*continued*)

- *Funders:* Annually, or at the end of each funding cycle.
- *Donors:* Every two years, or at the point of the analysis regarding a large capital campaign.
- *Referrers:* Every six months.   ■

 HANDS ON: When you develop asking materials and reports (such as a report of a survey), put right on the cover of the report the date that it was administered *and the date of the next surveying.* For example, if I surveyed staff to ascertain their job satisfaction, I might put down that the survey was completed in June 2010, with an update of the survey due in two years, or June 2012. By putting the deadline of the update on the report, you are more likely to remember to do the survey again.   ■

An asking schedule will do much to eliminate unneeded duplication and unnecessary harassment of the people you should value most: your key markets.

Targeting Your Marketing Effort

Throughout this book I have urged you to target many of your marketing efforts on your most crucial markets. We have reviewed the Pareto Principle (80/20 Rule) a number of times, and its application for your organization. But now you are going to put a plan together, one where you commit your inevitably limited resources to try to do everything for everyone. Some of your marketing team (and your board) will want you to interview everyone, or do focus groups on a certain market segment, or develop promotional materials for every tiny niche. Everyone will have their pet idea, their personal priority. How can you do all of this with only so much time and only so much money?

You can't, and thus you need to prioritize and target the most crucial markets and the big-ticket items to get the most for your money and time. Let's look first at what I mean by crucial markets and then at the all-important and all-expensive big-ticket items.

Your Most Crucial Markets

Let's make sure that you and I are on the same wavelength about your most important markets. In Chapter 6, we talked about focusing on the target markets and how the 80/20 Rule and strategic plan linkage are both important. They still are, and we will review them and add a political consideration for your marketing team to evaluate.

- *Pareto Principle based on current income.* To review, the 80/20 Rule states that 80 percent of your income comes from 20 percent of your customers. Thus it makes excellent empirical sense to focus your marketing efforts on your biggest customers. And, as we learned in Chapter 6, this applies not only to income, but also to your services: 80 percent of your client/student/patient/member/parishioner encounters almost certainly come from just 20 percent of those market groups. So make sure some of your focus goes to that 20 percent.
- *Crucial future markets.* However, many readers feel that they are too dependent on one group, often government, for their ongoing financial wellbeing. You may be among them, and intent on reducing the percentage of your total income or service encounters from this one group. To do that, you will hopefully not shrink overall, but increase the income and encounters from other groups, groups of customers who may not currently be in your 20 percent club. That means that you should focus a portion of your marketing efforts outside the 20 percent as dictated by your strategic plan. Where do you see opportunities to serve? If you find them outside of your 20 percent, fine! Just remember to allocate your marketing budget accordingly.
- *Markets that identify with you.* For most nonprofit organizations, certain customer groups are a crucial part of their identity. Most parochial schools, for example, take non-Catholic students, but even as the percentage of non-Catholics in the student body grows, the staff would be naive not to continue to market the educational opportunities that the school affords within the Catholic community. Are there markets that truly identify with your organization? For example, in many communities, blood donations are closely related to the American Red Cross. The YMCA is closely associated with swimming safety and summer camps for youth, and the American Cancer Society with cancer awareness, screening, and research. Do you have core markets that are critical to your community image as well as your internal self-image? Even if they are small markets, can you afford not to market to them?

Big-Ticket Marketing Items

Big-ticket items are the ones that use up the most time or the most money. They are the ones that you cannot realistically apply to each and every market evenly.

- *Surveys.* Surveys, while they do not have to be exorbitantly expensive, do cost money and really take a lot of time. It will be worse for the first cycle of surveying, as you learn to ask the questions in the correct manner and order. If you are surveying regularly (and I hope that you are), repeat cycles should take much less time, but not much less money. As noted in Chapter 8, online surveys are far less expensive than paper or in-person surveys, but they exclude people who can't or don't want to get online.

- *Focus groups.* These are flat-out expensive, costing between $2,000 and $10,000 each, depending on your facilitator, the setting, and the size of the group. This is why most organizations survey first, and then hone in on only the most crucial issues in their focus groups.

- *Personal contact. Time* is the cost here. If you follow the ideas that I gave you in Chapter 11, you will see how much of your week this can absorb. Even though you will be spreading the personal contact part of marketing throughout the entire marketing team, this is still a time-costly part of the mix.

- *Marketing materials.* I hope that I made my point in Chapter 9 that marketing materials do not have to be inordinately expensive. But they do cost something, and it probably does not make sense to have specialty items for even the smallest market (unless you expect that segment to grow). But do not just develop a single general-interest piece. Have different materials for your different target markets.

- *Your web site.* There are, of course, expenses involved in maintaining and regularly improving your web site. Let me step back: There'd *better* be expenses associated with this crucial contact point. Don't accept a free, minimal web site that is just a front page and no more. Today, you need to use your web site as outreach, as an educational forum, as a staff and volunteer recruitment location, and as a place for people to donate funds. You can get volunteer help for some of this (as I told you in Chapter 10), but web sites are far too important to do on the cheap.

As you go about the development of your marketing plan, remember to focus, focus, focus. You and the rest of the team will want to do everything for everyone. You can't, so learn the discipline of focusing.

Speaking of the marketing plan itself, that is our next subject.

A Marketing Plan Outline

I want to provide you with an outline that you can use tomorrow as you begin the development of your marketing plan. However, I have seen a lot of plans and I have seen too many that share some common faults. Therefore, before we get into the actual plan contents, I am compelled to provide you with some planning definitions, and my suggestions on what the best marketing plan cycle is. Then I'll show you my suggested outline.

Definitions

If you have been in management more than about two hours, you have probably been to a planning workshop or seen an article on planning. That's good. What's *not* good is the 5,578 different definitions that people seem to use for the four core components of a plan: *goals, objectives, action steps,* and *outcome measures.* At the risk of becoming number 5,579, here are my stabs at the semantics of planning:

- *Goal:* A goal is a long-term statement of intended outcome. It may or may not be quantified. It may or may not have a deadline. The adjective *long-term* is the most crucial part of the description.
  Goal Example: *The Carter County Ballet will regularly revise its marketing materials to demonstrate its ability to meet the wants of its target markets.*

- *Objective:* A shorter-term statement of outcome that supports the goal, has a deadline, has a measurable outcome, and has a person assigned the responsibility for that outcome.
  Objective Example: *The director of marketing will review, revise, and refresh all printed and electronic marketing materials every two years, completing the initial review no later than September 30, 2011.*

- *Action Step:* A short statement of work with a measurable outcome, deadline, and responsible person listed. It must support an objective. These statements are most likely to show up in one-year plans. To most readers they would sound like work plan statements.
  Action Step Example: *In June 2011, the director of marketing will review the target markets and compare the array of marketing materials to ensure that all target markets have materials specializing in their wants and needs.*

- *Outcome Measure:* A measurable statement of *real* outcome. Both objectives and action steps need them, but far too many "outcome" measures that I see in plans are really process measures. An example of a process measure as opposed to an outcome measure would be: "Meet with 40 potential donors each month" as opposed to "Secure two donations of at least $1,000 each month." The first measures activity, and while that activity may eventually lead to donations, it doesn't mandate it. It is a process measure. The second statement mandates a real outcome. Don't get caught in the process trap. It will deflate the value of your plan immediately.

These definitions are what I have in mind when I see a plan. The need for deadlines should be obvious: Work expands to fill the time allowed for it. If you don't have a deadline, it will take forever. The need for a person assigned the responsibility is also crucial to a plan that will be actually implemented. If you name a person (as opposed to a committee, or even no one), and if that person has had a chance to review the plan before it is finalized, you have, in essence, a contract that the objective or action step will be achieved. The person named can (and definitely should) be held accountable for the implementation of the objective or action step.

The Planning Cycle

One question that is sure to come up with your marketing team as you begin the planning process is this: How long a horizon should the plan have? In other words, for what timeframe should the plan be written? There are a lot of different opinions on this. Let me review the advantages and disadvantages of the most common choices organizations make:

- *A five-year plan written every five years.* I think that five years is far too long to wait to rewrite any plan. Too much changes too fast to wait this long. I agree with a five-year horizon for a strategic plan, however, because I have found that forcing people to think out five years for their goals tears them away from the temptation of the immediate crisis. But for a marketing plan, five years is a bit long.
- *A three-year plan written every three years.* About right on both the horizon and the rewrite, but is trouble to get detailed enough to give staff and board members guidance week to week or month to month.
- *A one-year plan.* We already have work plans. We need a longer-term vision.
- *A three-year plan written every three years with one-year components done annually.* Now we're talking. This has the best of both the three-year plan—the long-term view—and the one-year plan—the immediacy of the work. Additionally, by writing the annual portion every 12 months, you can stay up with rapidly changing trends while still being guided by a longer-term view.

Remember as well that you should always coordinate your marketing planning with your organization's strategic plan. If your strategic planning cycle is five years, you may have a challenge getting on a three-year cycle for marketing. But overall, I think that the three-year period for marketing is best.

Annotated Marketing Plan Outline

The following outline is intended to give you guidance as your marketing team attacks the planning process. It should ensure that you include all the important parts of a comprehensive marketing plan. The sections noted are in the order that I think is the most effective, but if you feel the need to switch or combine some, that's fine.

MISSION STATEMENT I always like to lead with the mission. It reminds both you and your reader who you are and what you are all about. We are talking, after all, about mission-based marketing. If your organization's board of directors has not reviewed your mission statement in the past few years, now is a good time to make sure that it is up-to-date and still relevant to the services you provide and the markets that you serve.

EXECUTIVE SUMMARY This section (which goes first, but should be written last) should *summarize,* not simply repeat, the remainder of the plan. Included here should be a *short* description of your organization's markets, services, and target markets, a *brief* listing of the core wants of your markets, and a reiteration of at least the goals, and perhaps even the objectives, of the plan. No more. A summary should be just that—a summary.

INTRODUCTION: PURPOSE OF THE PLAN Tell the reader why this plan was written, who its intended audience is, how the plan is to be used, what body developed it, and when your board adopted it.

DESCRIPTION OF MARKETS Whom do you serve? Where are they? Are they growing or shrinking? What changes and trends are there in your markets? What is happening in the macroeconomy, on a state or national level, that will affect your markets? Who is your competition? What do they do better or worse than you do? Put your information in text, tables, charts, or graphs—however you feel you can best communicate your situation.

DESCRIPTION OF SERVICES What services do you currently provide to what market segments? How many clients/students/customers do you have in each as opposed to 5 or 10 years ago? What growth do you project? What new services are you planning to initiate during the term of the plan?

ANALYSIS OF MARKET WANTS First and foremost, demonstrate that you have asked people what they wanted. Did you survey, interview, run focus groups, or ask informally? Then tell the reader what you have learned. Finally, discuss how you meet the wants that you identified.

TARGET MARKETS AND RATIONALES   From all the markets your committee has identified, you have to focus on a few target markets. Tell the reader what those markets are, and provide the rationales for why you chose those markets as opposed to others.

MARKETING GOALS AND OBJECTIVES   Goals and objectives should be included in a three-year plan. For the one-year plan, you need to get down to the action-step level.

APPENDICES   Whatever "dense" data you feel that you need to support your rationales goes here, as should copies of your marketing surveys and other items that don't need to be in the body of the document. Don't make this part of the plan the thickness of the Los Angeles telephone directory, however. Be reasonable. The vast majority of the people who will read this plan either work for you or are on your board. Thus, if one or two of them want a copy of a survey, focus group report, marketing piece, or market analysis, they can ask for it. Don't (literally) burden every reader with all the arcane documentation you can think of. People don't measure the value of the plan by its weight. Think through what they need in their hands and what can be put on your web site or provided electronically. Remember, if any document is too big, people may not read it at all.

Examples of Goals and Objectives

The following goals and objectives are actual ones from a rehabilitation center that works with individuals with disabilities in the Midwest. The goal actually comes from their strategic plan, and it proved to be the core of their eventual marketing plan. What you see in the following is just part of the plan, and they did an excellent job.

You can see the flow of activity from goal to objective to action step. You can see an assigned agent, a deadline, and a measurable outcome. Use these to compare to your draft goals and objectives. Do they measure up?

> GOAL 4: Become a market-driven organization.
>> *Objective 4-1:* Identify and quantify 10 key markets that The Center serves by 10/1/20_ (Director of Communications and Marketing.)
>>> *Action Step 4-1-1:* Develop a list of key markets and determine the top 10 markets (4/17/20_ – 6/30/20_; Director of Communications and Marketing).
>>> *Action Step 4-1-2:* Research each of the 10 markets to determine how large each market is in our primary service area,

how many we serve, and how many need services (1/2/20_ – 3/29/20_; Director of C&M).

Objective 4-2: Investigate systematically the needs, wants, and preferences of our markets with initial assessment completed no later than June 20_ (Director of Communications and Marketing).

Action Step 4-2-1: Spend time finding out as much about each of our market's needs, wants, and preferences by conducting focus groups, looking at previously gathered information, talking with individuals, sending questionnaires, and using any other forms of information gathering that we can afford or tap into. This will be done on the following schedule:

1. Adult consumers—April & May 20_
2. Vocational rehabilitation counselors & VA referrers—June & July 20_
3. Parents—August & September 20_
4. Employers—October & November 20_
5. Schools—December 20_, January 20_
6. Doctors—February & March 20_
7. Other rehab. providers—April & May 20_
8. Case managers/health-care networks—June & July 20_
9. Influencers/advocates—August & September 20_
10. Persons with barriers to employment—October & November 20_(April 20_ – November 20_; Director of C&M, Marketing Manager).

Objective 4-3: Identify 10 key competitors and assess their strengths and weaknesses (1/2/20_ – 3/29/20_; Director of C&M, Marketing Manager, President, Vice President, Vocational & Children's Programs Coordinators).

Action Step 4-3-1: The Center staff makes a list of 10 key competitors and what we think are their strengths & weaknesses (1/2/20_ – 1/22/20_; staff named above in objective).

Action Step 4-3-2: Question consumers, referrers, community leaders, board members, and any other appropriate sources to receive their opinions about specific competitors (1/22/20_ – 2/29/20_; Director of C&M, Marketing Manager).

Action Step 4-3-3: Compile information gathered in above two steps in a report which will provide a comprehensive look at The Center's competition which can be used in future marketing decisions (3/1/20_ – 3/22/20_; Director of C&M).

As you write your plan, keep in mind the need for outcomes, deadlines, and assigned responsibility. When the goals and objectives are in draft stage, circulate the work and let people comment. Then, complete the entire plan (using the outline provided in this section) and get the entire board to review, comment, and adopt it.

Marketing Planning Software

Before you begin your planning you may want to explore the current crop of strategic and marketing planning software. As this book goes to press, the best, most flexible of these is MarketPlan Pro, from PaloAlto software: www.paloalto.com. This software walks you through the key questions and gives you the prompts you need to research the answers you need. It is a business tool and has more financial input than you may need, but you can skip that if you like.

However, like all software, what's available, and its features, change and improve regularly. Google the search term "marketing planning software," go to vendor sites, and download a trial version. Ask for references. See what your peer organizations use. And, check my web site for the latest as well: www.missionbased.com. Planning software can help, but it doesn't substitute for the hard work and thinking that the plan requires.

Recap

In this chapter you have learned how to get marketing ideas put into reality: by developing a marketing plan. This plan will be the tool you use to ensure that your organization truly utilizes all the new marketing skills that you have obtained by reading this book. Without the plan, you may or may not be able to do this.

First, we went over how to assemble your marketing team, including who should be on the team and what their responsibilities should be. I even gave you a list of the things your team should attempt to accomplish in the first six months, although for many groups the list may be a stretch. But you need to set your goals high so that you accomplish more than the minimum.

Then, we turned to the development of an asking schedule, and I provided you with a sample template as well as some general guidelines for how often to ask groups such as staff, funders, customers, and referral sources.

Next, I showed you how to apply the skill that I have repeatedly discussed: focusing on your target markets. This is crucial now that you are about to develop your marketing plan, and I gave you three criteria—the 80/20 Rule, your strategic plan, and the markets that identify you—on which to base your prioritization.

Finally, we got to the plan itself. I provided you with definitions of goals, objectives, action plans, and outcomes, as well as an annotated outline that you can use in your planning efforts.

You have learned a lot in reading this book. Now is the time to put that knowledge into action in a coordinated and effective manner. Develop your team and write your plan. It is a lot of work, but the rewards for your organization and for the people you serve will be great. Don't skip the planning. You will regret it if you do.

Discussion Questions

1. Do we have the right people on our marketing team? Should we add or delete anyone?
2. How can we develop an asking schedule? Should we survey and do focus groups? How can we train staff to ask, ask, ask?
3. What about an information loop? How do we ensure that what the staff hears gets to where it needs to go?
4. Should we develop (update) our marketing plan, and if so, by when? Who should be responsible for this?

Final Words

You are ready to move ahead. You have the tools, the motivation, and the capability to make the journey to becoming a market-driven and, of course, still mission-based organization. And although the outcome is not assured, the need to do so is unarguable. A great number of people are depending on you to take the lead.

As you go through the process, you will meet barriers, and I have tried to give you the ways to avoid or, if they are unavoidable, to surmount them. You will tire; you'll be frustrated and unsure at times. That is completely natural and, I am sure, already part of your daily and weekly work cycle. I hope that this book has given you not just the tools, but also the motivation to get back up and keep at it. That was my goal in writing it, because your mission is so, so important to the people you serve as well as to your entire community.

The next 10 years will bring unimaginable change to every part of our economy, and our little corner, the nonprofit world, will be no exception. The nonprofit players in your community will change drastically year after year as new organizations spring up and some of the oldest and most tradition-bound fall by the wayside or into mission-impotence from stubborn refusal to see what the community wants and then respond to it. "We've always done things this way" will be the clarion call of the doomed organization, even when what they have done is good, well-intentioned, and charitable.

The people your organization serves depend on you to be there to provide those services to them. You need to depend on them to guide you with their wants, to show you where the opportunities to serve are, and together to move your organization, your mission, and your community to new heights of effectiveness, wellbeing, and success.

Our communities will always need our nonprofits. We all depend on and benefit from the special kinds of people who work and volunteer for such organizations to be the philanthropic cement in our society—the positive role models, the keepers of the faith, the hope, and the charity that define our humanity. In 10 years, however, we won't need nonprofits that look like the ones we count on today. We will need organizations that respond to us as we will be then. Your organization can be such a nonprofit if you ask, listen, and respond. In doing so, you will do much to ensure your ability to continue doing your mission.

Best of luck on your journey. A lot of people are depending on you to make it a successful one.

Index